THE
Women
OF THE
TORAH

THE
Women
OF THE
TORAH

COMMENTARIES
FROM THE TALMUD,
MIDRASH, AND KABBALAH

BARBARA L. THAW RONSON

JASON ARONSON INC.
Northvale, New Jersey
Jerusalem

This book was set in 11 pt. New Baskerville by Hightech Data Inc., and printed and bound by Book-mart Press, Inc. of North Bergen, NJ.

10 9 8 7 6 5 4 3 2 1

Library of Congress Cataloging-in-Publication Data

Ronson, Barbara L. Thaw, 1955-
    The women of the Torah : commentaries from the Talmud, midrash,
and kabbalah / by Barbara Thaw Ronson.
        p. cm.
    Includes bibliographical references.
    ISBN 0-7657-9991-X (alk. paper)
    1. Women in the Bible. 2. Women in rabbinical literature.
3. Bible. O.T.—Criticism, interpretation, etc. 4. Bible. O.T.—
Criticism, interpretation, etc., Jewish. 5. Rabbinical literature—
History and criticism. I. Title.
BS680.W7R66 1998
221. 9'22'082—dc21   97–33197

Printed in the United States of America. Jason Aronson Inc. offers books and cassettes. For information and catalog write to Jason Aronson Inc., 230 Livingston Street, Northvale, NJ 07647-1726, or visit our website: http://www.aronson.com

Dedicated in honor and memory of my
Aunt Ruth and my grandmothers,
Dinah and Anna.

Dedicated also to my mother and father
as a prayer for their
continuing good health.

And a special thank you to my husband, Steve,
for his enduring patience, good humor, and
relentless questioning of the beliefs
we hold as Truth.

Contents

Even a simple maidservant at the Red Sea saw more of the Divine than the Prophet Ezekiel in all his visions . . .

—Zohar III 94a,
Mechilta Beshallach

Introduction

"**W**ho is wise? He who knows the consequences of his actions."[1] Viewed through the lens of the ancient Talmudic, Midrashic, and Kabbalist commentaries, this book examines, in Biblical sequence, the scriptural passages related to our ancestral mothers, wives, and daughters. The chosen Rabbinic excerpts, clearly documented, offer insightful glimpses into the question of what it may mean to be truly feminine, truly wise—illuminating how actions and deeds which appear to be malevolent or at the very least misguided when viewed superficially, may in fact have been engineered to produce the greatest good.

"Observe this. The garments worn by a man are the most visible part of him, and senseless people looking at the man do not seem to see more in him than the garments. But in truth the pride of the garments is the body of the man, and the pride of the body is the soul. Similarly the Torah has a body made up of the precepts of the Torah . . . and that body is enveloped in garments made up of worldly narrations. . . . Woe to the sinners who consider the Torah as mere worldly tales, who only see its outer garment. . . . Just as wine

---

1. Babylonian Talmud, *Tamid* 32a

cannot be kept save in a jar, so the Torah needs an outer garment. That garment is made up of the stories and narratives, but it behooves us to penetrate beyond."[2]

Thus admonishes the Zohar, the most well known and influential book of Jewish mysticism. But penetrate beyond into what?

Rabbinic tradition tells us that when Moses stood at Mount Sinai he received much more than the written Torah; he was given what has come to be known as the Oral Torah, the unwritten law, a body of knowledge, keys to interpretation that Moses then taught to his immediate successor, Joshua. Joshua meticulously passed it on to the elders, the elders passed it on to the prophets, the prophets to the scribes, and so on down through the generations until it reached our earliest rabbis. It is taught that the Torah was received by Moses in multiple ways—through its simple external meanings, through the numerical values assigned to letters and words, and through the meanings derived from the shapes of the letters.

Moses Cordovero, a master of Kabbalah, has compared each letter to a sublime and majestic palace. These letters are not merely convenient, empty symbols that represent agreed upon sounds. Each component of each letter, its shape, its crown, its extensions are representatives of quite specific mystical ideas, reflections on paper, in man's world, of the primal emanations of God.[3]

Glance into a Torah scroll. Most surprisingly, unlike our printed versions of the Bible, the actual Torah, written on parchment, is penned without any indication of the beginning

2. (Zohar, Vol. V:152a)
3. Moses Cordovero, *Pardes Rimonim,* chapter 2.

and end of each verse—there are no vowels, no punctuation marks! The rabbis teach that this is meant to aid us in discovering the multiple levels of hidden meaning. There is an esoteric tradition, expounded upon by Ramban, a Spanish 12th century rabbi and Kabbalist, that the Torah was originally delivered even without breaks between the words themselves. The teaching states that the words of the Torah, when divided differently, separate themselves into the Divine Names. The written Torah was given to Moses in the form which expressed the commandments, but orally it was transmitted to him in the form which revealed the Names of God.[4] These names are said to conceal the mystery of the forces of all creation.

History in the Span of a Breath

The familiar word, *rabbi,* which literally means "my master" or "teacher," didn't actually make its appearance until the first century of the Common Era,[5] but the role played by the rabbis as community leaders, teachers, and interpreters of Scripture, was filled by a variety of predecessors; the priests, elders, and prophets all fulfilled a kind of interpretive role. Different opinions are voiced by different historians and writers regarding the origin of the idea itself of interpretation of sacred text and the impetus for the rise of Rabbinic Judaism. The sections that follow are not specific to the topic at hand, an investigation devoted solely to the women in Scripture, but I wish to provide a foundation on which to stand, to more

---

4. Jacob Newman, *The Commentary of Nahmanides on Genesis Chapters 1–6* (Leiden: E. J. Brill, 1960), 27–28.
5. James L. Kugel and Rowan A. Greer, *Early Biblical Interpretation* (Philadelphia: The Westminster Press, 1986), 64.

fully breathe in the essence and spirit of the profound body of knowledge herein presented. My purpose here is to simplify the picture not by drawing personal conclusions regarding why certain key events occurred, but to place into a historical context the powerful works that I will subsequently refer to.

For the sake of clarity let us return to what is taken to be the beginning of recorded Jewish history, and within the span of a breath, to approach the eras in which the great commentaries—Talmud, Midrash, and Kabbalah—make their formal and informal appearances.

Some four thousand years ago, it is surmised, Abraham, the first Hebrew, and his wife Sarah left their home in Mesopotamia, today part of Iraq, and headed for Canaan. Joseph, Abraham's great grandson, is sold into slavery, and his father, Jacob, leads the family of twelve tribes down into Egypt. After Joseph's death, the Hebrews find themselves enslaved there until Moses, divinely appointed, leads them out of bondage. Standing at the foot of Mount Sinai, the Israelites receive the Torah. After the death of Moses, Joshua, his successor, leads the tribes out of the desert and back into Canaan, the land promised to Abraham, to his son Isaac, and his grandson Jacob.

The eleventh century B.C.E. gives rise to the Age of the Judges, and a century later, Saul is anointed as the first king of the Israelites. David and his son Solomon—the builder of the first Holy Temple—subsequently adorn the throne. But under the reign of Solomon's son, Palestine breaks up into the two kingdoms of Judah and Israel. The warnings of the eighth century prophets go unheeded, and the northern kingdom of Israel finds herself conquered by the Assyrians; the ten tribes comprising the kingdom are exiled and irrevocably dispersed. Then in the seventh century B.C.E., the Assyrian

Empire meets her own demise at the hands of the Babylonians.

Having now reached the sixth century B.C.E. we begin to slow down in our rapid, skeletal overview, devoid of the exploration of probable causes. The events that now take place seem to be crucial in shaping the need for a new form of interpretation of God's law. Nebuchadnezzar, the king of Babylonia, invades the kingdom of Judah and on the ninth day of the Hebrew month of Av in the year 587 B.C.E. destroys the city of Jerusalem and Solomon's Temple. The Judaeans (members of the tribes of Judah and Benjamin) are for the first time exiled from their new homeland and deported to Babylonia. Then, only fifty years later, the powerful Babylonian Empire is sideswiped by Persia and wiped off the face of the map.

In the first year of his reign, Cyrus, the king of Persia, issues a surprising proclamation: "The Lord God of Heaven has given me all the kingdoms of the earth and has charged me with building Him a house in Jerusalem, which is in Judah. Anyone of you of all His people—may his God be with him, and let him go up to Jerusalem that is in Judah and build the House of the Lord God of Israel, the God that is in Jerusalem" (Book of Ezra 1:2–3). Many exiled Judeans return to their homeland, and the Temple is rebuilt.

The book further records that a man named Ezra, a "priest, scholar in the law of the God of Heaven" is later dispatched by the currently ruling king, Artaxerxes, to return to Judah to aid in the rebuilding of the new Jewish community. "And you, Ezra, by the Divine wisdom you possess, appoint magistrates and judges to judge all the people in the province of Beyond the River who know the laws of your God and to teach those who do not know them" (7:25). Twelve years after his return to Judea, a decisive event takes place that many scholars believe marks the birth of a form of scriptural study that was to hold fast and flower for hundreds of years. "The entire people assembled as one man in the square before the Water Gate, and they asked Ezra the scribe to bring the scroll of the Teaching of Moses with which the Lord had charged Israel. On the first day of the seventh month, Ezra the priest brought the congregation, men and women and all who could listen with understanding. He read from it, facing the square before the Water Gate, from the first light until midday . . . . The ears of all the people were given to the scroll of the Teaching . . . and the Levites explained the Teaching to the people, while the people stood in their places. They read from the scroll of the Teaching of God, translating it and giving the sense; so they understood the reading" (Nehemiah, chapter 8).

The Interpreters of Scripture—Who Were They and Why Did They Do It?

The most obvious need for biblical interpretation arose because of the problem of language. While in Babylonian exile, the Jews began to abandon the Hebrew language of their homeland and to speak the tongue of their new home, Aramaic. Aramaic is a semitic language that bears quite a few similarities to Hebrew, but is distinct enough to be unintelligible to anyone not specifically schooled in it. In addition, the spoken Hebrew of those left behind in Judea differed from the written, literary Hebrew of the Bible. The spoken language had been tainted by contact with other dialects, and the meanings of many ancient biblical words were no longer consistent with current usages of the very same words and idioms.[6]

---

6. James L. Kugel and Rowan A. Greer, *Early Biblical Interpretation* (Philadelphia: The Westminster Press, 1986), 28–31.

Another impetus for interpretation arose with the desire of the returning exiles to precisely understand the meaning of God's dictates as revealed in the sacred writings that had been preserved and resurrected. Many laws were unclear, not specific enough to be enacted in their new society.[7] Sometimes contradictions seemed to exist between one book of the Bible and another in regard to specific dictates. This type of interpretation of Scriptural law has come to be known as "halakhah," from the Hebrew root *halakh,* meaning "to walk," that is, the path one must walk to be most precisely aligned with God's Will.

A third major incentive was one directly related to the subject matter of this book—the quest to make sense out of the seeming iniquities committed by our biblical ancestors,[8] to find their meanings on levels deeper than the most external, to solve inconsistencies and to fill out the sparse information often provided regarding actions taken and decisions made by our mothers and fathers. In a continuing quest to unearth these secrets, to shed light on their own dilemmas by viewing themselves as a reflection of their forebears, a vast body of literature grew up through the ensuing centuries which has come to be known as "aggadah," literally meaning "lesson" or "tale" or "that which is told." In the restored Judean community, both halakhah and aggadah together provided a guide to conduct that the individual felt would help him live his life in accordance with his divine potential.

In Ezra's time and for many years after, law and philosophy, halakhah and aggadah, were taught side by side, usually by the same teachers in a form known as "midrash," a method

7. Ibid., 31–33.
8. Ibid., 33.

of study in which Scripture was followed and probed verse by verse.[9] The word *midrash* comes from the root *d'rsh* which, in its biblical usage means "to search," "to seek," "to examine," or "to investigate."[10] Today, the term *midrash* is inexactly used to refer to only aggadah; it has somewhat erroneously come to mean any interpretive subject matter that is nonlegal in nature.

In regard to the ascent of Rabbinic Judaism, scholars often point to a series of events that took place in the first century, C.E., after the fall of the Persian Empire, and after the defeat of Greece by the Romans: 66 C.E.—the first Jewish uprising against Roman domination is waged; 70 C.E.—the Romans, under Titus, conquer Jerusalem and destroy the rebuilt Temple; 135 C.E.—following the unsuccessful Bar Kochba revolt, Judea is devastated by the Roman forces and declared off-limits to Jews. Our historians believe it was at this point that the undeniable realization arose that for the Jewish religion to survive, it could no longer be centered around Temple and sacrifice, could no longer depend on centralized rituals alone to sustain, unite, and inspire. On the heels of tragedy, the rabbis began the task of collecting and laying down the full scope of the law for the community, and an institution was born that would flourish until the middle of the eleventh century, the Academy. The first academy was created in Jabneh, Israel, by Rabbi Johanan b. Zakkai, and numerous other academies were later established in both Israel and Babylon.

---

9. R. Dr. H. Freedman and Maurice Simon, "Foreword by R. Dr. I. Epstein," in *The Midrash Rabbah,* vol. 1 (London, Jerusalem, New York: Soncino Press, 1977).
10. Cecil Roth, ed., *Encyclopedia Judaica* (Jerusalem: Keter, 1972), 1507.

The Talmudic word for academy is *yeshivah,* which literally means "sitting," and refers to the set arrangement of seating assigned to the sages and their pupils who participated in the studies, debates, and rulings.[11] Commonly, the head of each academy was previously the disciple of the head who preceded him,[12] so a chain of correctly transmitted ideas was established. These were schools of Oral Law, and all knowledge was transmitted solely in a verbal manner. The idea of the school is an ancient one; Rabbinic tradition tells us that even the biblical patriarchs and their sons studied in the yeshiva. Tractate *Yoma* teaches that a yeshiva existed during the Egyptian bondage as well as during the forty years spent wandering in the desert.[13]

The Rabbinic teachers who lived until the end of the second century c.e. are called the "tannaim"; *tanna* means "repeater" or "teacher" in Aramaic. These are the sages who are cited in our earliest teaching text, the "mishna," which for many centuries to come was transmitted in its oral form. *Mishna* is the Hebrew word for "repetition" or "recitation." From these tannaim also came the "targums," Aramaic translations of the Bible. Within the academies, the extensive work of the tannaim was further carried on by the "amoraim"; *amora* means "discusser," "speaker," or "interpreter" in Aramaic. This elaborative work is known as the "Gemara," a text filled not only with commentary but with all the articulations of the sages, from proverbs to parables.

The "Talmud," which includes both Mishna and Gemara, is the great product of the academies in both Israel and

11. Ibid., 199.
12. Ibid., 756.
13. Ibid., 199, Babylonian Talmud, *Yoma* 28b.

Babylonia. *Talmud* is the Hebrew word and *Gemara* the Aramaic word for "study." The Jerusalem Talmud was completed around 400 C.E., and the Babylonian Talmud was independently completed about 500 C.E. When Babylonia became a world metropolis, it was their version that became the scriptural authority for all Jewry. In this current work, I refer only to the Babylonian Talmud for commentary.

The Babylonian Talmud is made up of the oral discussions and discourses as they were delivered in the academies. Explorations of both legal and nonlegal topics are interspersed throughout; one third is halakhah, two thirds aggadah. In the Jerusalem Talmud only one sixth is devoted to aggadah because, in Palestine, a completely distinct class of philosophical, nonlegal literature developed alongside the halakhah.[14] Along with the Babylonian Talmud, it is this extraordinary, separate aggadic body of literature, the midrashim (pl. of midrash), that I will often refer to in the coming pages.

It cannot be overemphasized that all the work of the academies was carried on orally; it was, in fact, forbidden to commit anything to writing. The disciples of the amoraim, the schools of the savoraim, were responsible for perpetuating the work of their mentors until the middle of the sixth century C.E., at which time, due to persecutions and barbaric invasions, the rule forbidding writing was finally retracted.

The Babylonian Talmud is recorded in both Aramaic and Rabbinic Hebrew. Rabbinic Hebrew, which includes Greek and Latin words, is not equivalent to modern Hebrew which, in turn, is not equivalent to Biblical Hebrew.[15] In later genera-

---

14. Ibid., 762.
15. Hayim Nahman Bialik and Yehoshua Hana Ravnitsky, "Introduction by David Stern," in *The Book of Legends* (New York: Schocken Books, 1992), xviii.

tions, as in the restored kingdom of Judea, a language barrier needed to be surmounted. Commentaries on the Talmud came into existence, the most popular and generally authoritative being those by the eleventh century French Rabbi Shlomo Itzhaki, also known as Rashi, an acrostic of his name. Another commentator I will make frequent reference to in my effort to discern the hidden meanings of Scripture is Rabbi Moshe ben Nachman, also known as Ramban, a scholar, philosopher, poet, and physician born in twelfth century Spain.

The Babylonian Talmud is composed of material that was collected from many different academies during different periods of time. The collections of purely aggadic material, the nonlegal midrashim, present an even greater difficulty in terms of unequivocally dating them, because each collection contains ideas and creations from vastly different eras. Due to the injunction against writing anything down, these collections don't begin to appear until the fifth and sixth centuries.

There are two main types of midrash. The exegetical midrash is a commentary on one of the books of the Bible, with each of its chapters, verses, or words pondered and explored. The homiletical midrash collection is divided into chapters, each filled with discourses and maxims on a particular theme or point. In the earliest homiletical midrashim, a device known as a "proem" is often employed; a verse from an entirely different source is cited and serves as the introduction to the homily. The amoraim favored this device to rivet the attention of their listeners and to emphasize the profound unity of all the biblical books.[16] Unfortunately, the compilations that have come down to us do not contain the full sermons,

---

16. Cecil Roth, ed., *Encyclopedia Judaica* (Jerusalem: Keter, 1972), 1510.

rather only the central ideas espoused, which tends to make them difficult for the modern reader to comprehend.

The collections that will be drawn upon in this current volume hail from what is referred to by scholars as the Early (400 C.E.–640 C.E.) and Middle (640 C.E.–1000 C.E.) Periods of midrashic compilation. The oldest collections of midrash that we have, all exegetical in nature, are the Mekhilta, an exposition of the Book of Exodus; Sifra, on the Book of Leviticus; and the Sifrei, two collections based on the Books of Numbers and Deuteronomy. Genesis Rabbah is an ancient exegetical commentary on the book of Genesis. Also from this Early Period we receive Lamentations Rabbah, Esther Rabbah, Song of Songs Rabbah, and Ruth Rabbah, exegetical commentaries on these respective books of the Bible. Leviticus Rabbah, also dated from this period, is homiletical in nature.

From the Middle Period we receive the Midrash on Proverbs, Ecclesiastes Rabbah, the Midrash on Psalms, Exodus Rabbah, Pirke de Rabbi Eliezer (the Chapters of . . .), and Midrash Tadshe, all exegetical in nature. The Tanhuma and Pesikta Rabbati are Middle Period collections based upon a homiletical format.[17] Great intervals of time separate the initial creation of the commentaries and their subsequent committal to writing and deposit into published collections. Because of this, we see multiple versions of the very same axioms and tales scattered throughout and hidden within the vast sea of Rabbinic literature, in both the Babylonian Talmud and Jerusalem Talmud and in the numerous later volumes. In this current work, when reference is made to any particular commentary, I offer only the most well-known or easily accessible sources available in English translation.

---

17. Ibid., 1509–1513.

Fifty Gates of Understanding (The Esoteric)

Our rabbis have taught that "fifty gates of understanding were created in the world, and all of them, except one, were transmitted to Moses."[18] These gates are said to hold the knowledge of everything revealed and everything concealed—the essence of and force behind every aspect of every level of creation—from the minerals and plants up to the secrets of the human soul, from the earth and its seasons up through the secrets of the heavens. The last gate, the highest one, the fiftieth one, perhaps pertains to our Creator, Ramban surmises, the knowledge of Whom has never been transmitted to any living being.

The wisdom of the forty-nine gates was transmitted to and received by Moses, enabling him to contemplate and understand the mysteries of all creation. But just exactly *how* was this knowledge transmitted to him? Through some long-lost treatise or now-legendary manual? No, say our Sages. It was relayed through the Torah—*our* Torah. All these secrets are said to be hidden within the body of the sacred text—expressed either explicitly or indirectly, via its literal words or by subtle implication, by the numerical values of the words, or by the form of the letters which are sometimes written in their usual manner and which sometimes appear with minor deviations from the norm.[19] The great academies that flourished in Israel and Babylon were not the only schools that thrived during the Rabbinic period. Side by side and often shrouded in mystery were schools devoted to unveiling these mystical meanings hidden within every holy letter of the Torah.

---

18. Babylonian Talmud, *Rosh Hashanah* 21b.
19. Jacob Newman, *The Commentary of Nahmanides on Genesis Chapters 1–6* (Leiden: E. J. Brill, 1960), 23–24.

Who exactly were the teachers of these esoteric schools, and who were the students? We find that many of the Rabbis who were engaged with the creation of the Talmud also were engaged with the mysteries. The Zohar (Book of Splendor), the most influential mystical text, is a verse-by-verse reading of the Pentateuch which strives to derive the kabbalistic teachings directly from Scripture. But prior to its publication in 1295, the most significant text was the Bahir, also known as the Midrash of Rabbi Nehuniah ben Hakana—a man who was not only a leading mystic in the first century, but also a Talmudic sage![20] Both Eliezer the Great, author of the midrash, Pirke de R. Eliezer, and the illustrious Rabbi Akiba, were disciples of Rabbi ben Hakanah; Rabbi Akiba is himself quoted three times in the Bahir. There are numerous examples of such overlap. Rabbi Yohanan ben Zakkai, the sage responsible for creating the first academy in Jabneh after the second Temple's destruction, instructed a Rabbi Yehoshua, who, in turn, was also a disciple of Rabbi ben Hakanah.[21] But these schools of Kabbalah were not always led by well-known Talmudic sages; sometimes they were directed by community leaders and sometimes by masters whose names have been long lost to us.[22]

The Hebrew word *Kabbalah* is taken from the root, *kabal,* meaning "to receive." As was true within the academies, mystical schools also taught their mysteries orally with personal manuscripts, "hidden scrolls" kept only by the school heads to ensure accurate transmission. School members were sworn

---

20. Aryeh Kaplan, *The Bahir* (York Beach, ME: Samuel Weiser, 1979), ix, xi.
21. Ibid., xvii–xviv. Aryeh Kaplan, Introduction in *Sefer Yetzirah* (York Beach, ME: Samuel Weiser, 1990), xv–xvii.
22. Aryeh Kaplan, Introduction in *The Bahir* (York Beach, ME: Samuel Weiser, 1979), xv.

to secrecy, promising not to divulge the mysteries to outsiders. Oftentimes, the community within which the school functioned had no idea that it even existed.[23] These forums for mystical study did not spring into existence in the first century. According to the Kabbalists, our ancient ancestors not only knew the Torah before it was given by virtue of the Divine or Holy Spirit, but also knew its esoteric meanings and modeled their lives upon the laws and patterns of the hidden, supernal universes, the ladder that connects man with his Creator.

The Zohar, to which I'll refer throughout the current work, has provoked much debate regarding its actual genesis. The Zohar manuscript was first circulated in eleventh century Spain by a Moses de Leon who claimed that the discourses contained within were actually obscure teachings that originated in the second century in the Galilean circle of a Rabbi Shimon bar Yohai. The many Kabbalists who subscribe to this theory believe that after the Roman decree forbidding the teaching of Torah, and after the murder of Rabbi Akiba who defied this decree, Rabbi bar Yohai, a disciple of Akiba, fled with his son to a cave in the mountains. During the thirteen years they remained in hiding, Elijah the Prophet appeared twice a day, revealing to him the secrets of the Zohar (these secrets also having been known to Akiba and all the sages before him). Rabbi Shimon bar Yohai then committed it to writing using both Aramaic and Hebrew.

Others maintain that the Zohar is a pseudepigraphic work compiled and enhanced by de Leon out of mystical sources readily available to him—the Bahir, the classic Rabbinic midrashim, and the commentaries of his contemporaries.

---

23. Ibid., xv.

(Pseudepigraphic works are books that are narrated by a living author who attributes the words and discourses contained within to long-deceased ancients; these books are a subcategory of apocalyptic literature, the term coming from the Greek word for "revelation.")

In 1492, the Jewish population was expelled from Spain, with many mystics settling in Safed, Israel. Due to a resurgent interest in the value and significance of esoteric illuminations of Scripture, Kabbalah and especially the Zohar once again became a central feature of life and study for the Rabbis, with many additional books of commentary being produced. Rabbi Moses Cordovero's works, for example, originate in this place and time. Then again in the eighteenth century, the Hasidic movement, greatly influenced by the Zohar, developed in Poland and the Ukraine.

A Small Door—Final Notes on This Volume

Upon first being introduced to the often poetic Rabbinic commentaries and philosophical discourses, they can appear to be rather random embellishments of Scriptural verse, flights of fancy, or hair-splitting exercises executed without rhyme or reason. In actuality, none of the teachings were arrived at without recourse to certain immutable principles, as well as predetermined rules governing the very art of exegesis. The interpretation of halakhah or law was, at first, presided over by seven rules, later expanded to thirteen by Rabbi Ishmael in the first century. Aggadah, all nonlegal commentary, was rigidly regulated by thirty-two basic rules which were formulated by his contemporary, Rabbi Jose ha-Gelili.

Among the thirty-two principles is the system of primary gematria, wherein the numerical values assigned to each letter reveal previously unseen meanings about the words they form and about the relationship they bear to other words to which, on the surface, they may appear to be completely disconnected. In addition to this basic system, the sages of the Talmud, Midrash, and Kabbalah utilize other more complex forms of gematria to wrest meaning from the text. The rabbis teach that the values assigned to the Hebrew letters, as well as some of the systems themselves, were among those keys to interpretation received directly by Moses on Mount Sinai.

As previously mentioned, the Torah scroll contains no punctuation, which allows for multiple interpretations of any particular verse, phrase, or word. Certain words in Scripture are even meant to be pronounced in one way although written in another. The Maharal of Prague teaches that the verbal version indicates the obvious, most external aspects of the word, whereas the written version can reveal its veiled elements.[24] To the masters, the very shapes of the letters disclosed the concealed.

There's a Talmudic admonition that a student should always study the precise wording of his master;[25] the words and phrases chosen by the teacher often contain significance not obvious to the pupil. Taking this injunction to heart, I have on the whole paraphrased only those commentaries and ideas espoused by different rabbis, in different words, in different sources. Most excerpts from the Zohar have been directly and exactly quoted.

The sages based many of their commentaries on the literal meanings of words, words which present-day translators of Scripture often modify to render the Biblical phrases and verses more understandable or pleasing to the modern ear. My aim is not to explain how all the commentaries were ar-

---

24. Matityahu Glazerson, *Letters of Fire* (Spring Valley, NY: Feldheim Publishers, 1991), 120–121.
25. Babylonian Talmud, *Berakoth* 47a.

rived at (although oftentimes this may be simplistically alluded to), but I did, nonetheless, choose to utilize the older, standard English translations of the Five Books of Moses which seem to be more aligned with the exact meanings discerned by the rabbis, and from which they drew their conclusions.

The Zohar compares the Torah to a maiden who is isolated in the hidden chamber of a palace. She has an admirer who, for love of her, ceaselessly wanders about the palace, passing by her gate. The maiden, aware of him, one day opens a small door in her chamber just for a moment, just long enough to reveal her face and withdraw it. But now the man knows that she too feels the pangs of love, and even more than before, he longs to know her, heart and soul. "It is the same with the Torah, which reveals her hidden secrets only to those who love her. She knows that he who is wise of heart daily haunts the gates of her house. What does she do? She shows her face to him from her palace, making a sign of love to him, and straightway returns to her hiding place again. No one understands her message save he alone, and he is drawn to her with heart and soul and all his being. Thus the Torah reveals herself momentarily in love to her lovers in order to awaken fresh love in them. Now this is the way of the Torah. At first, when she begins to reveal herself to a man, she makes signs to him. Should he understand, well and good, but if not, then she sends for him and calls him 'simpleton,' saying to her messengers: 'Tell that simpleton to come here and converse with me' . . . When he comes to her she begins to speak to him, first from behind the curtain which she has spread for him about her words suitable to his mode of understanding, so that he may progress little by little. This is called 'Derashah.' [The derivation of the traditional laws from the letter of Scripture.] Then she speaks to him from behind a thin veil of a finger mesh, discoursing riddles and parables—which go by the name of Aggadah. When at last he is familiar with her she shows herself to him face to face and converses with him concerning all her hidden mysteries and all the mysterious ways which have been secreted in her heart from time immemorial. Then such a man is a true adept in the Torah, a 'master of the house,' since she has revealed to him all her mysteries, withholding and hiding nothing. She says to him: 'Seest thou the sign, the hint, which I gave thee at first, how many mysteries it contains?' He realizes then that nothing may be added to nor taken from the words of the Torah, not even one sign or letter" (Zohar, Vol. III:99a–99b).[26]

In Hebrew, the Bible bears the acronym *TaNaKh*, which stands for "Torah"—made up of the Five Books of Moses; "Nevi'im"—Prophets, made up of thirteen individual books including the Book of Joshua, the Judges, the two Books of Samuel, and the two Books of Kings; and finally "Ketuvim"— the Writings, which include among others the Psalms, Proverbs, the Song of Songs, Lamentations, Ecclesiastes, and the books of Ruth and Esther.

I did not choose to view the Bible as an historical document, seeking to uncover its sometimes cryptic meanings based upon the societal dictates of the times in question. My wish was to explore the Bible by perceiving it solely as a timeless divine doctrine—to illuminate the value and significance of Prayer, the individual woman's relationship to her Creator (informing her relationship with family and neighbor), and to discover and highlight the idea of Woman that exists independently of the era she finds herself born into.

---

26. Harry Sperling and Maurice Simon, *The Zohar* (London: Soncino Press, 1984), pp. 301–302.

In studying the women of Scripture in conjunction with the Rabbinic commentaries, I found that a certain pattern of themes appears to recur: the issue of infertility and the overwhelming wish for a child; the mystery of prayer and the unrelenting effort to communicate with one's Creator—to be heard and to hear; the significance accorded one's given name and its meaning in regard to Destiny; the transformation of Destiny; the often miraculous answering of the barren woman's prayers; the ideas of beauty and love; the ability to prophecy, to discern the truth, and the inherent struggle to stand up for one's vision; the final outcome for the long-term good of the family and nation, the carrying out and victory of God's Will against any and all odds.

Please regard these designations solely as a simplistic framework to hold the vast and uncontainable. Every word of explanation I posit seems to underscore the impossibility of conveying the grandeur of the works of the sages and the immensity of the divine treatise they devoted their entire lives to studying. Throughout the text, I have made a consumate effort to avoid imposing personal opinion; I have chosen to allow the commentaries to speak for themselves, to allow the reader to be struck by his or her own impressions. This book is an expression of a personal quest to deepen and enhance my understanding. My studies have brought me many moments of delight; my wish is solely to share with you this fleeting glimpse through the crack in a small door.

> ... The egg of the ant is not as small compared with the
>   Highest Sphere
> As my wisdom is small and my sense defective measured
>   against
> the hidden matters of the Torah,

which are stored up in her house, concealed in her
    room.
For every precious thing, every marvel, every deep secret
    and all glorious wisdom
is hidden within her, locked up in her treasure store;
by a hint, by a word . . . (Ramban)[27]

27. Jacob Newman, *The Commentary of Nachmanides on Genesis Chapters 1–6* (Leiden: E. J. Brill, 1960), 20.

A Note on the Text

Ail translations of excerpts from classic texts that appear within quotation marks have been supplied with permission by the following publishers:

The Babylonian Talmud: R. Dr. I. Epstein, *The Babylonian Talmud* (London, Jerusalem, New York: Soncino Press, date per volume).

JPS TANAKH. Excerpts from the JPS TANAKH, copyright 1985, reprinted by permission of The Jewish Publication Society.

The Midrash on Proverbs: Burton Visotzky, *The Midrash on Proverbs* (New Haven and London: Yale University Press, 1992).

The Midrash Rabbah: R. Dr. H. Freedman and Maurice Simon, *The Midrash Rabbah* (New York: Soncino Press, 1977).

Midrash Tanhuma: John T. Townsend, *Midrash Tanhuma— S. Buber Recension* (Hoboken, NJ: Ktav, 1989).

The Pentateuch and Haftorahs: Dr. J. H. Hertz, C. H., *The Pentateuch and Haftorahs: Hebrew Text, English Translation, and Commentary by the Late Chief Rabbi* (London: Soncino Press, 1956).

Pesikta Rabbati: William G. Braude, *Pesikta Rabbati* (New Haven and London: Yale University Press, 1968).

Pirke de Rabbi Eliezer: Gerald Friedlander, *Pirke de Rabbi Eliezer* (New York: Sepher-Hermon Press, 1981).

Ramban's Commentary: R. Charles b. Chavel, *Ramban—His Life and Teachings* (New York: Philipp Feldheim, Inc., 1960).

Rashi's Commentary: Rev. M. Rosenbaum and Dr. A. M. Silbermann, *Pentateuch with Rashi's Commentary, Genesis and Exodus* (New York: Hebrew Publishing Co., date per volume). Reprinted by permission of the Publishers, Hebrew Publishing Co., P.O. Box 930157, Rockaway Beach, NY 11693-0157. Copyright ©. All rights reserved.

The Zohar: Harry Sperling and Maurice Simon, *The Zohar* (London: Soncino Press, 1984).

All excerpts that do *not* appear within quotation marks express the author's rendition of these commentaries, the translations and meanings having been culled from multiple sources, both written and oral.

Twenty three Good Women in Israel
and nine belonging to other nations
are mentioned in the Bible;
the women of Israel are:

Sarah, Rebekah, Rachel, Leah, Jochebed, Miriam,
Deborah, the Wife of Manoah, Hannah,
Abigail, the Wise Woman of Tekoah,
the Widow Whom the Prophet Elijah Helped,
the Shunamite Woman, Huldah, Naomi, Jehosheba,
the Wife of One the Prophets whom Elisha helped,
Esther, the Five Daughters of Zelophehad.

Those of the other nations are:

Hagar, Osenath, Zipporah, Siphrah,
Puah, Bathya, the Daughter of Pharaoh,
Rahab, Ruth, Jael.
— Midrash Tadshe, 21

Seven prophetesses are named in the Bible:

Sarah, Miriam, Deborah, Hannah,
Abigail, Huldah, and Esther.

Among those women granted the power
of prophecy, most of our Sages also include:

Rebekah, Rachel, and Leah

I

The Women of the Five Books of Moses

Bereshith—the first of the Five Books of Moses, its Hebrew name taken from the first word of the text, "In the beginning."

Originally entitled Sefer Maaseh Bereshith, the Book of Creation, having been rendered into Greek as Genesis, meaning "origin."

Genesis, chapter 9, verses 18–19: "The sons of Noah who came out of the ark were Shem, Ham, and Japheth—Ham being the father of Canaan. These three were the sons of Noah, and from these the whole world branched out."

The sages tell us that ten generations had lapsed between the time of Adam and Eve and the birth of Noah, and that it took another ten generations before Abraham, a descendant of Shem and the man destined to be the first father of the Jewish people, breathed his first breath.

Our story begins some four thousand years ago in Mesopotamia, now part of Iraq—the northern part being inhabited by Assyrians, the southern part by Babylonians. We commence our inquiry into Rabbinic insight and commentary at the point in Scripture where the universal history of man gives way to the more directed focus of the history of the Israelites.

How ancient and far removed a world are we really entering? The rabbis tell us that everything, all the events that befell our forefathers and mothers were but a foreshadowing of the path ordained for their descendants. Tanchuma Lech Lecha

9: "Whatever has happened to the patriarchs is a sign to the children." How, then, and to what extent are our own individual beginnings, our individual and collective possibilities now echoing within the wishes, the prayers, the trials of these men and women who lived and died in lands so utterly, so deceptively, far away?

Sarah

The Book of Genesis, Chapter 11,
one of the four most beautiful women in the world
and one of the seven prophetesses.

"In all that Sarah says to thee, listen to her voice"

C hapter 11:27. Now these are the generations of Terach. Terach begot Abram, Nahor and Haran; and Haran begot Lot. 28. And Haran died in the presence of his father Terach in the land of his nativity, in Ur of the Chaldees. 29. And Abram and Nahor took to themselves wives: the name of Abram's wife was Sarai; and the name of Nahor's wife, Milcah, the daughter of Haran, the father of Milcah and the father of Yiscah. 30. And Sarai was barren; she had no child.

11:27 "Terach begot Abram."

Scripture tells us that our first forefather was born to a man named Terach, and the Talmudic sages (Talmud, *Baba Bathra* 91a) add that his mother was Terach's first wife, Amatlai. Tradition has it that the powerful King Nimrod, having been warned by his astrologers that a male child would one day grow to surpass him in power and greatness and would negate his idolatrous religion, ordered that all newborn boys be put to death. Amatlai hid her son in a cave, leaving him to God's mercy. When he emerged twenty days later, his reasoning enabled him to immediately grasp the meaning of God.

Numerous permutations of this legend exist, efforts to recount the unknown events filling the Patriarch's early years.

What does Scripture tell us about the woman destined to be our first matriarch, the partner of the individual whose very existence was a threat to the mightiest king of that generation? On the surface, no genealogy, whatsoever, seems to be provided. In fact, the first and only detail clearly provided in the text about this extraordinary woman (whose name will be changed six chapters hence, under God's instruction, to the more familiar form, Sarah) is that she is unable to bear children! So the quest for understanding begins.

11:29 ". . . the name of Abram's wife was Sarai; and the name of Nahor's wife, Milcah, the daughter of Haran, the father of Milcah and the father of Yiscah."

Haran, one of Abram's brothers, has two daughters, Milcah and Yiscah; Milcah marries Abram's other brother, Nahor. But who is Yiscah? The Rabbis believe that Yiscah is none other than Sarai herself.

The name Yiscah comes from the root *sakkah*, which means "to see" or "to look," and embodies two aspects of our first foremother, as a child, as well as an elderly woman—her ability to prophecy and her possession of an extraordinary beauty which drew everyone who passed her to look at her, to gaze.

TALMUD, SANHEDRIN 69b: Yiscah was Sarai, and why was she called Yiscah? Because she foresaw the future by holy [divine] inspiration."

TALMUD, *MEGILLAH* 14a: What is the meaning of divine inspiration? It is the ability to discern by means of the Holy Spirit.

RASHI: Whenever Abraham listens to "the voice of Sarah" in the Scriptural text, he is listening to the holy or prophetic spirit within her. We can even infer from an upcoming chapter wherein we witness Abraham's admonishment by God, "in all that Sarah says unto thee, listen to her voice" (21:12), that Sarah was even superior to Abraham in her powers of divination, her ability to discern correct action from wrong.

What's in a name? "A rose by any other name would smell as sweet." Perhaps so. But the Sages found evidence of Divine Providence in the names given to individuals and nations. The Kabbalists teach that all of creation was brought into being by various combinations of the holy Hebrew letters, and that every living thing is sustained purely by virtue of its holy name. The Baal Shem Tov, the founder of Hasidism, expounds that through its name the very essence of a person or thing can be discerned. "And out of the ground the Lord God formed every beast of the field and every fowl of the air, and brought them unto the man to see what he would call them" (Genesis 2:19). Although names are given by people, the rabbis felt that it is always the Divine which causes the correct name to be chosen.

The sages thus made a study of the analysis of given names as a key to uncovering and understanding the nature and task assigned to individuals and groups. The Maharal of Prague states that when a parent names a child, it is a prophecy.

Naamah was Noah's wife. Why, ask the Rabbis, was she called Naamah? Because her deeds were pleasant (naamah) (Genesis Rabbah 23:3). Ramban further teaches that she was well known in her generation because of her righteousness and the righteousness of her offspring. Lot's wife, who meets her death, her transformation into a pillar of salt, by disobeying Divine command and looking back over her shoulder at the destruction of her home in Sodom, was named Edith, meaning "witness."

Likewise, of tremendous significance in Scripture is the event where an individual undergoes a sudden name change, whether initiated by man, by an angel, or by God. As we move through Scripture we will study the divinely ordained names that our ancestors bear, and the meanings that they carry within like invisible flags.

Chapter 11:31. And Terach took his son Abram, his grandson, Lot, the son of Haran, and his daughter-in-law Sarai, the wife of his son Abram, and they set out together from Ur of the Chaldees to go into the land of Canaan; but when they had come as far as Haran, they settled there. . . . Chapter 12:1. Now the Lord said unto Abram, "Get thee out of thy country, and from thy kindred and from thy father's house unto the land that I will show thee. 2. And I will make of thee a great nation, and I will bless thee and make thy name great. . . . 5. And Abram took Sarai his wife and Lot his brother's son, and all their substance that they had gathered and the souls that they had made in Haran; and they went forth to go into the land of Canaan, and into the land of Canaan they came.

12:1 "Get thee out of thy country."

RASHI ON THE TANHUMA: The literal translation of "get thee out" is "go for thyself," meaning that Abram should leave his father's home for his own good. "There I will make of you a great nation, whilst here you will not merit the privilege of having children. Furthermore, I shall make known your character throughout the world."

GENESIS RABBAH 39: Traveling at that time held three disadvantages—it broke up family life, reduced one's wealth, and lessened one's renown. To willingly uproot his family, Abram required three blessings, three promises: the promise of children, wealth, and a respected name.

But at the time that Abram leaves Haran with his lovely wife, she is already well past middle age, and this alluring promise of children is, of course, underscored by the bare fact of Sarai's infertility.

12:5 "And Abram took Sarai . . . and the souls they had made in Haran.

This verse is taken by some Kabbalists to refer to Abram's ability to actually create life, reminiscent of later accounts and legends attesting to the creation of a "golem." These commentators go on to explain that the plural, "they made," shows us that Abram intentionally avoided working alone, like God, but worked together with Shem who taught Abram the even earlier mysteries. (The oldest of all the existent Kabbalistic texts is the Sefer Yetzirah, the Book of Creation, which includes extensive teachings on the mystery and significance of the Hebrew letters, and according to Rabbi Aryeh Kaplan, appears to be a meditative instruction manual designed to increase the initiate's powers of concentration and thus lead him into realms where powers outside the natural order are contacted and developed. The Zohar attributes the teachings to Abraham himself.)

During the Talmudic period, some Sages rejected the usefulness of the esoteric mysteries. The head of the academy in Tiberius after Rabbi Yochanan's death was a Rabbi Elazar ben Padat. He responds to the literal exegesis of verse 12:5.

PESIKTA RABBATI 43 AND GENESIS RABBAH 39:14: "If all the inhabitants of the world should undertake to create a single gnat they would be unable to do so therefore how can you speak of 'the soul that they had made in Haran'? Is it conceivable that Abraham and Sarah created souls?" According to the Midrash on Psalms 3:2, R. Elazar was not rejecting the idea of these supernatural possibilities, rather, he felt that the keys were lost and buried within the Torah, that the paragraphs of the Torah are not in their correct order. If they were, anyone who read them would be able "to create a world, resurrect the dead, and perform miracles." So why doesn't Scripture therefore simply use the word *converted* as opposed to the oblique phrase *had made*? R. Padat explains that Scripture is teaching us that bringing a pagan close to God is akin to creating him. Why then does Scripture state that "they" had made, as opposed to that "he" had made? R. Hunia explains that both man and wife were equally involved in this spiritual endeavor; that Abram converted the men to the faith in one God, and Sarai converted the women. "It was by their conversion of men and women that Abram and Sarai are said to have created souls—brought them in under the wings of the Presence."

> *When the Chasidic Rabbi of Zans and his young son paid a visit to the Rabbi of Belz, they found the Rabbi and his wife quietly sitting at a simple table in a bare white room. Rabbi Zan's son later said that, to him, the pious pair appeared to be the embodiment of Adam and Eve before the Fall. . . . And what of that meager room? It looked like Paradise.*[28]

Chapter 12:10. There was a famine in the land, and

---

28. Martin Buber, "Adam and Eve", *Tales of the Hasidim. The Later Masters* (New York: Schocken Books, 1975), p. 207.

Abram went down to Egypt to sojourn there, for the famine was severe in the land. 11. And it came to pass, when he was come near to enter into Egypt, that he said unto Sarai his wife, "Behold, now I know that thou art a fair woman to look upon. 12. And it will come to pass, when the Egyptians will see thee, that they will say: This is his wife; and they will kill me, but thee they will keep alive. 13. Say, I pray thee, thou art my sister; that it may be well with me for thy sake, and that my soul may live because of thee." 14. And it came to pass, that when Abram was come into Egypt, the Egyptians beheld the woman that she was very fair. 15. And the princes of Pharoah saw her and praised her to Pharoah, and the woman was taken into Pharoah's house. 16. And he dealt well with Abram for her sake; and he had sheep and oxen and he-asses and men-servants and maid-servants and she-asses and camels. 17. And the Lord plagued Pharoah and his house with great plagues because of Sarai, Abram's wife. 18. And Pharoah called Abram and said, "What is this that thou hast done to me? Why didst thou not tell me that she was thy wife? 19. Why saidst thou: 'she is my sister?', so that I took her to be my wife; now therefore behold thy wife, take her, and go thy way." 20. And Pharoah gave men charge concerning him, and they brought him on the way, and his wife, and all that he had.

We have here the very first portion of Scriptural text wherein Sarai plays a central role. The peculiar incident narrated here is not unique within the Book of Genesis. It will recur in chapter 20, involving Sarai and Abram and a different monarch, and it will repeat itself, yet again, with Isaac and Rebekah.

The rabbis have two questions. Why does Abram suddenly comment after so many years of marriage on his wife's beauty, and how is the peculiar lie he requests that she go along with, to be understood? In analyzing Sarai's other appellation, Yiscah, we found that one of the meanings of its root, *sakkah*, is "to look" or "gaze," and Sarai was so-named because everybody gazed at her beauty, which even into old age never left her.

GENESIS RABBAH 40:4, ZOHAR I 81b: Abram suddenly comments on Sarai's fair looks because due to the extreme modesty ruling their intercourse, he never fully realized the extent of her beauty. In addition, despite the physical exertion and drain of traveling, Sarai unexpectedly retained her radiant grace.

What of the wife-sister motif? Documents excavated from the town of Nuzi, which was located in Mesopotamia and culturally associated with Haran, the neighboring birthplace of Abram, reveal the existence of an institution described as wife-sistership. This title afforded the bearer higher social status and superior privileges and protections than would be granted an ordinary wife. What are the meaning and implications of this incident aside from its most external explanation?

ZOHAR I 81b–82a: Abram "saw with her the Shekhinah [the Holy Spirit]. It was on this account that Abram made bold to say subsequently, 'she is my sister,' with a double meaning: one the literal, the other figurative, as in the words 'Say to Wisdom, Thou art my sister' (Proverbs 7:4). Abram knew that all the Egyptians were full of lewdness. It may therefore seem surprising that he was not apprehensive for his wife, and that he did not turn back without entering the country. But the truth is that he saw with her the Shekhinah and was therefore confident. 'That it may be well with me for thy sake': These words were addressed to the Shekhinah."

The Shekhinah represents the female forces of Providence, the Holy Spirit, the Divine Presence when it manifests on Earth. She is said to have been present when the ten commandments were given at Mount Sinai. She dwelled within the holy Temple in Jerusalem and is said to visit or rest upon a man or woman who is experiencing prophetic revelation. She is sometimes called Sister, sometimes Daughter, sometimes Bride or Queen. She is the daughter of the Divine emanations of Wisdom and Understanding, the sister and bride of the male forces that feed her.

The Kabbalists describe five universes, each lower one a reflection of the one above it, each further removed from God's source, each universe an additional garment for His overwhelming light. Our physical universe is contained within the lowest of these worlds, so man finds himself in a position of struggle and difficulty in his efforts to find God, hidden within the mundane.

Each universe is patterned on a structure called the Tree of Life, a representation of God's ten Divine emanations, the ten sefirot or vessels, all capable of holding God's light and transmitting it.

In the system of Kabbalah, the second Divine emanation or sefira, Chochmah-Wisdom, is personified as the Father, Abba. The third sefira, Binah-Understanding, is personified as the Supernal Mother, Imma. When they unite, the Mother bears six sons and one daughter. The six sons are the next six sefirot, collectively called the Small Face, Zer Anpin. The final sefira, Malkhut-Kingship, is the female, Nukva, of Zer Anpin. She is also Zer Anpin's bride. Zer Anpin and Nukva are therefore brother and sister, but eventually, they become bride and groom as well.

For harmony to reign in the universe of the Sefirot and to enable blessings to flow down to man, the six sefirot of Zer Anpin must unite with Malkhut. This level of attachment, wherein brother and sister become man and wife, represents the highest level of union attainable in the supernal universe of the Divine emanations. Due to its extreme holiness, the Torah strictly forbids it among human beings. It is this sacred relationship that the two patriarchs allude to when they call their wives, "sister," thereby indicating that their own earthly marriages are structured spiritually on the pattern of the supernal one.

> *"The righteous shall flourish like the palm tree..."* *(Psalms 92:13). Rabbi Isaac asked: Why is the righteous man compared to a palm tree? If a palm tree is cut down, it takes a very long time for one to again grow; if the world loses a righteous man, it takes a long time before another arises to take his place. And just as a palm tree does not grow unless the male is accompanied by the female, so, too, the righteous can flourish only when they are male and female together, like Abram and Sarai. (Zohar I: 82a)*

12:14 "And it came to pass that when Abram was come into Egypt..."

But where was Sarai?

GENESIS RABBAH 40:5: Abram had hidden her inside a locked box. When they arrived at the customs house, the officer demanded that he pay the customs dues, and Abram willingly agreed to. "'You carry garments in that box,' said he. 'I will pay the dues on garments.' 'You are carrying silks,' he asserted. 'I will pay on silks.' 'You are carrying precious stones.'

'I will pay on precious stones.' 'It is imperative that you open it and we see what it contains,' he insisted. As soon as he opened it, the land of Egypt was irradiated with her lustre."

ZOHAR I:82a: "When it was opened, a light like that of the sun shone forth."

GENESIS RABBAH 40:5: It is taught that Eve's image is transmitted to the beauties of each generation, serving as a standard by which Beauty, itself, is measured. But not only did Sarai attain to Eve's divine beauty, she even surpassed it. . . . After opening the box, Pharoah's princes proceed to outbid one another to gain possession of the woman, but when Pharoah is apprised of Sarai, she is brought into his palace to become one of his wives.

ZOHAR I:82a: "Assuredly God is a shield to the righteous to save them from falling into the power of men, and so God shielded Abram that the Egyptians should not have power to harm him and his wife. For the Shekhinah did not leave Sarai all that night."

GENESIS RABBAH 51:2: "And the whole of that night, Sarai lay prostrate on her face, crying: 'Sovereign of the Universe! Abraham went forth (from his land) on Thine assurance, and I went forth with faith; Abraham is without this prison, while I am within!' Said the Holy One, blessed be He, to her: 'Whatever I do, I do for thy sake, and all will say—It is because of Sarai, Abram's wife . . .'

The whole of that night an angel stood with a whip in his hand; when she ordered, 'Strike,' he struck, and when she ordered 'Desist,' he desisted. And why such severity? Because she told him: 'I am a married woman,' yet he would not leave her."

12:16 "And he dealt well with Abram for her sake."

The Hebrew phrase meaning, "for the sake of" Sarai or "because of" Sarai can also be translated "by the word of" Sarai, which is how the rabbis derive their midrashim regarding both her urgent prayer to God and her words with the angel. This entire incident emphasizes how everything repeatedly revolves around Sarai, how all the blessings and all the interventions were granted not for Abram's sake, but for his wife's.

TALMUD, *BABA METZIA* 59a: Blessings dwell in a man's house only on account of his wife. In Egypt, Pharoah lavished gifts on Abram even before the truth of their marital relationship was revealed.

12:17 "And the Lord plagued Pharoah and his house with great plagues, because of Sarai."

RAMBAN ON GENESIS 12:10: Every event which befalls the Patriarchs will subsequently befall their children. Abram goes down to Egypt on account of famine and drought, but the Egyptians, without cause, oppress him by taking his wife. God avenges this act by afflicting the House of Pharoah with plagues, but the ruler responds by sending Abram and Sarai away with all sorts of gifts! Abram thus learns that one day his descendants would travel to Egypt on account of famine, they would be persecuted, their woman would be forcibly taken from them, and God, as He did now, would avenge them with plagues. Released from bondage, they would carry away with them all variety of riches.

PIRKE DE RABBI ELIEZER, CHAPTER 26: "In that night, when our mother Sarah was taken, it was Passover night...."

ZOHAR 1:82a: "Woe to the sinners of the world who do not know and do not observe the work of the Holy One, blessed be He, nor do they reflect that all which takes place in the world is from God, who knows from the outset what will be at the end. . . . He looks ahead and lays a train now for developments in the distant future. Thus had not Sarai been taken to Pharoah, he would not have been plagued, and it was his castigation which caused the subsequent castigation of the Egyptians. The word 'great' is applied here to the plagues inflicted on Pharoah and also to the 'signs and wonders which God showered upon Egypt,' to indicate that here, as there, were ten plagues, and that just as God performed wonders for Israel by night, so He performed wonders for Sarai by night."

ZOHAR I:82b: "At midnight, all the truly righteous arise to read the Torah and to sing psalms, and we have learnt that the Holy One, blessed be He, and all the righteous in the Garden of Eden listen to their voices, and in consequence a certain grace is imparted to them by day. . . . Hence it is that the praises which are sung at night constitute the most perfect praise. So when God was slaying the firstborn in Egypt, the Israelites in their houses were singing praises and psalms to Him. See now, King David used to get up in the middle of the night. . . . He did not remain sitting or lying in his bed, but he literally rose and stood up to compose psalms and praises. . . .

In the night when Sarai was with Pharoah, the angels came to sing praises before God, but God said to them, 'Go all of you, and deal heavy blows on Egypt, in anticipation of what I intend to do subsequently.' "

GENESIS RABBAH 41:2: Pharoah and his entire household contracted leprosy; "even the beams of his house were smitten."

PIRKE DE RABBI ELIEZER, CHAPTER 26: Despite these afflictions, Pharoah gave Sarai silver, man-servants, and the land of Goshen for a possession. It is for this reason that the children of Israel lived in the land of Goshen—it was the land of their mother.

GENESIS RABBAH 45:1: Pharoah was so awed by the miracles that had been done on Sarai's behalf, that when he sent her off, he also gave her his own daughter as a handmaid, declaring that it would be better for his daughter to be a maid in Abram's house than to be a mistress in another's. His daughter's name was Hagar.

Chapter 15:1. After these things, the word of the Lord came unto Abram in a vision, saying, "Fear not, Abram, I am thy shield, thy reward shall be exceedingly great." 2. And Abram said, "Oh Lord God, what wilt Thou give me seeing I go childless, and he that shall be possessor of my house is Eliezer of Damascus?" 3. And Abram said, "Behold, to me Thou hast given no seed, and lo, one born in my house is to be mine heir." 4. And behold, the words of the Lord came unto him, saying, "This man shall not be thine heir, but he that shall come forth out of thine own bowels shall be thine heir." 5. And He brought him forth abroad and said, "Look now toward Heaven and count the stars, if thou be able to count them." And He said unto him, "So shall thy seed be." 6. And he believed in the Lord. . . .

15:2 "God, what wilt Thou give me, seeing I go childless?"

Why did I bother leaving my homeland, Abram bemoans, for what purpose did I listen to You, if, in the end, I have no heir?

TALMUD, *SHABBAT* 156a: Abram was a proficient, influential astrologer in his day, and through his consultation with the stars, he believed himself to be unfit to bear a child. In response to Abram's anxious conclusion, God admonishes him not to be overly dependent on his astrological predictions, on what he thinks he knows so well.

RASHI ON 15:5: According to the literal meaning of the text, Abram is brought outside and instructed to look up at the stars, but God is actually reprimanding him: "Go forth from (give up) your astrological speculations that you have seen by the planets that you will not raise a son; Abram indeed may have no son, but ABRAHAM will have a son; Sarai may not bear a child, But SARAH will bear. I will give you other names, and your destiny [*mazel* meaning both "planet" and "luck"] will be changed." Scripture has chosen to use a very specific form of the Hebrew word for *look*, "habet," within the phrase, "look now toward heaven." This word signifies the act of looking down from above, suggesting that God brought Abram up, out of the terrestrial sphere, and elevated him above the stars.

The Kabbalists teach that the righteous, through prayer, can transcend the destiny predetermined by the constellation of birth.

Chapter 16:1. Now Sarai, Abram's wife, bore him no children; and she had a handmaid, an Egyptian, whose name was Hagar. 2. And Sarai said unto Abram, "Behold, now, the Lord hath restrained me from bearing; go in, I pray thee, unto my handmaid; it may be that I shall be builded up through her." And Abram hearkened unto the voice of Sarai. 3. And Sarai, Abram's wife, took Hagar the Egyptian, her handmaid, after Abram had dwelt ten years in the land of Canaan, and gave her to

Abram, her husband, to be his wife. 4. And he went in unto Hagar, and she conceived; and when she saw that she had conceived, her mistress was despised in her eyes. 5. And Sarai said unto Abram, "My wrong be upon thee: I gave my handmaid unto thy bosom, and when she saw that she had conceived, I was despised in her eyes. The Lord judge between me and thee." 6. And Abram said to Sarai, "Behold, thy maid is in thy hand; do to her that which is good in thine eyes." And Sarai dealt harshly with her, and she fled from her face.

16:1 "Now Sarai, Abram's wife, bore him no children."

First Sarah, then Rebekah, and after her, Rachel, three of the four matriarchs, all grieving for a child. But why? "Give me children, or else I die!" Rachel will cry out to her husband, Jacob. Why were the matriarchs barren? What meaning, what Divine purpose, if any?

GENESIS RABBAH 45:4: Their infertility was their only lack; the matriarchs possessed beauty and they possessed wealth. It was their desire for a child which forced them to remain in close partnership with their husbands, "to lean" on them, which would not have been the case had they been granted children early on.

But some of our rabbis had quite a different insight. They said that the affliction with barrenness is what, in fact, led our matriarchs closer to God, teaching them to turn upward for sustenance, and thereby allowing God to receive that which He, too, wants. "Why were the matriarchs barren? . . . Because the Holy One, blessed be He, yearns for their prayers and supplications. . . . Why did I make thee barren? 'Let Me see thy countenance, let Me hear thy voice' " (Song of Songs 2:14).

16:2 "Go in, I pray thee, unto my handmaid; it may be that I shall be builded up through her."

RASHI: "Builded up"? Sarah's words teach that "a person who has no children is not firmly established (literally built up: his name and future are not perpetuated) but is unstable (literally demolished).

16:3 "And Sarai took . . . her handmaid, and gave her to Abram . . . to be his wife."

GENESIS RABBAH 45:3 AND RAMBAN: Hagar is not being handed over to Abram merely as a concubine, but as another wife, highlighting the respect Sarai always demonstrated toward her husband. Although presenting a handmaid to one's husband was legal acceptable behavior at that time, Sarai voluntarily granted to Hagar all the rights and privileges of a full-fledged wife.

GENESIS RABBAH 45:3: In addition, Sarai persuades Hagar to go to her husband with a willing heart; she is, after all, going to be united with a very holy man.

16:4 ". . . and when she saw that she had conceived, her mistress was despised in her eyes."

GENESIS RABBAH 45:4: Hagar conceives after the first intimacy with Abram, but she responds to the blessing with slander and hatred. Whenever Hagar received visitors, she would say to them that her mistress Sarai was not what she seemed to be, that her appearance of righteousness was an illusion. The proof?: I conceived in only one night; all those years with Abram, and still she hasn't conceived!

Anticipating the miraculous birth of Isaac to Sarai, R.

Hanina b. Pazzi counters Hagar's hateful sentiments: "Thorns are neither weeded nor sewn, yet of their own accord they grow and spring up, whereas how much pain and toil is required before wheat can be made to grow!"

16:5 "And Sarai said unto Abram, "My wrong be upon thee."

GENESIS RABBAH 45:5: Sarai chooses not to argue directly with Hagar, but instead turns to her husband for assistance in the matter. The phrase, "my wrong"/"hamassi," literally means "what is stolen from me." Sarai is accusing her husband of remaining silent on her behalf, and thereby "robbing" her of the protective words he should have spoken.

In the previous chapter, Abram questioned God, "What wilt Thou give me, seeing I go hence childless?" The rabbis here give Sarai an opportunity to voice her opinion about her husband's exchange with the Lord, implicating it as the very source of the problem at hand. "I have a grievance against thee [Abram]. For imagine two men incarcerated in prison, and as the king passes, one of them cries out, 'Execute justice for me!' The king orders him to be released, whereupon his fellow prisoner says to him, 'I have a grievance against you, for had you said, 'Execute justice for US,' he would have released me, just as he released you; but now that you said, 'Execute justice for ME,' he released you, but not me. Similarly, hadst thou said, 'WE go childless,' then as He gave thee a child, so would He have given me; since however thou saidst, 'And I go childless,' He gave thee a child but not me."

16:5 "The Lord judge between me and thee."

TALMUD, *BABA KAMA* 93a: "Woe to him who cries for

Divine intervention, even more than to him against whom it is invoked! . . . Punishment is meted out first to the one who cries, and is more severe than for the one against whom justice is invoked."

GENESIS RABBAH 45:5: Our foremother, Sarai, was destined to live to the age of one hundred seventy-five, just like her husband Abram, but because of her undue cry for justice, forty-eight years were taken from her life.

16:6 "Do to her that which is good in thine eyes."

GENESIS RABBAH 45:6: Hagar is now Abram's wife, therefore he takes no actions that would harm her, but because of her slanderous words against Sarai, neither does he do anything to help her. He allows Sarai to do with her what she will, and the rabbis tell us that Sarai responded to the situation by requiring Hagar to do work demeaning and unsuited to her new, higher status.

RAMBAN: Both Abram and Sarai were guilty parties in this incident, and as an act of Divine retribution, God will hear Hagar's affliction and will grant her a son, "a wild ass of a man," (Genesis 16:12), forever destined to plague the descendants of Abram and Sarai with all manner of torments.

Chapter 16:7. And the angel of the Lord found her by a fountain of water in the wilderness, by the fountain in the way to Shur. 8. And he said, "Hagar, Sarai's handmaid, whence camest thou, and whither goest thou?" And she said, "I flee from the face of my mistress Sarai." 9. And the angel of the Lord said unto her, "Return to thy mistress, and submit thyself under her hands." 10. And the angel of the Lord said unto her, "I will greatly multiply thy seed, that it shall not be num-bered for multitude." 11. And the angel of the Lord said unto her, "Behold, thou art with child, and shalt bear a son; and thou shalt call his name "Ishmael," because the Lord hath heard thy affliction. 12. And he shall be a wild ass of a man: his hand shall be against every man, and every man's hand against him; and he shall dwell in the face of all his brethren." 13. And she called the name of the Lord that spoke unto her, Thou art a God of Seeing; for she said, "Have I even here seen Him that seeth me?" 14. Therefore the well was called Beer-lahai-roi; behold, it is between Kadesh and Bered. 15. And Hagar bore Abram a son; and Abram called the name of his son, whom Hagar bore, Ishmael. 16. And Abram was fourscore and six years old, when Hagar bore Ishmael to Abram.

GENESIS RABBAH 45:7: "If one man tells you that you have ass's ears, do not believe him; if two tell it to you, order a halter." Despite the higher status that Hagar was previously awarded, she is consistently referred to in Scripture as Sarai's handmaid. Abram says, "Behold, thy *maid* is in thy hand"; the angel, here, addresses her as "Hagar, Sarai's *handmaid*, and Hagar, in turn, acquiesces with this viewpoint regarding her true status by responding to the angel's question with, "I flee from the face of my *mistress* Sarai."

Hagar has wandered toward the fortification that shielded the Eastern border of Egypt from raiding bedouins, being drawn, the rabbis say, back to her native land. At this point, the text relates that an angel appears to her, directing her to return to Sarai and Abram.

GENESIS RABBAH 45:7: How many angels appeared to the lost handmaid? At least four or five . . . "Come and see how great is the difference between the earlier generations and the later ones!" When an angel appeared to Manoah and his wife, foretelling the birth of their son, Samson (Judges 13:22), Manoah responds with tremendous fear, "We shall surely die, because we have seen God!" On the other hand Hagar, a mere handmaid, sees four or five angels and completely lacks any trepidation!

RASHI: Abram's household consisted of seers, and Hagar's lack of fear stemmed from having seen Divine messengers quite regularly while living there!

GENESIS RABBAH 45:10: Hagar expresses gratefulness for being permitted to see angels, even now, when all alone.

The angel instructs her to name the forthcoming child Ishmael, which means, "God hears," signifying God's attentiveness to her plight.

GENESIS RABBAH 45:8: Only three other children in the entire Bible were given names before they were actually born: Isaac (Gen. 17:19), Solomon (I Chron. 22:9), and Josiah (I Kings 13:2).

RASHI ON 16:15: Abram was not with Hagar when the angel spoke to her, yet, it is written that Abram, himself, gave the child the preordained name. ". . . the Holy Spirit rested upon him [Abram], and he called him Ishmael."

PIRKE DE RABBI ELIEZER, CHAPTER 32: "Why was his name called Ishmael ['God will hear']? Because in the future the Holy One, Blessed be He, will hearken to the cry of the people arising from the oppression which the children of Ishmael will bring about in the land in the last days [before the coming of the Messiah]."

Chapter 17:1. And when Abram was ninety years old and nine, the Lord appeared to Abram, and said unto him, "I am God Almighty (El Shaddai); walk before Me, and be thou whole-hearted. 2. And I will make My covenant between Me and thee, and will multiply thee exceedingly." 3. And Abram fell on his face; and God talked with him, saying: 4. "As for Me, behold, My covenant is with thee, and thou shalt be the father of a multitude of nations. 5. Neither shall thy name any more be called Abram, but thy name shall be Abraham; for the father of a multitude of nations have I made thee. 6. And I will make thee exceeding fruitful, and I will make nations of thee, and kings shall come out of thee . . ." 15. And God said unto Abraham, "As for Sarai thy wife, thou shalt not call her name Sarai, but Sarah shall her name be. 16. And I will bless her, and moreover I will give thee a son of her; yea, I will bless her, and she shall be a mother of nations; kings of peoples shall be of her."

Back in chapters 12 and 15, God promised Abram that he would ultimately bless him with heirs and with greatness. Here, in chapter 17, God finally seals his covenant with Abram and demonstrates the embarkation upon this new phase of Divine relationship by revoking the birthname of the patriarch and that of his wife. Abram becomes Abraham; Sarai is amended to Sarah. Sarai is, in fact, the only woman in the Torah to have her name directly altered by God.

Sarai means "my princess" as in "a princess to me, and not to others," *Sarah*, the rabbis tell us, is a more comprehensive form of the regal name.

TALMUD, *BERAKHOT* 13a: "At first she became a princess to her own people, but later she became a princess to all the world."

Throughout the text of Genesis and the commentaries of the rabbis, we are repeatedly shown how Abraham, our key figure, takes a subordinate position in relation to his wife. When in the custody of Pharoah, God responds to Sarah's prayers with, "Whatever I do, I do for *thy* sake, and all will say, "it is because of Sarai, Abram's wife" (Genesis Rabbah 41:2). Scripture, itself makes a point of saying that Pharoah "dealt well with Abram for HER sake" (Genesis 12:16). The rabbis note that Sarah always held sway over Abraham: "In all that Sarah says to thee, listen to her voice" (21:12).

GENESIS RABBAH 47:1: "A virtuous woman is a crown to her husband" (Proverbs 12:4). Who else is this a description of but Sarah? asks Rabbi Aha. "Her husband was crowned through her, but she was not crowned through her husband," he declares. What does the rabbi mean by his bold and seemingly one-sided assertion? He is making use of the principle of gematria. The name Sarai, which ends with the Hebrew letter *yud* and has a value of ten, was changed to Sarah, which ends with the letter *heh* and has a value of five. God took the *yud* he removed from Sarai and divided it into two *heh*'s, two five's. One *heh* was given to Sarai, turning her name into Sarah; the other *heh* was given to Abram, turning his name into Abraham. It is only *after* God changes the patriarch's name that He says to him, "For the father of a multitude of nations have I made thee." It was thus, through Sarah, (through the *yud* previously in her name), that Abraham was "crowned," exalted and honored!

> *A man who loves his wife as himself, and honors her more than himself—to him the Scriptural promise is pronounced: "Thou shalt know that thy tent is in peace" (Job 5:24). (Talmud, Yebamot 62b).*

17:16 "And I will bless her."

RASHI: God's blessing to Sarah was that she would once again become youthful; she would experience a rejuvenation.

ARYEH KAPLAN, NOTES ON THE BAHIR: "The word *berakhah* (blessing) is closely related to the word *berekh*, meaning 'knee.' Just as bending the knee lowers the body, so the concept of berakhah lowers God's essence so that He can relate to the universe and be comprehended through His acts. . . .

An important concept here, which shall be encountered many times, is the Kabbalistic idea that before there is an 'awakening from on high,' there must first be an 'awakening from below.' That is, before any spiritual sustenance is granted, there must first be some effort on the part of the recipient . . . The word 'blessing' primarily refers to sustenance given as a result of an 'awakening from below . . .' "[29]

RAMBAN ON GENESIS 17:1: According to the mystics, there are seventy two different names for God. Why is God referred to as "El Shaddai" in the first verse of the current chapter? Ramban teaches that it is with this particular Divine Name that miracles are performed for the righteous, "hidden miracles," miracles that appear to be consistent with the laws of nature, but are nonetheless the result of prayer and upright behavior. God now assures Abraham that He will override his ruling constellation of birth and will grant him a son.

Chapter 17:17. Then Abraham fell upon his face, and

---

29. Aryeh Kaplan, *The Bahir* (York Beach, ME: Samuel Weiser, 1979), 91–92.

laughed, and said in his heart, "Shall a child be born unto him that is a hundred years old? And shall Sarah, that is ninety years old, bear?" 18. And Abraham said unto God, "Oh that Ishmael might live before Thee!" 19. And God said, "Nay, but Sarah thy wife shall bear thee a son; and thou shalt call his name Isaac; and I will establish My covenant with him for an everlasting covenant for his seed after him. 20. And as for Ishmael, I have heard thee; behold, I have blessed him, and will make him fruitful, and will multiply him exceedingly; twelve princes shall he beget, and I will make him a great nation. 21. But My covenant will I establish with Isaac, whom Sarah shall bear unto thee at this set time in the next year." 22. And he left off talking with him, and God went up from Abraham.

17:18 "Oh that Ishmael might live . . ."

GENESIS RABBAH 47:4: "Imagine a king who wished to increase his friend's allowance: 'I intend to double your allowance,' the king informed him. 'Do not fill me with a false hope,' he rejoined, 'pray only that you do not withhold my present allowance!' "—Allow Ishmael to live, and I will not wish for another son!

RASHI ON 17:17: Abraham is not expressing doubt at the possibility of God granting him and his wife the impossible, but he is, rather, questioning their worthiness. It was not unusual, says Rashi, for previous generations to beget at the age of even five hundred years, but by Abraham and Sarah's day, "the length of life had already become shorter and a diminution of strength had come upon people."

Chapter 18:1. And the Lord appeared unto him by the

terebinths of Mamre, as he sat in the tent door in the heat of the day; 2. and he lifted up his eyes and looked, and behold, three men stood over against him; and when he saw them, he ran to meet them from the tent door, and bowed down to the earth, 3. and said, "My lord, if now I have found favor in thy sight, pass not away, I pray thee, from thy servant . . . 6. And Abraham hastened into the tent unto Sarah, and said, "Make ready quickly three measure of fine meal, knead it, and make cakes." 7. And Abraham ran unto the herd, and fetched a calf tender and good, and gave it unto the servant; and he hastened to dress it. 8. And he took curd, and milk, and the calf which he had dressed, and set it before them; and he stood by them under the tree, and they did eat. 9. And they said unto him, "Where is Sarah thy wife?" And he said, "Behold, in the tent." 10. And He said, "I will certainly return unto thee when the season cometh round; and, lo, Sarah thy wife shall have a son." And Sarah heard in the tent door, which was behind him. 11. Now Abraham and Sarah were old, and well stricken in age; it had ceased to be with Sarah after the manner of women. 12. And Sarah laughed within herself, saying, "After I am waxed old shall I have pleasure, my lord being old also?" 13. And the Lord said unto Abraham, "Wherefore did Sarah laugh, saying, Shall I in truth bear a child, who am old? 14. Is anything too hard for the Lord? At the set time I will return unto thee, when the season cometh round, and Sarah shall have a son" 15. Then Sarah denied, saying, "I laughed not"; for she was afraid. And He said, "Nay; but thou didst laugh." 16. And the men rose up from thence, and looked out toward Sodom. . . .

18:2 ". . . And behold, three men stood over him."

ZOHAR I:100b–101b: "When Abraham was still suffering from the effects of the circumcision [Gen. 17:10 'This is My covenant between Me and you and thy seed after thee: every male among you shall be circumcised.'], the Holy One sent him three angels, in visible shape, to inquire of his well-being. You may perhaps wonder how angels can ever be visible . . . Abraham, however, assuredly did see them, as they descended to earth in the form of men. And, indeed, whenever the celestial spirits descend to earth, they clothe themselves in corporeal elements and appear to men in human shape. Now Abraham, although he was in great pain from his wound, ran forward to meet them so as not to be remiss in his wonted hospitality. R. Simeon said: 'Assuredly he saw them in their angelic forms, since it is written: And he said, Adonai, [my Lord] which shows that the Shekhinah had come with them [the Shekhinah, the Holy Spirit, is often addressed by that Divine Name], and that the angels accompanied her as her throne and pillars . . . and Abraham, now that he was circumcised, saw what he could not see before.' At first he took them for men, but afterwards he became aware that they were holy angels who had been sent on a mission to him."

RAMBAN ON GENESIS 18:1: The human senses are not able to perceive the angels, therefore, whenever an angel is described as being heard or seen in Scripture, it is by virtue of a vision or a dream and is referred to by our Sages as an "opening of the eyes." Furthermore, these visions are not an indication that the individual has achieved the level of a prophet. Ramban goes on to remind us that Hagar, for example, is not included in the Talmud's list of prophetesses, although Scripture records her episode with an angel in the desert. On the other hand, when Scripture refers to the angels as "men," these angels have been clothed in a special holy "garment," and can be perceived only by those men and women who have achieved a certain degree of piety.

GENESIS RABBAH 50:2: And behold, three men . . . "One angel does not perform two missions, nor do two angels together perform one mission."

RASHI: Three angels—"one to announce to Sarah the birth of a son, one of overthrow Sodom, and one to cure Abraham."

GENESIS RABBAH 50:2: Three angels—Michael was the bearer of good news for Abraham, Gabriel was sent to destroy Sodom, and Rafael's mission was to rescue Lot, Abraham's nephew who lived with his family in the condemned city.

> *The angel, Michael, is related to the sefirah of Chesed-Love. His name Mi Kael, literally means "Who is like El?" [El being the Divine name associated with the Divine Emanation of Love.] Gabriel is related to the sefirah of Gevurah-Strength. His name, Gavri El, means "the strength of God." He is the angel of Justice, the restraint of love. The angels, with their very names, proclaim that the source of their power lies not within themselves, but stems from God.*

18:9 "And they said unto him, 'where is Sarah, thy wife?' "

ZOHAR I:101b–102a: "Did not the celestial angels know that she was in the tent? The fact is that angels do not know of happenings in this world save what is necessary for their mission. From the angels one can hide himself, but not from God. The angel asked, 'Where is Sarah, thy wife?'. . ."

If we look carefully, we'll notice that sometimes in Scripture small dots have been placed right above certain letters within certain words—notations which do nothing to alter the pronunciation or external meaning. The sages explain that when they appear, these dots offer additional interpretive clues.

GENESIS RABBAH 48:15: If the number of dotted letters within a word exceeds the number of ordinary (plain) letters, it is the dotted ones that are placed together and interpreted as a word, and vice versa if the number of plain letters exceeds the dotted ones. In verse 28:9, 'and they said unto him, where is Sarah,' the dotted letters in the word meaning "unto him" exceed the plain, and thus only the dotted letters are grouped and interpreted.

ZOHAR I:101b: In the word meaning "unto him"/"elav," spelled "aleph," "lamed," "yud," "vav," there are dots over the letters "aleph," "yud," and "vav," which surprisingly spell the word *ayo*, "where is he," as opposed to the expected "where is she." "This is a reference to the Holy One, who is above." The next word in the verse is "ayeh," meaning "where," which, in this case, is written in its feminine form. What is Scripture's intent? "... To emphasize the bond of union between the male and the female, which is the secret of true faith."

18:10 "And Sarah heard in the tent door, which was behind him."

ZOHAR I:103a: Literally, the verse translates as "And Sarah heard in the tent door, and *he* was behind him. "We would have expected to read, "and *she* was behind him." The "door of the tent" is yet another reference to God's Divine presence on earth, the Shekhinah. Sarah actually hears "the door of the tent," the voice of the Shekhinah, uttering the strange promise. The "he" refers to God Himself, standing just behind, confirming the declaration.

ZOHAR I:103b: ". . . The Holy One makes Himself known to everyone according to the measure of his understanding and his capacity to attach himself to the spirit of Divine Wisdom." It is only through the supernal grades, the sefirot, the Divine Emanations, that a knowledge of God and communication with Him is possible for man. ". . . Through those gates, which are doors for the soul, the Holy One makes Himself known. For there is a door within door, grade behind grade, through which the glory of the Holy One is made known. Hence here 'the tent door' is the door of righteousness . . . and this is the first entrance door: through this door a view is opened to all the other supernal doors. He who succeeds in entering this door is privileged to know both it and all the other doors, since they all repose on this one."

Verses 12–15 record how Sarah laughed upon hearing the news that she would be granted a child. God first questions Abraham about his wife's reaction, and then Sarah, herself. Rather than condemning Sarah, analysis of these verses provides the rabbis with additional insights into the sacred relationship and understanding shared by the couple.

18:12 "And Sarah laughed within herself."

RAMBAN: The word for "laugh" that is used in this verse implies derision. When Scripture means to describe joyous laughter, it speaks of the laughter as originating in the mouth, not in the heart. So, why, he asks, doesn't Sarah believe the prophecy of the angels of God, and why does she deny having laughed? In front of her husband, God accuses Sarah for disbelieving in the unimaginable! . . . "Is anything too hard for the Lord?"

GENESIS RABBAH 48:19: "This may be compared to a man who had in his hand two parts of a chain, and went to a smith and asked him, 'Can you repair these?' 'I can make them from the outset,' he replied, 'and you think that I can not repair them!' So here God said, 'I can create man from the beginning, yet you would say that I cannot restore them to their youth!' "

18:13 "And the Lord said unto Abraham, 'Wherefore did Sarah laugh saying: Shall I, in truth, bear a child, who am old?' "

GENESIS RABBAH 48:18: Examine the text; Sarah did not *exactly* say this—she had implicated both herself *and* her husband, implying that *both* of them were beyond childbearing age. "Bar Kappara said: Great is peace, for even Scripture made a misstatement in order to preserve peace between Abraham and Sarah."

18:14 "At the set time I will return unto thee, when the season cometh round."

ZOHAR I:102b: Instead of "*I* will return," we would have expected the angel to say, "*He* will return," referring to God, "since the visitation of barren women is in the hand of the Almighty Himself and not in the hand of any messenger. . . . 'Three keys there are which have not been entrusted to any messenger, namely, of childbirth, of the resurrection, and of rain.' But the truth is that the words, 'I will return' were spoken by the Holy One, blessed be He, who was present there."

18:14 "And Sarah shall have a son."

ZOHAR I:103a: When God informs Abraham that Sarah will bear a child, He does not merely say, *"Thou* shalt have a son," rather He specifically states that *"Sarah* shall have a son." Why? To assure Abraham that this promised child will absolutely not be from Hagar or from any other woman, save Sarah.

ZOHAR I:103a: This child was destined to truly be a son to Sarah. Due to him, she will be anguished to the depths of her soul, due to him she will lose her life, due to him she will be exalted every Rosh Hashanah—"the time when the Holy One sits in judgement on the world, for on that day the Israelites read the portion: 'And the Lord remembered Sarah as He had said.' (21:1)"

18:16 "And the men rose up from thence and looked out toward Sodom."

After Abraham's failed efforts to dissuade God from destroying the cities of Sodom and Gomorrah, and after the merciful rescue by the angels of Lot and his daughters from within the condemned city, Abraham journeys south with his wife, right into the arms of a second lustful monarch.

Chapter 20:1. And Abraham journeyed from thence toward the land of the South, and dwelt between Kadesh and Shur; and he sojourned in Gerar. 2. And Abraham said of Sarah his wife, "She is my sister." And Abimelech king of Gerar sent, and took Sarah. 3. But God came to Abimelech in a dream of the night, and said to him, "Behold, thou shalt die, because of the woman whom thou hast taken; for she is a man's wife." 4. Now Abimelech had not come near her; and he said, "Lord, wilt Thou slay even a righteous nation? 5. Said he not himself unto me: She is my sister? and she, even she herself said, He is my brother. In the simplicity of my heart and the innocency of my hands have I done this." 6. And God said unto him in the dream, "Yea, I know that in the simplicity of thy heart thou hast done this, and I also withheld thee from sinning against Me. Therefore suffered I thee not to touch her. 7. Now therefore restore the man's wife; for he is a prophet, and he shall pray for thee, and thou shalt live; and if thou restore her not, know thou that thou shalt surely die, thou, and all that are thine." 8. And Abimelech rose early in the morning, and called all his servants, and told all these things in their ears; and the men were sore afraid. 9. Then Abimelech called Abraham, and said unto him, "What hast thou done unto us? And wherein have I sinned against thee, that thou hast brought on me and on my kingdom a great sin? "Thou hast done deeds unto me that ought not to be done." 10. And Abimelech said unto Abraham, "What sawest thou, that thou hast done this thing?" 11. And Abraham said, "Because I thought: Surely the fear of God is not in this place; and they will slay me for my wife's sake. 12. And moreover she is indeed my sister, the daughter of my father, but not the daughter of my mother; and so she became my wife. 13. And it came to pass, when God caused me to wander from my father's house, that I said unto her: This is thy kindness which thou shalt show unto me; at every place whither we shall come, say of me: He is my brother." 14. And Abimelech took sheep and oxen, and men-servants and women-servants, and gave them unto Abraham, and restored him Sarah his wife. 15. And Abimelech said, "Behold, my land is before thee: dwell where it pleaseth thee." 16. And unto Sarah he said,

"Behold, I have given thy brother a thousand pieces of silver; behold, it is for thee a covering of the eyes to all that are with thee; and before all men thou art righted." 17. And Abraham prayed unto God; and God healed Abimelech, and his wife, and his maid-servants; and they bore children. 18. For the Lord had fast closed up all the wombs of the house of Abimelech, because of Sarah Abraham's wife. Chapter 21:1. And the Lord remembered Sarah as He had said.

20:2 "And Abraham said of Sarah, his wife, 'She is my sister.'"

ZOHAR I:111b–112a: "It is a dictum of our teachers that a man should not rely on miracles, and even if the Holy one, blessed be He, has once performed a miracle for him he should not count on it another time, for miracles do not happen everyday. And whoever runs into obvious danger may therefore exhaust all his merit previously accumulated. . . . Now, seeing that Abraham had already had once a miraculous deliverance when he journeyed into Egypt, why did he put himself now again into a similar difficulty by saying, 'she is my sister'? The answer is that Abraham did in no way rely on himself, but he saw the Shekhinah constantly in the abode of Sarah, and that emboldened him to declare, 'she is my sister.' . . . All his words contained mystic allusions." Abraham is referring to his relationship with the Shekhinah, his inseparable attachment to her. "Observe that on the first occasion, when they went down to Egypt, he called her 'my sister' in order to cleave all the more firmly to the true faith, and not to be led astray. . . . For Abimelech and all the inhabitants of the land followed strange worship, and therefore Abraham, entering there, made bold to say 'my sister' claiming thereby the same dissoluble kinship as between brother and sister. For the marital bond can be dissolved, but not that between brother and sister. So whereas all the people of that land were addicted to the worship of the stars and constellations, Abraham, the true believer, avowed 'she is my sister,' as much as to say, 'We two will never separate.' "

Throughout the chapters on Sarah and Abraham, the rabbis find evidence of the perfect realization of the holy communion achieved by this couple here on earth—a counterpart and reflection of the holy communion between the male and female forces in the universes above.

Sarah, who, at the age of sixty-five was still extremely beautiful, is now years later coveted and once again taken by a king.

TALMUD, *BABA METZIA* 87a: Her skin once again became smooth, the wrinkles disappeared, and beauty returned to its place.

And as in the previous episode with Pharoah, God plagues the king's household "because of Sarah," at Sarah's bidding, by her word.

20:18 "For the Lord had fast closed up all the wombs of the house of Abimelech."

PIRKE DE RABBI ELIEZER, CHAPTER 26: "And Abimelech became impotent, and all the women of his house became barren, even to the smallest insect. . . . And the angel Michael descended and drew his sword against him. Abimelech said to him: Is this a true judgement and a true sentence to slay me as I had no knowledge?"

In the Scriptural text, Abimelech is reprimanded by God, not only for taking the married woman, but for then taking credit for *choosing* not to sin with her.

RASHI ON 20:6: "It is true that at first you had no intention of sinning, but you cannot claim innocency of hands—because *I permitted thee not!*" It was God who withheld him from sinning, God who did not grant permission for the act, God who did not permit Abimelech even the *possibility* of touching her.

When Abimelech returns Sarah to her rightful husband, giving Abraham monetary compensation, Abimelech remarks that the gifts will be evidence of respect.

RASHI ON 20:16: "These will put a covering over the eyes of all who are with thee so that they shall not hold you in light esteem. But had I sent you back empty-handed, they might have said, 'After he abused her he sent her back,' now . . . they will understand that I have sent you back *against my own will, forced to do so by a miracle.*' "

TANHUMA, BUBER 4.27: Abimelech placed a royal garment on Sarah, so that anyone seeing her would believe she was a queen and would, therefore, be afraid to woo her.

PIRKE DE RABBI ELIEZER, CHAPTER 26: The angel Michael said to Abimelech, "Restore the man's wife, for he is a prophet. . . . And he shall pray for thee, and thou shalt live. . . . Abraham arose and prayed before the Holy One, blessed be He, and said before Him: 'Sovereign of all the Worlds! Thou hast created the whole world to increase and multiply; let Abimelech and all the females of his household increase and multiply.' The Holy One, blessed be He, was entreated by him, as it is said, 'And Abraham prayed unto God, and God healed Abimelech and his wife and his maidservants, and they bore children.' "

GENESIS RABBAH 52:13: This is the very first time we ever hear of anyone praying not for himself, but for another!

RASHI ON 21:1: ". . . Whoever prays for mercy on behalf of another, when he, himself, is also in need of that very thing for which he prays on the other's behalf, will himself receive a favorable recompense from God." This, Rashi believes, is why Scripture places "And the Lord remembered Sarah" immediately after Abraham's prayer for Abimelech.

TANHUMA, BUBER 4.36: "The ministering angels said to the Holy One: Sovereign of the world, Abraham is healing others, but he himself needs healing. . . . The Holy One said: He is worth having me give him children. Look at the work of the Holy One! It is not like the work of flesh and blood. A human promises to give a gift to his companion. Sometimes he gives it; sometimes he does not give it. But the Holy One is not like that. When He promises to do something good, he immediately does something good."

Chapter 21:1. And the Lord remembered Sarah as he had said, and the Lord did unto Sarah as He had spoken. 2. And Sarah conceived, and bore Abraham a son in his old age, at the set time of which God had spoken to him. 3. And Abraham called the name of his son that was born unto him, whom Sarah bore to him, Isaac. 4. And Abraham circumcised his son Isaac when he was eight days old, as God had commanded him. 5. And Abraham was a hundred years old, when his son Isaac was born unto him. 6. And Sarah said, "God hath made laughter for me; everyone who heareth will laugh on account of me." 7. And she said, "Who would have said unto Abraham, that Sarah should give children suck? For I have borne him a son in his old age." 8. And the child grew and was weaned. And Abraham made a great feast on the day Isaac was weaned.

21:1 "And the Lord remembered [pakad] Sarah".

Sarah is a ninety-year-old woman. Why does God, now, grant her a child?

PESIKTA RABBATI 43:6: "The Holy One, blessed be He said: I act as trustee. Whatever a man deposits with Me, I return to him."

GENESIS RABBAH 53:5: The word for "deposit" is *pikadone*; the word for "remembered" is *pakad*. Do not only read it as "And the Lord remembered Sarah," read it: And the Lord returned what Sarah had deposited. "Sarah laid up with Him a store of pious acts and good deeds; therefore the Lord returned to her (the reward) for these."

GENESIS RABBAH 53:6: "This woman who had entered the houses of both Pharoah and Abimelech and yet emerged undefiled—surely it was but right that she should be remembered [conceive]."

TANHUMA, BUBER 4.31: "Some say: Sarah was not bearing, and others say: Abraham was not begetting; nevertheless, she trusts in the Lord. The Holy One said to her: Since you have put your trust in Me, by your life, I am visiting you."

GENESIS RABBAH 53:3: Although Sarah feared that she would not bring up children, still she praised God. " 'What! Am I to lose faith in my Creator! Heaven forfend! I will not lose faith in my Creator.' . . . Said the Holy One, blessed be He to her, 'Since thou didst not lose thy faith, I, too, will not give thee cause to lose faith.' But rather, 'And the Lord remembered Sarah.' "

TANHUMA, BUBER 4.34: ". . . The Holy One sat in judgement and said to His ministering angels: Does Sarah deserve to bear a son? When they all agreed and said 'Yes,' the Holy One set His seal after theirs."

TANHUMA, BUBER 4.36: "The Holy One scratched for her a mark on the wall. He said to her: When the sun comes to here, you shall bear. . ."

21:2 "And Sarah conceived and bore Abraham a son."

TANHUMA, BUBER 4.37: "There is an analogy here between her conception and her giving birth. Just as her conception was painless, so was her giving birth painless."

> *Unto the woman He said: I will greatly multiply thy pain and thy travail; in pain thou shalt bring forth children. (God to Eve, Genesis 3:16.)*

21:3 "And Abraham called the name of his son . . . Isaac."

In Hebrew, Isaac is Yitzchok and is most commonly thought to have been derived from the word for "laughter"/"tzichok." But Sarah, who laughs with derision at the prophecy and later laughs with joy at the birth, was not the one to actually name the child, therefore our sages believe that the name, in fact, signifies some entirely different ideas.

GENESIS RABBAH 53:7: The second syllable in the name, "chok," means "law" or "gift." The name [Yitz-chok] signifies that "Law had gone forth" (yatza chok) to the world, "a gift was made to the world." Look further. The first letter in the name, *yud*, whose value is ten, corresponds to the ten commandments. The second letter, the *zaddik*, has a value of ninety, referring to Sarah's age at the time of his birth; the third letter, the *kuf*, whose value is one hundred, refers to the age of his father. The last letter, the *chet*, valued at eight, refers to Isaac's circumcision, performed when he was eight days old.

> *What is the significance of the number eight? The Kabbalists define the three dimensional universe as consisting of six directions: Up-Down, North-South, East-West. The Maharal of Prague states that this is the reason that the world was created in six days, one day for each direction. The seventh day, the Sabbath, is the central point, binding together all the other days and supporting them. The eighth day, the day required for the covenant of circumcision, takes us, then, one step entirely beyond the physical and into the realm of the spiritual.*

21:6 "And Sarah said, 'God hath made laughter for me.'"

The first chapter of Genesis: "and God made the two great lights; the greater light to rule the day and the lesser light to rule the night; and the stars." Just as the word *made* describes how God gave light to the world, so, too, in this verse, within Sarah's words, *made* implies the addition of more light for the world. At Isaac's birth, brilliance was added to all heaven and earth.

21:6 "Everyone who heareth will laugh with me."

GENESIS RABBAH 53:8: "If Sarah was remembered, what did it matter to others? But when the Matriarch Sarah was remembered [gave birth], many other barren women were remembered with her; many deaf gained their hearing; many blind had their eyes opened, many insane became sane."

21:7 "Who would have said . . . that Sarah should give children suck?"

Sarah had only one child. Why, ask the rabbis, does Scripture record it as "children," in the plural? Abraham made a celebration, a great feast. . .

RASHI: "Great," because all the great men of that generation, Shem, Eber, and Abimelech were in attendance.

GENESIS RABBAH 53:10: "Great," because God, Himself, was present.

Nevertheless the miraculous birth provoked ridicule.

TANHUMA, BUBER 4.37 AND PESIKTA RABBATI, 43: The nations of the earth were skeptical: That old man and woman picked up a foundling from the street and now they're pretending it's their own! Perhaps the boy is the handmaid's child! And to make things worse, they've made a feast to publicly establish their absurd claim. . . . So what did these women do? They brought their own children to Sarah and asked her to suckle them.

GENESIS RABBAH 53:9: Abraham said to Sarah, " 'This is not a time for modesty, uncover your breasts so that all may know that the Holy One, blessed be He, has begun to perform miracles.' She uncovered her breasts and the milk gushed forth as from two fountains, and noble ladies came and had their children suckled by her, saying, 'We do not merit that our children should be suckled with the milk of that righteous woman.' "

TANHUMA BUBER 4.38: "All the Egyptian women's children whom Sarah suckled, all of them became proselytes."

GENESIS RABBAH 53:9: "The Rabbis said: Whoever came for the sake of heaven became God-fearing"; her milk infused within them the spirit of righteousness. Even those who did not come "for the sake of heaven," but only out of curiosity, to see if there had actually been a miracle, were rewarded with greatness in this world. But when they stood apart from the others at Mt. Sinai, refusing to partake in the acceptance of the Torah, the gift of that influential power was taken away from them.

GENESIS RABBAH 53:9: The Hebrew word for children is *banim*. Don't read it as *banim*, suggest the rabbis, read it instead as *banaim*/"builders." Sarah suckled builders! Those whom Sarah suckled grew up to become the individuals responsible for building up the world.

PESIKTA RABBATI 43: "... all Gentiles throughout the world who fear God spring from the children who drank of the milk of Sarah."

Chapter 21:9. And Sarah saw the son of Hagar the Egyptian, whom she had borne unto Abraham, making sport. 10. Wherefore she said unto Abraham, "Cast out this bondwoman and her son; for the son of this bondwoman shall not be heir with my son, even with Isaac." 11. And the thing was very grievous in Abraham's sight on account of his son. 12. And God said unto Abraham, "Let it not be grievous in thy sight because of the lad, and because of thy bondwoman; in all that Sarah saith unto thee, hearken unto her voice; for in Isaac shall seed be called to thee. 13. And also of the son of the bondwoman will I make a nation, because he is thy seed."

21:9 "And Sarah saw the son of Hagar, the Egyptian . . . making sport."

ZOHAR I:118b: After Isaac's birth, Ishmael is never referred to by name as long as he lived under Abraham's roof, but only as "the son of Hagar, the Egyptian." "Dross cannot be mentioned in the presence of gold"; it is not fitting for Ishmael's name to be spoken in Isaac's presence.

> *In the center of the heaven there is an illumined path, which is the celestial dragon, and in it are fixed multitudes of little stars which are charged to keep watch over the secret deeds of human beings. In the same way myriads of emissaries go forth from the primeval celestial serpent, by whom Adam was seduced, to spy out the secret deeds of mankind. Whoever, therefore, strives to live a life a purity is assisted from on high, and is encircled by the protecting hand of his Master, and is called saintly. On the other hand, when a man seeks to pollute himself, hosts of demons, who lie in wait for him, hover over him and surround and pollute him, so that he is called unclean. They all walk in front of him and cry, "Unclean, unclean." (Zohar II: 125a–125b)*

PIRKE DE RABBI ELIZER, CHAPTER 30: Sarah's request to send away Ishmael and Hagar was more grievous to Abraham than all the misfortunes which had previously plagued him, ". . . this matter was exceedingly evil in his eyes."

So, what motivated Sarah's demand? What did Sarah see?

GENESIS RABBAH 53:11: When Sarah saw Ishmael "making sport," she was watching him engage in idolatry, building altars, catching and sacrificing locusts. To other rabbis, the term *sport* or mockery, refers to inheritance only. When everyone was busy rejoicing at Isaac's birth, Ishmael looked at them with derision: You are all fools, for I am the firstborn in this household, and I will receive my due.

21:10–21:11 "Cast out this bondwoman. . . . And the thing was very grievous in Abraham's sight."

PIRKE DE RABBI ELIEZER, CHAPTER 30: That night, God appeared to Abraham and said, "Dost thou not know that Sarah was appointed to thee for a wife from her mother's womb? She is thy companion . . . Sarah is not called thy handmaid, but thy wife; neither is Hagar called thy wife, but thy handmaid. All that Sarah has spoken she has uttered truthfully. Let it not be grievous in thine eyes."

ZOHAR I:118b: "The Scripture really speaks in praise of Sarah. For what she saw was that he [Ishmael] was indulging in idolatrous practices. Hence she said: 'Surely this is not the son of Abraham, who follows in the footsteps of Abraham, but the son of Hagar the Egyptian, who is reverting to the type of his mother.' . . . It cannot be supposed that Sarah was moved by jealousy of her or of her son. For if so, the Holy One would not have supported her by saying, 'In all that Sarah saith unto thee, hearken unto her voice.' . . . Hence the words of Sarah, 'For the son of this bondwoman shall not be heir,' as much as to say: 'I know that he will never enter the fold of the true faith and that he will have no portion with my son either in this world or in the world to come.' Therefore God supported her, since He wished to keep the holy seed carefully separated, for that was the end for which He created the world, as Israel was already in His thought before the creation of the world. It was for that reason Abraham appeared in the world, so that the world could be sustained for his sake. Abraham and Isaac together upheld the world, yet they were not firmly established until Jacob [Isaac's future son] came into the world. . . . From Jacob the holy people gradually emerged into the world [the twelve tribes will sprout from Jacob and his wives], and so the whole of existence became duly established according to the holy pattern. Hence God said, 'In all that Sarah saith unto thee, hearken unto her voice; for in Isaac shall seed be called to thee'; that is, in Isaac and not in Ishmael."

If your wife is short, bend down to her and hear her whisper [to invite her counsel]. *(Talmud,* Baba Metzia *59a)*

Chapter 21:14. And Abraham rose up early in the morning; and took bread and a bottle of water, and gave it unto Hagar, putting it on her shoulder, and the child, and sent her away; and she departed, and strayed in the wilderness of Beer-sheba. 15. And the water in the bottle was spent, and she cast the child under one of the shrubs. 16. And she went, and sat her down a good way off, as it were a bowshot away; for she said, "Let me not look upon the death of the child." And she sat over against him, and lifted up her voice, and wept. 17. And God heard the voice of the lad; and the angel of God called to Hagar out of heaven, and said unto her, "What aileth thee, Hagar? fear not; for God hath heard the voice of the lad where he is. 18. Arise, lift up the lad, and hold him fast by thy hand; for I will make him a great nation." 19. And God opened her eyes, and she saw a well of water; and she went, and filled the bottle with water, and gave the lad drink. 20. And God was with the lad, and he grew; and he dwelt in the wilderness, and became an archer. 21. And he dwelt in the wilder-

ness of Paran; and his mother took him a wife out of
the land of Egypt.

PIRKE DE RABBI ELIEZER, CHAPTER 30: "Abraham rose
up early and wrote a bill of divorce, and gave it to Hagar, and
he sent her and her son away from himself, and from Isaac,
his son, from this world and from the world to come."

It is taught that it was solely due to the merit of his father
that the water in their bottle lasted as long as it did; when
Ishmael and Hagar reached the border of the wilderness,
Hagar began to revert to the idolatrous practices she had been
brought up with, and it was then that the water in the bottle
became suddenly exhausted.

21:16 "And she went and sat her down a good way off, as it were, a bowshot away."

GENESIS RABBAH 53:13: "A bow shot away" or more literally, "as the shot of a bow." The rabbis play on the phrase *ki
metawe*, meaning "as the shot," connecting it with *kee
metaheth*, meaning "one who criticizes." Here is a woman
criticizing God's sense of justice. Just yesterday Hagar was
Divinely promised fruitfulness (Gen 16:10), and today her only
son lies dying of thirst!

When Hagar previously fled from Sarah, Scripture records,
"The Lord heard thy affliction." Now, having strayed after
idols, even though she cries to God for help, it is not Hagar's
prayers that are answered, but her son's.

PIRKE DE RABBI ELIEZER, CHAPTER 30: Ishmael, faint
with thirst "cast himself beneath the thorns of the wilderness,
so that the moisture might be upon him." And he prayed
" 'Oh Sovereign of the World, if it be Thy pleasure to give

me water to drink, give me to drink and let not my soul depart because of thirst; for death by thirst is unnatural and it is harder than all other kinds of death.' The Holy One, blessed be He, heard his prayer."

GENESIS RABBAH 53:14: When a sick person prays on his own behalf, his prayers are more effective than those of anyone else.

GENESIS RABBAH 53:14, RASHI: The ministering angels denounced and challenged God's decision to offer aid to Ishmael: Are You planning to provide a well of water for a man who will one day destroy Your children with thirst?" (The angels, explains Rashi, are referring to an episode recorded in the Book of Isaiah, chapter 21, that will take place when Nebuchadnezzar leads the Israelites into exile, fruitlessly begging for relief from their thirst. The verse in Isaiah implicates the caravans of the Dedanites. Dedan was Keturah's son, and Keturah is identified by the rabbis as none other than Hagar, the mother of Ishmael. The Arab tribes are regarded as having descended from Ishmael.) God turns to His condemning angels and demands an answer to a question of His own: Tell Me, what is Ishmael right now? Righteous or guilty? Righteous, they answer. "I judge man only as he is at the moment," said He.

21:19 "And God opened her eyes."

MAIMONIDES: In Hebrew, the phrase meaning "to open the eyes," is always used throughout Scripture in a metaphorical sense; it never literally refers to the physical regaining of sight, but rather to the reception of new sources of knowledge.

GENESIS RABBAH 53:14: "All may be presumed blind, until the Holy One, blessed be He, enlightens their eyes."

21:19 "And she saw a well of water."

PIRKE DE RABBI ELIEZER, CHAPTER 18: "Ten things were created on the eve of the Sabbath in the twilight: the mouth of the earth, the mouth of the well, the mouth of the ass, the rainbow, the Mannah [the Divine sustaining food in the wilderness], the Shamir [a stone-cutting worm], the shape of the alphabet, the writing and the tables of the law, and the ram of Abraham."

21:19 "And she went and filled the bottle with water."

GENESIS RABBAH 53:14: The rabbis perceive this action on Hagar's part as a demonstration of her insufficient faith; she is afraid that the Divine aid just dispensed would be withdrawn, would vanish, as quickly as it had come.

GENESIS RABBAH 53:15: "Rabbi Isaac said: Throw a stick into the air, and it will fall back to its place of origin." When the boy grew, Hagar took a wife for him from among the daughters of Egypt, her native land.

What of Abraham, so distressed by the forced departure of his son?

PIRKE DE RABBI ELIEZER, CHAPTER 30: When Abraham sent Hagar away, he bound a water barrel around her waist, allowing it to drag behind her, so that he would know which way they went. A tale is told that three years after their departure, Abraham related to Sarah that he wished to go and see his son again, swearing to her that when he arrived at Ishmael's dwelling, he wouldn't even descend from his camel.

When Abraham arrived at midday, he found Ishmael's wife, alone. "Where is Ishmael?" he asked. "He's gone with his mother to pick the fruit of the palms." Abraham then asked her for a little bread and water to soothe him after his arduous journey. But the woman responded that she had neither bread nor water. Before turning to leave, Abraham spoke these parting words to the woman: "When Ishmael comes home, tell him this story—A certain old man came from the land of Canaan to see thee, and he said, 'Exchange the threshold of thy house, for it is not good for thee.' " When Ishmael heard the story, he understood his father's words, and his mother, Hagar, took a different wife for him.

Three years later, Abraham again went to visit Ishmael, and again his wife was alone. But this time, when Abraham asked for bread and water, she graciously delivered it. "Abraham arose and prayed before the Holy One, blessed be He, for his son, and thereupon, Ishmael's house was filled with all good things of the various blessings. When Ishmael came home, his wife told him what had happened, and Ishmael knew that his father's love was still extended to him."

A pious man married a pious woman, but when they found themselves unable to bear children, and feeling that they were being of no service to God, they chose to separate. The pious man went and married a wicked woman, and she made him wicked. The pious woman married a wicked man and she made him righteous and good. . . . All depends on the woman, our Rabbis teach. (Genesis Rabbah 17:7)

Chapter 22:1. And it came to pass after these things, that God did prove Abraham, and said unto him: "Abraham"; and he said, "Here am I." 2. And He said, "Take now thy son, thine only son, whom thou lovest, even Isaac, and get thee into the land of Moriah; and offer him there for a burnt-offering upon one of the mountains which I will tell thee of." 3. And Abraham rose early in the morning, and saddled his ass, and took two of his young men with him, and Isaac his son; and he cleaved the wood for the burnt-offering, and rose up, and went unto the place of which God had told him.

22:1 "And it came to pass after these things that God tried Abraham."

PIRKE DE RABBI ELIEZER, CHAPTER 31: God revealed Himself to Abraham, and He said: " 'Take now thy son, thine only son, whom thou lovest, even Isaac.' And Abraham, having pity upon Isaac, said before Him: 'Sovereign of all worlds! Concerning which son dost Thou decree upon me? Is it concerning the son lacking circumcision, or the son born for circumcision?' He answered him: 'Thine only son.' He rejoined: 'This one is the only son of *his* mother, and the other son is the only son of *his* mother.' He said to him: 'The one thou lovest.' He said to Him: 'Both of them do I love.' He said to him: 'Even Isaac. And offer him there for a burnt offering.' "

GENESIS RABBAH 55:2: "The Lord trieth the righteous" (Psalm 11:5). "Rabbi Jonathan said: A potter does not examine defective vessels, because he cannot give them a single blow without breaking them. What then does he examine? Only the sound vessels, for he will not break them even with many blows. Similarly, the Holy One, blessed be He, tests not the wicked but the righteous. . . . Rabbi Eliezer said: When a man possesses two cows, one strong and the other feeble, upon which does he put the yoke? Surley upon the strong one."

So, Abraham is put to his final test, commanded to sacrifice his longed-for son.

PESIKTA RABBATI 40:6: Abraham lifted the knife and the angels cried out to God: "It is an anomaly on Thy part to have Isaac slaughtered. Thereupon the Holy One, blessed be He, said to Michael: Why dost thou stand still? Do not let Abraham go on!"

Chapter 22:20. And it came to pass after these things, that it was told Abraham, saying, "Behold, Milcah, she also hath borne children unto thy brother Nahor: 21. Uz his firstborn, and Buz his brother, and Kemuel the father of Aram; 22. And Chesed, and Hazo, and Pildash, and Jidlaph, and Bethuel." 23. And Bethuel begot Rebekah; these eight did Milcah bear to Nahor, Abraham's brother. 24. And his concubine, whose name was Reumah, she also bore Tebah, and Gaham, and Tahash, and Maacah.

22:20 ". . . after these things . . ."

RASHI ON GENESIS RABBAH 56: Upon returning from the trying event at Mount Moriah, Abraham is accosted with the realization that had Isaac actually been slain, he would have died before having had children. Abraham now intentionally ponders the problem of finding the proper wife for his son. "This is what is meant by 'after these things' or words—namely after the words that expressed the thoughts aroused by the binding of Isaac."

22:20 "After these things it was told Abraham . . . 'Milcah, she also hath borne children . . .' "

GENESIS RABBAH 57:1: While he was still on Mount Moriah, Abraham's troubled mind is set at ease; he is informed that the divinely ordained mate for his son has been born.

Abraham was one of three sons. His brother Haran had two daughters, Sarai and Milcah. As we know, Abram married Sarai. Milcah married Nahor, and here, Scripture informs us that their marraige was fruitful.

RAMBAN: Just as we had not been previously informed of the outcome of the marraiges performed in Abraham's hometown, so, too, is Abraham now first informed. The distance between Mesopotamia and Canaan was not very great, therefore if Haran and Milcah had borne children in their younger years, Abraham would have known of it before the present moment. When Abraham left Haran, he was seventy-five years old; Nahor and Milcah were also well past the prime of life. It seems, to our rabbis, that just as a miracle had been performed for Sarah, so too had one been performed for her sister, "Milcah, she also . . ."

RASHI: In fact, Milcah's offspring were equal in all respects to those Abraham was ordained to have. Milcah, herself, bears eight children, and four children are borne by Nahor's concubine. So it would be with Abraham's future line—eight children would be born of the principal wives, Rachel and Leah, and four would be born to their handmaids, Zilpah and Bilhah.

22:23 "And Bethuel begot Rebekah."

Milcah had eight children, but Scripture tells us about the offspring of only one of them, Bethuel, the youngest, entirely ignoring the other seven. Bethuel has two children, a boy and a girl. At this point, Scripture fails to mention the existence of the son, naming only his daughter. This entire chapter, say our rabbis, was, in fact, written only to reveal the genealogy of the woman destined to be our second matriarch, Rebekah.

GENESIS RABBAH 58:2: " 'The sun also riseth and the sun goeth down' (Ecclesiastes I:5). Rabbi Abba said: Do we then not know that the sun rises and the sun goes down? But the meaning is that before the Holy One, blessed be He, causes the sun of one righteous man to set, he causes the sun of another righteous man to rise. . . . Before the Holy One, blessed be He, allowed Sarah's sun to set, He caused that of Rebekah to rise. Thus we first read, 'Behold Milcah, she hath also borne children (Bethuel begot Rebekah), and after that, 'And the life of Sarah was a hundred years. . . .' "

Chapter 23:1. And the life of Sarah was a hundred and seven and twenty years; these were the years of the life of Sarah. 2. And Sarah died in Kiriath-arba, the same is Hebron in the land of Canaan; and Abraham came to mourn for Sarah, and to weep for her. 3. And Abraham rose up from before his dead, and spoke unto the children of Heth, saying: 4. "I am a stranger and a sojourner with you; give me a possession of a burying-place with you, that I may bury my dead out of my sight." 5. And the children of Heth answered Abraham, saying unto him: 6. "Hear us, my lord: thou art a mighty prince among us; in the choice of our sepulchres bury thy dead; none of us shall withhold from thee his sepulchre, but that thou mayest bury thy dead." . . . 8. And he spoke with them, saying, "If it be your mind that I should bury my dead out of my sight, hear me, and entreat for me to Ephron the son of Zohar, 9. that he may give me the cave of Machpelah, which he hath, which is in the end of his field; for the full price let him give it to me in the midst of you for a possession of a burying-place." 10. Now Ephron was sitting in the midst of the children of Heth; and Ephron the Hittite answered Abraham in the hearing of the children of Heth, even of all that went in at the gate of his city, saying: 11. "Nay, my lord, hear me: the field give I thee, and the cave that is therein, I give it thee. . . . 17. So the field of Ephron, which was in Machpelah, which was before Mamre, the field, and the cave which was therein, and all the trees that were in the field, that were in all the border thereof round about, were made sure 18. unto Abraham for a possession in the presence of the children of Heth. . . . 19. And after this, Abraham buried Sarah his wife in the cave of the field of Machpelah before Mamre the same is Hebron in the land in Canaan. Chapter 24:1. And Abraham was old, well stricken in age, and the Lord had blessed Abraham in all things.

Immediately following the account of the binding of Isaac, Scripture informs us that Sarah has died. Does this juxtaposition hold any significance?

PIRKE DE RABBI ELIEZER, CHAPTER 32: When the Devil, Sammael, saw Abraham peacefully returning from Mount Moriah with his son by his side, his anger was reignited, for he realized that his attempts to foil Abraham had been unsuccessful. To rectify the outcome, Sammael paid a visit to Sarah before her husband and son had reached home. "Hast thou not heard what has happened in the world? She said to him: No. He said to her: Thy husband, Abraham, has taken thy son Isaac and slain him and offered him up as a burnt-offering upon the altar. She began to weep, to cry aloud three times, corresponding to the three sustained notes (of the shofar) and she gave forth three howlings, corresponding to the three disconnected short notes, and her soul fled, and she died."

In the Tanhuma, Satan disguises himself as Isaac, and in Leviticus Rabbah and Ecclesiastes Rabbah, it is Isaac, himself, who tells his mother what has just happened up on Mount Moriah. But in all the different renditions, Sarah's life is suddenly terminated.

23:1 "And the life of Sarah was a hundred and seven and twenty years."

GENESIS RABBAH 45:5: Sarah dies at the age of one hundred twenty-seven. The Rabbis teach that Sarah was destined to reach her husband's age of one hundred seventy-five, but forty-eight years were intentionally robbed from her because of the seemingly small iniquity she committed of disputing with Abraham over Hagar's misdeeds and then declaring aloud to her husband and to God, "The Lord judge between me and thee!"

The Sages, in no way, use this to diminish her extraordinary level of righteousness. In fact, it's a tribute to her superior level of righteousness that Sarah is judged so harshly for what might be seen as a rather small iniquity had it been committed by someone else.

RASHI: The Hebrew word for year/*shanah* is inserted after every term in verse 23:1, so that the verse literally reads, "one hundred years and seven years and twenty years." Scripture means for us to take each term by itself; the word *years* is repeated to indicate that all of her years were equally good.

GENESIS RABBAH 58:1: "At the age of twenty she was as at the age of seven in beauty, and at the age of one hundred, she was as at the age of twenty in sin." [The Heavenly Court, before the time of Revelation, does not punish transgressions before the age of twenty.]

THE MAHARAL OF PRAGUE: At the age of one hundred she possessed the beauty of a twenty year old, and at twenty she was like a seven year old in sin.

GENESIS RABBAH 58:7: Everybody who knew of Sarah's death closed their houses to go and show their respect for her, and as a reward, they did not, themselves, pass away until participating in the funeral rites of Abraham, forty-eight years later.

23:2 "And Sarah died in Kiriath-arba."

GENESIS RABBAH 50:4: Kiriath-arba literally means "the city of four," so called because four righteous couples would be buried there—Adam and Eve, Abraham and Sarah, Isaac and Rebekah, and Jacob and Leah.

ZOHAR II:124b: "Of Sarah alone among all women do we find recorded the number of her days and years and the length of her life and the place where she was buried. All this was to show that the like of Sarah was not to be found among all the women of the world."

Rachel and the Ignorant Shepherd

At the time of Vespasian, Kalbua Savua was one of the three wealthiest men in Jerusalem. Among his many workers was a poor, uneducated and unassuming shepherd. But Kalbua's beautiful daughter, Rachel, recognized something in this man, some capability, some potential, however unnameable, and she fell in love with him. One day she approached the shepherd with a proposition. If he'd agree to attend a school of study, she'd agree to become his wife. The man joyously consented, and the two, knowing that her father would disapprove of the match, mar-

ried in secret. When Kalbua eventually discovered the betrothal, in anger he drove Rachel and her husband out of his home vowing that the couple would never benefit from any of his wealth.

Rachel and her new husband, now subject to abject poverty, made their home in a straw bin. One cold, winter night, a stranger appeared at the door begging for a little bit of straw to place beneath his wife, who had just given birth. And the couple, without hesitation, gave up part of their only possession to a man who seemed to have even less than they had. The stranger, teach our sages, was Elijah the Prophet.

Eventually, Rachel told her husband that the time had come for him to begin his studies, and her husband, now a forty-year-old man, reacted with embarrassment. "They'll all laugh at me, a grown man who knows nothing, not even the alphabet!" Rachel asked her husband to bring her an ass with an injured back, and when he brought it, she covered its wounds with healing herbs, and together they led the useless animal to the marketplace. That first day, everyone who saw the pitiful animal laughed at it. The second day they laughed at it. But on the third day, they no longer laughed. "Go now and study," Rachel said to her husband. "Today they'll laugh, but tomorrow they will no longer laugh, and the day after that they'll say, 'That is his practice,' and pay you no heed."

Rachel's husband entered a children's schoolhouse and began, along with them, to learn the letters of the alphabet. In time he learned the entire Torah and progressed from the schoolhouse to the Academy of R. Eliezer and R. Joshua. And under their instruction he learned one law, then another and another. After receiving each bit of knowledge, he went off to contemplate all its in-

ner meanings, asking more and more questions, until he surpassed even his teachers, who no longer could provide him with answers. The uneducated shepherd was granted the title of Rabbi, and after twelve years of study, he knew it was time to return home. Twelve thousand of his own disciples returned along with him; he was the great Rabbi Akiva, the one sage, the rabbis teach, who was permitted to enter Paradise alive and to emerge unharmed.

News of the visit of the great Rabbi preceded him and all the town came out to greet him. Rachel's father, Kalba Savua, seeing his daughter's poverty, regretted his decision to withhold his wealth, and he approached the Rabbi to ask to be released from his vow. "Would you have made such a vow if you had known that your daughter's husband was to become a great man?" "No," answered Savua. "Had he known just one law, I would not have uttered such a vow." And Rabbi Akiva revealed to the man that he, himself, was Rachel's husband. The man kissed the Rabbi's feet and gave him half of his wealth. When Rachel heard that her husband was finally home, she rushed out to find him. Seeing her shabby clothes, the neighbors tried to coerce her to borrow some clothes and to make her appearance more presentable, but she refused. Disheveled, she approached her husband and fell at his feet, but his disciples shoved the poor woman away from their noble Rabbi. Akiba, recognizing his wife, his loyal companion, harshly berated his disciples. "Let her alone," he said. "Mine and yours, everything that we have, is due to her. . . ."[30]

30. For variations on this tale see: Micha Joseph Bin Gorion, *Mimekor Yisrael* (Bloomington and Indianapolis: Indiana

23:19 "Abraham buried Sarah his wife in the cave of the field of Machpelah."

ZOHAR II:127a–128b: "Abraham recognized the cave of Machpelah by a certain mark, and he had long set his mind and heart on it. For he had once entered that cave and seen Adam and Eve buried there. He knew that they were Adam and Eve because he saw the form of a man, and whilst he was gazing a door opened into the Garden of Eden, and he perceived the same form standing near it. Now, whoever looks at the form of Adam cannot escape death. For when a man is about to pass out of the world he catches sight of Adam and at that moment he dies. Abraham, however, did look at him, and saw his form and yet survived.

. . . Abraham used to offer up his prayer daily, and in so doing used to proceed as far as that field, which emitted heavenly odors. Whilst there he saw a light issuing from the cave, so that he prayed on that spot, and on that spot the Holy One communed with him. On that account Abraham now asked for it, having always longed for it since then. Why did he not ask for it before that time? Because the people would not listen to him, as he had no obvious need for it. Now that he needed it, he thought it was time to demand it. Observe that had Ephron seen inside the cave what Abraham saw, he would never have sold it to him. But he never saw there anything, since such things are never revealed except to their rightful owner. It was thus revealed to Abraham and not to

University Press, 1990), 552–558; Moses Gaster, *Maaseh Book* (Philadelphia: Jewish Publication Society, 1929), 117–121; Hyman E. Goldin, *The Book of Legends, Talmudic Period* (New York: Hebrew Publishing Co., 1929), 248–254.

Ephron . . . who had no part or portion in it, and who therefore only saw darkness in it; and for that reason he sold it.
Nay, he even sold him more than he had mentioned in his
original request . . . as he felt indifferent to the whole thing,
not realizing what it was."

24:1 "And Abraham was old."

TANHUMA, BUBER 5.3: "When Sarah died, old age sprang
upon Abraham and he was called elderly."

TANHUMA, BUBER 5.4: "Come and see. From Adam even
to Abraham there are twenty generations, but there is no mention of old age written about any of them except about him
[Abraham]. . . . The Holy One gave him this grey crown which
is an ornament for when one becomes old. And when did it
come over him? When he practiced righteousness. . . ."

GENESIS RABBAH 58:9: "The Holy One, blessed be He,
said to him: 'It is My function to dispense Love; since thou
hast embraced My function, come and don My raiment.'" The
Sages considered the act of burying the dead to be a supreme
act of kindness and love, because it is a kindness which cannot be repaid.

TANHUMA, BUBER 5.2: "The beginning of the Torah is
steadfast love, its middle is steadfast love, and its end is steadfast love" (Ecclesiastes Rabbah 7:2). The Holy One made thirteen bridal canopies for Adam and Eve. The Holy One
adorned Eve with twenty-four ornaments. Not only that, but
He took her by the hand and brought her to Adam. . . . Thus
the beginning of the Torah is steadfast love. Its middle also
is steadfast love. Where is it shown? 'Then Rebekah's nurse,
Deborah died' (Genesis 35:8), 'and its name was called Weep-

ing Oak,' for Jacob was sitting there and weeping over her. The Holy One said: Jacob is sitting and grieving. He appeared to him visibly . . . 'and blessed him.' And its end is steadfast love as seen in the case of Moses, for when he passed away, He buried him. . . . Abraham persisted in clinging to a measure of steadfast love. The Holy one said to him: This measure was Mine and you have taken it. By your life, I am making you old like Me."

24:1 "And the Lord had blessed Abraham in all things."

Chapter 24 of the Book of Genesis begins with an affirmation regarding the fullness of the first Patriarch's life; Abraham had been granted all the obvious things that a man values—wealth, respect, longevity, an equal partner, and children.

GENESIS RABBAH 59:7: Abraham had triumphed over his "evil inclination," he lived to see his son Ishmael reformed in his ways, his wealth remained undiminished, and Abraham was blessed in that God never again tested him.

Regarding Ishmael, Scripture refers to his lifetime in the same way it does to Sarah's—"And these are the years of the life of Ishmael—a hundred years and thirty years and seven years" (Gen. 25:17). Ramban teaches that the reason for this account of Ishmael is that he became a righteous, repentant man, and Scripture speaks of him in the same way it speaks of all righteous people.

Despite all the blessings that had been endowed upon Abraham, he did, in fact, still lack one important thing. His son was as yet unmarried, and Abraham needed to guarantee the continuance of his lineage, aligned with the spiritual quest to which his life had been devoted.

Rebekah

The Book of Genesis, Chapter 24.

"Upon me be thy curse, my son."

Chapter 24:2. And Abraham said unto his servant, the elder of his house, that ruled over all that he had, "Put, I pray thee, thy hand under my thigh. 3. And I will make thee swear by the Lord, the God of heaven and the God of the earth, that thou shalt not take a wife for my son of the daughters of the Canaanites, among who I dwell. 4. But thou shalt go unto my country, and to my kindred, and take a wife for my son, even of Isaac." 5. And the servant said unto him, "Peradventure the woman will not be willing to follow me unto this land; must I needs bring thy son back unto the land from whence thou camest?" 6. And Abraham said unto him, "Beware thou that thou bring not my son back thither. 7. The Lord, the God of heaven, who took me from my father's house, and from the land of my nativity, and who spoke unto me, and who swore unto me, saying: Unto thy seed will I give this land; He will send His angel before thee, and thou shalt take a wife for my son from thence. 8. And if the woman be not willing to follow thee, then thou shalt be clear from this my oath; only thou shalt not bring my son back thither." 9. And the servant put his hand under the thigh of Abraham his master, and swore to him concerning this matter. 10. And the servant took ten camels, of the camels of his master, and departed; having all goodly things of his master's in his hand; and he arose, and went to Aramnaharaim, unto the city of Nahor.

24:4 "Go unto my country ... and take a wife for my son."

For help in the matter, Abraham turns to his servant; Eliezer, however, was not an ordinary servant, not an ordinary man.

GENESIS RABBAH 59:8, 59:10: Eliezer "ruled over all that he had"—the inner Scriptural meaning is that he was master over all his passions, just as his master, Abraham, was. And when Abraham sends Eliezer on this quest, he assures him that an angel of God will accompany him on his journey. Rabbi Dosa taught that actually, two angels were appointed to Eliezer—one whose mission would be to accompany him to Haran, the other to bring Isaac's divinely appointed mate out to meet the servant when he arrived at the city well.

Chapter 24:11. And he made the camels to kneel down without the city by the well of water at the time of evening, the time that women go out to draw water. 12. And he said, "O Lord, the God of my master Abraham, send me, I pray Thee, good speed this day, and show kindness unto my master Abraham. 13. Behold, I stand by the fountain of water; and the daughters of the men of the city come out to draw water. 14. So let it come to pass, that the damsel to whom I shall say: Let down thy pitcher, I pray thee, that I may drink; and she shall say: Drink, and I will give thy camels drink also; let the same be she that Thou hast appointed for Thy servant, even for Isaac; and thereby shall I know that Thou hast shown kindness unto my master." 15. And it came to pass, before he had done speaking, that, behold, Rebekah came out, who was born to Bethuel the son of Milcah, the wife of Nahor, Abraham's brother, with her pitcher upon her shoulder. 16. And the damsel was very fair to look upon, a virgin, neither had any man known her; and she went down to the fountain, and filled her pitcher, and came up. 17. And the servant ran to meet her, and said, "Give me to drink, I pray thee, a little water of thy pitcher." 18. And she said, "Drink my Lord"; and she hastened, and let down her pitcher upon her hand, and gave him drink. 19. And when she had done giving him drink, she said, "I will draw for thy camels also, until they have done drinking." 20. And she hastened, and emptied her pitcher into the trough, and ran again unto the well to draw, and drew for all his camels. 21. And the man looked steadfastly on her; holding his peace, to know whether the Lord had made his journey prosperous or not. 22. And it came to pass, as the camels had done drinking, that the man took a golden ring of half a shekel weight, and two bracelets for her hands of ten shekels weight of gold; 23. and said, "Whose daughter art thou? tell me, I pray thee. Is there room in thy father's house for us to lodge in?" 24. And she said unto him, "I am the daughter of Bethuel the son of Milcah, whom she bore unto Nahor." 25. She said moreover unto him, "We have both straw and provender enough, and room to lodge in." 26. And the man bowed his head, and prostrated himself before the Lord. 27. And he said, "Blessed be the Lord, the God of my master Abraham, who hath not forsaken His mercy and

His truth toward my master; as for me, the Lord hath led me in the way to the house of my master's brethren."

24:14 "Let this same be she that Thou hast appointed . . . for Isaac."

Eliezer asks God for a specific sign by which he will recognize the woman chosen for Isaac.

RASHI: The sign he, himself, chooses, is intended to convey vital information about the girl's worthiness to enter into the house of Abraham and Sarah. Is she charitable? (The Talmud tells us that a man must feed his animals before he, himself, sits down to a meal; Eliezer sought evidence of a tender heart.)

GENESIS RABBAH 60:4: In the Bible, only three men were answered by God even before they had completed vocalizing their requests: Moses—"And it came to pass, as he made an end of speaking these words, that the ground did cleave asunder" (Numbers 16:31); Solomon—"Now when Solomon had made an end of praying, the fire came down from heaven" (Chronicles II 7:1); Eliezer—"And it came to pass before he'd done speaking, that, behold, Rebekah came out."

PIRKE DE RABBI ELIEZER, CHAPTER 16: "And everything is revealed before the Holy One, blessed be He. A daughter of kings [a commentary on her father, Bethuel's, status], who in all her life had never gone forth to draw water, went out to draw water in that hour. And the girl, who did not know who the man was, accepted (the proposal) to be married to Isaac. Why? Because she had been destined for him from her mother's womb . . . ."

GENESIS RABBAH 60:5: All of the women drew water from

the well, but only for Rebekah did the water rise up of its own accord to meet her. "Said the Holy One, blessed be He, to her, 'Thou hast provided a token for thy descendants: as the water ascended immediately it saw thee, so will it be for thy descendants [wandering in the desert]; as soon as the well sees them, it will immediately rise.'"

24:17 "And the servant ran to meet her."

GENESIS RABBAH 60:6: He anticipated and welcomed her kind actions.

> *R. Joshua walked along the highway, traveling toward the city. When he entered the city, he met a little girl who was standing and filling her pitcher from a well. He said to her, "Give me some water to drink." She said, "I will give water to both you and your ass." After he had finished drinking and was turning to go on his way, he said, "My daughter, you acted just like Rebekah." She said, "I acted like Rebekah, but you, sir, did not act like Eliezer."* (Lamentations Rabbah I. I, 19)

24:22 "The man took a golden ring . . . and two bracelets for her hands."

GENESIS RABBAH 60:6, RASHI: The Hebrew word for bracelet signifies something that is united or joined. The bracelets were also meant to be symbolic of the two tablets of stone as yet to be given at Mount Sinai, their ten shekels weight to correspond to the ten commandments written upon them.

All these symbolic gifts were intended to underscore the idea that the prime purpose of marriage is to be in service of God. Eliezer is so confident that God's hand had guided him to the correct woman, that he presents Rebekah with these gifts even *before* he inquires after her name and family.

> Chapter 24:28. And the damsel ran, and told her mother's house according to these words. 29. And Rebekah had a brother, and his name was Laban; and Laban ran out unto the man, unto the fountain. 30. And it came to pass, when he saw the ring, and the bracelets upon his sister's hands, and when he heard the words of Rebekah his sister, saying, "Thus spoke the man unto me," that he came unto the man; and behold; he stood by the camels at the fountain. 31. And he said, "Come in, thou blessed of the Lord; wherefore standest thou without?—for I have cleared the house, and made room for the camels." 32. And the man came into the house . . . 33. And there was set food before him to eat; but he said, "I will not eat, until I have told mine errand." And he said, "Speak on." 34. And he said, "I am Abraham's servant. 35. And the Lord hath blessed my master greatly; and he is become great; and He hath given him flocks and herds, and silver and gold, and men-servants and maid-servants, and camels and asses. 36. And Sarah my master's wife bore a son to my master when she was old . . . .

Eliezer goes on to recount for Rebekah's family the details of his journey, his oath to Abraham, the purpose of his trip, and all the events that have taken place since his departure.

RASHI ON 24:42 AND ON GENESIS RABBAH 60: "Rabbi Acha said: The ordinary conversation of the Patriarch's servant is more pleasing to God than even the Torah [religious discourse] of their children, for the chapter of Eliezer [the account of his journey] is repeated in the Torah [it is written twice, once as part of the narrative, and repeated as part of Eliezer's conversation], whereas many important principles of the Law are derived only from slight indications given in the text."

The Rabbis perceive Eliezer's quest to find Isaac's "appointed" wife, their return journey together to Canaan, and the culminating marriage between Isaac and Rebekah to have been Divinely directed from beginning to end.

24:42 "And I came this day unto the fountain."

PIRKE DE RABBI ELIEZER, CHAPTER 16: Eliezer experienced the first of the miracles while traveling from Kiriath-arba to Haran. A trip which normally would have taken seventeen days, takes Eliezer only three hours' time.

GENESIS RABBAH 60:6, 59:11: Eliezer wishes to convey to Rebekah's family that God has been with him on this expedition from start to finish. This miracle of the contracted distance was a sign to him, even prior to meeting Rebekah at the well and having been led directly to his intended destination, that God was beside him. "The Lord hath led me in the right way" (Gen. 24:48), that is, the designated way, the correct way.

Eliezer tells his story, exactly as it happened, and Scripture records his tale word for word in vivid, precise detail. Not *exactly*, say the rabbis. In the retelling, Eliezer alters some small details.

RAMBAN: "And before I had done speaking to my heart, behold, Rebekah came forth with her pitcher on her shoulder; and she went down unto the fountain and drew" (24:45). Eliezer says that Rebekah "drew" the water—He does not tell them about the miracle of the water rising in the well because he sensed that they would not believe him.

24:47 "I asked her and said, 'Whose daughter art thou?' And she said, 'The daughter of Bethuel, Nahor's son, whom Milcah bore unto him.' And I put the ring upon her nose and the bracelets upon her hands."

Remember that Eliezer, in actuality, gave her the gifts *before* inquiring after her lineage. Again, Eliezer speaks cautiously so as to assure the successful culmination of his mission; her family would have found his actions shocking and incomprehensible. Eliezer's actions proceeded under Divine protection and guidance, but he was wise enough to keep his knowledge and understanding concealed.

Chapter 24:49. "And now if ye will deal kindly and truly with my master, tell me; and if not, tell me; that I may turn to the right hand, or the left." 50. Then Laban and Bethuel answered and said, "The thing proceedeth from the Lord; we cannot speak unto thee bad or good. 51. Behold, Rebekah is before thee, take her, and go, and let her be thy master's son's wife, as the Lord hath spoken." 52. And it came to pass, that, when Abraham's servant heard their words, he bowed himself down to the earth unto the Lord. 53. And the servant brought forth jewels of silver, and jewels of gold, and raiment, and gave them to Rebekah; he gave also to her brother and to her mother precious things. 54. And they did eat and drink, he and the men that were with him, and tarried all night; and they rose up in the morning, and he said, "Send me away unto my master." 55. And her brother and her mother said, "Let the damsel abide with us a few days at the least ten; after that she shall go." 56. And he said unto them, "Delay me not, seeing the Lord hath prospered my way; send me away that I may go to my master." 57. And they said, "We will call the damsel, and inquire at her mouth." 58. And they called Rebekah, and said unto her, "Wilt thou go with this man?" And she said, "I will go." 59. And they sent away Rebekah their sister, and her nurse, and Abraham's servant, and his men. 60. And they blessed Rebekah, and said unto her, "Our sister, be thou the mother of thousands of ten thousands, and let thy seed possess the gate of those that hate them." 61. And Rebekah arose, and her damsels, and they rode upon the camels, and followed the man. And the servant took Rebekah, and went his way.

24:49 ". . . tell me that I may turn to the right hand or to the left."

RASHI, GENESIS RABBAH 60:9: What are the unspoken implications of Eliezer's words? He is asking whether he may take Rebekah with him, or whether he must now seek a wife for Isaac from among the daughters of Ishmael who dwelt "to the right hand" of Abraham, or from among the daughters of Lot who dwelt to "the left."

24:50 "The thing proceedeth from the Lord."

RASHI: Laban and Bethuel admit that from Eliezer's story it appears as though Rebekah was, indeed, chosen by Divine decree. They, therefore, have no choice in the matter, they are not at liberty to refuse.

GENESIS RABBAH 60:12: Rebekah herself cannot be forced to comply, and when they put the question to her, Bethuel and Laban cannot believe that Rebekah actually wishes to go. "I will go," (24:58) she replies, meaning, "In spite of you, whether you wish it or not."

24:60 "Be thou the mother of thousands."

Before she leaves home, her family sends her off with a blessing for fertility. The rabbis, however, paint her brother, Laban, in a very unfavorable light, creating midrash after midrash to reveal his coarse and devious nature. As we will subsequently learn, despite the blessings of her family, Rebekah will remain barren for twenty long years after her marriage to Isaac.

GENESIS RABBAH 60:13: "Why was Rebekah not remembered (with children) until after *Isaac* prayed for her? So that the heathens might not say: Our prayer bore fruit."

24:56 "Delay me not."

PIRKE DE RABBI ELIEZER, CHAPTER 16: "The servant arose early in the morning and saw the angel standing and waiting for him in the street. He said to them: 'Do not hinder me, for the Lord has prospered my way, for behold, the man who came with me yesterday . . . he is standing and waiting for me in the street. . . .' At six hours of the day [noon] the servant went forth from Haran and he took Rebekah and Deborah, her nurse, and made them ride upon the camels. So that the servant should not be alone with the maiden by night, the earth was contracted before him, and in three hours [a repetition of the previous miracle], the servant came to Hebron at the time of the prayer of the afternoon."

Chapter 24:62. And Isaac came from the way of Beerlahai-roi, for he dwelt in the land of the south. 63.

And Isaac went out to meditate in the field at the eventide, and he lifted up his eyes and saw and behold, there were camels coming. 64. And Rebekah lifted up her eyes, and when she saw Isaac, she alighted from the camel. 65. And she said unto the servant, "What man is this that walketh in the field to meet us?" And the servant said, "It is my master." And she took her veil and covered herself. 66. And the servant told Isaac all the things that he had done. 67. And Isaac brought her into his mother Sarah's tent, and he took Rebekah, and she became his wife; and he loved her. And Isaac was comforted for his mother.

24:63 "And Isaac went out to meditate in the field at eventide."

ZOHAR II:132a: ". . . When he [Eliezer] reached Haran and met Rebekah "at the time of evening" it was the time of the afternoon prayer. Thus the moment [back in Canaan] when Isaac began the afternoon prayer coincided with the moment when the servant encountered Rebekah. So, too, it was at the very moment of his afternoon prayer that Rebekah came to Isaac himself. Thus all was fitly disposed through the working of the Divine Wisdom."

24:67 "And Isaac brought her into his mother Sarah's tent."

PIRKE DE RABBI ELIEZER, CHAPTER 32: Isaac was in mourning for his mother for a period of three years, ever since the event of his binding on Mount Moriah. He was then thirty-seven years old; at the time he married Rebekah, he was forty. Our rabbis teach that it was the appearance of Rebekah in Isaac's life that turned him away from his grief.

The rabbis point out that the literal translation of the Hebrew words in verse 24:67 convey hidden meaning. Literally,
the text states "And he brought her into the tent—Sarah, his
mother." Our rabbis take this to mean that Rebekah, in all
respects, was exactly "like" his mother.

GENESIS RABBAH 60:16: "You find that as long as Sarah
lived, a cloud hung over her tent [the Divine Presence]; when
she died, that cloud disappeared; but when Rebekah came, it
returned. As long as Sarah lived, her doors were wide open;
at her death that liberality ceased, but when Rebekah came,
that openhandedness returned. As long as Sarah lived, there
was a blessing on her dough, and the lamp used to burn from
the evening of the Sabbath until the evening of the following
Sabbath; when she died, these ceased, but when Rebekah
came, they returned. And so when he saw her following in
his mother's footsteps, separating her challah in cleanness and
handling her dough in cleanness . . ." he takes her for his wife,
and is comforted through his great love for her.

ZOHAR II:133a: "Rabbi Jose remarked: 'The letter *heh*
at the end of the word *haohelah* (into the tent) is a reference
to the Shekhinah, which now returned to the tent. For during the whole of Sarah's life the Shekhinah did not depart
from it, and a light used to burn there from one Sabbath eve
to the other; once lit, it lasted all the days of the week. After
her death the light was extinguished, but when Rebekah came
the Shekhinah returned and the light was rekindled'. Thus the
verse reads literally: 'And he brought her into the tent—Sarah
his mother,' the last phrase implying that Rebekah was in all
works a replica of Sarah his mother. Rabbi Judah said: 'Just
as Isaac was the very image of Abraham, so that whoever
looked at Isaac said, 'There is Abraham,' and knew at once that

'Abraham begot Isaac,' so was Rebekah the very image of Sarah.' " [When Sarah became pregnant, cynics concluded that the father must be Abimelech, being that she spent so many years with Abraham prior to the abduction, and had never conceived. So, in response, God shaped Isaac's features exactly like those of Abraham so that there could be no doubt that Abraham was, indeed, the father.—Rashi on the Tanhuma]

ZOHAR II:133a: "Rabbi Eleazar said: 'All this is truly said. But observe a deeper mystery here. For verily, although Sarah died, her image did not depart from the house. It was not, however, visible for a time, but as soon as Rebekah came it became visible again. . . . No one, however, saw her save Isaac, and thus we understand the words, 'and Isaac was comforted after his mother,' that is, after his mother became visible and was installed in the house again.' "

RAMBAN ON 24:67: This verse illustrates the tremendous honor Isaac bestowed upon his mother even after her death. Her tent was never taken down, and until Rebekah came, no woman was permitted to enter it.

ZOHAR II:133b: Not even Abraham entered her tent again after his wife's death, nor did he permit entrance to the woman he married after her, nor to the handmaids, nor to any other woman save Rebekah. "And Abraham gave all that he had unto Isaac," Scripture will state in the next chapter. This was Abraham's gift to his son; he left the tent entirely to Isaac so that everyday, he alone, could witness his mother's image.

25:1 "And Abraham took another wife, and her name was Keturah."

Rabbinic tradition has it that Keturah was none other than

Hagar, herself. The last we heard of Hagar was back in chapter 21 when she secured a wife for her son, Ishmael.

GENESIS RABBAH 61:4: Rabbi Nehemiah takes issue with the notion that it is Hagar whom we again meet. Why is it written, "And Abraham took *another* wife," he asks. Rabbi Judah replies that, this time, he took her by Divine command. But "Why?" asks Rabbi Nehuniah, "is she called Keturah?" Rabbi Judah explains that this is because she united nobility and piety/"kitrah" in herself.

PIRKE DE RABBI ELIEZER, CHAPTER 30: Her actions were beautiful, like incense, the Hebrew word for incense, *ketoreth*, being closely related to Keturah, her name.

ZOHAR II:133b: ". . . we know by tradition that though Hagar when she left Abraham went astray after the idols of her ancestors, yet in time she again attached herself to a life of virtue. Hence her name Keturah (literally, "attached"). Abraham then sent for her and took her to wife. From here we learn that a change of name acts as an atonement for sin, since that was the reason why her name was changed. The term *vayoseph* [translated here as "another," but literally, "and he added"] indicates not that Abraham took another wife, but that he took again his former spouse whom he had driven out on account of Ishmael, and who had now abandoned her evil practices, and had made a change in her name symbolical of her change of life."

R. Judah said: There are fourteen things which are stronger one than the other, and each one is dominated by the next. The ocean-deep is strong, but the earth dominates it because the deep is subservient to it. The earth is strong, but the mountains are stronger and dominate

---

it. The mountain is strong, but iron dominates it and breaks it. Iron is strong, but fire makes it melt away. Fire is strong, but water dominates it and extinguishes it. Water is strong, but the clouds carry it. The clouds are strong, but wind disperses them. The wind is strong, but a wall dominates it and withstands it. A wall is strong, but a man dominates and demolishes it. Man is strong, but trouble creeps over (and weakens) him. Trouble is strong, but wine dominates it and causes it to be forgotten. Wine is strong, but the Angel of Death dominates it and takes life away. Stronger (worse) than them all, however, is a bad woman. (Ecclesiastes Rabbah 7:26)

Chapter 25:19. And these are the generations of Isaac, Abraham's son: Abraham begot Isaac. 20. And Isaac was forty years old when he took Rebekah, the daughter of Bethuel the Aramean, of Paddan-aram, the sister of Laban the Aramean, to be his wife. 21. And Isaac entreated the Lord for his wife, because she was barren; and the Lord let Himself be entreated of him, and Rebekah his wife conceived. 22. And the children struggled together within her; and she said, "If it be so, wherefore do I live?" And she went to inquire of the Lord. 23. And the Lord said unto her, "Two nations are in thy womb, And two peoples shall be separated from thy bowels; And the one people shall be stronger than the other people; And the elder shall serve the younger." 24. And when her days to be delivered were fulfilled, behold, there were twins in her womb. 25. And the first came forth ruddy all over like a hairy mantle; and they called his name Esau. 26. And after that came forth his brother, and his hand had hold on Esau's heel; and his name was called Jacob. And Isaac was threescore years old when she bore them.

25:20 "... Rebekah, the daughter of Bethuel the Aramean of Paddan-Aram, the sister of Laban the Aramean ..."

This verse is curious to the rabbis. We already have been told that Bethuel is Rebekah's father and that Laban is her brother and that both are from Paddan-aram, so what is Scripture's purpose in restating the fact so repetitively, so emphatically? The rabbis play on the Hebrew word for Aramean/*arami*, which, by a slight transposition, reads as "ram'ai," meaning "rogue" or "cheat":

GENESIS RABBAH 63:4: "Her father was a rogue and her brother was a rogue and the people of her town were, likewise, rogues, and this righteous woman who came forth from among them might well be compared to 'a lily among thorns' (Song of Songs II:2)."

ZOHAR II136:b: She "came from a wicked environment, yet she did not follow their ways, but distinguished herself in good and righteous deeds."

ZOHAR II132:a: In describing the initial meeting between Rebekah and Eliezer, Scripture chooses to state that she "went out" instead of she "came out." Why? "The implication is that God brought her away from the people of the town and made her an exception to them."

RASHI: Scripture restates all these facts of Rebekah's origins just so that her praises can once again be proclaimed.

ZOHAR II:137a: "Isaac was derived from the side of

Abraham, who was the embodiment of supernal Grace [Chesed], and acted graciously towards all creatures, though he himself represented the attribute of Severity [Gevurah]. Rebekah, on the other hand, originated from the side of Severity, but broke away from her kith and kin and joined Isaac; and in spite of her origin, she was of a mild disposition and gracious bearing, so that in the midst of the severity which characterizes Isaac, she was as 'a lily among thorns.' And if not for her gentleness the world would not have been able to endure the severity inherent in Isaac. In this manner God constantly mates couples of opposing natures, one, for example, of a stern with one of a mild type, so that the world preserves its balance."

25:21 "And Isaac entreated the Lord for his wife, because she was barren."

As with Sarah before her, we again meet up with a righteous woman, praised and loved, who is burdened with infertility. What appears to be an immutable destiny, must again, somehow, be bypassed, overturned. The method? Prayer.

ZOHAR II:137a–137b: Isaac and Rebekah lived together for twenty long years, unable to bear children. Why? "God delights in the prayer of the righteous, who thereby attain to higher sanctity and purification. He therefore withholds from them their needs until they offer supplications."

PIRKE DE RABBI ELIEZER, CHAPTER 32: After these twenty years, Isaac takes Rebekah up to Mount Moriah, the place where he had been bound on the altar by his father, and it is there, that he prays to God on her behalf.

GENESIS RABBAH 63:5: Rabbi Johanan says that Isaac "poured out petitions in abundance."

25:21 "And the Lord let Himself be entreated of him, and Rebekah his wife conceived."

GENESIS RABBAH 63:5: Resh Lakish connects the word for *entreated*/"vaye'tar," with the word for *pitchfork*/"athra," and comments that Isaac successfully reversed Rebekah's destiny, just as a pitchfork overturns corn on the threshing floor.

ZOHAR II:137a: ". . . The term 'veye'tar' ('and he entreated') is akin to 'vayehtar' ('and he dug'), signifying that Isaac, in his prayer, dug a tunnel, as it were, leading right up to the supernal department appointed over fecundity. He thus arose above the planetary influences ('mazal') in the same way as Hannah in her prayer (Samuel I:10). Similarly, the term 'vaye'athar' ('and he let himself be entreated') implies that the Lord, Himself, cleared a way for Isaac's prayer, with the result that 'Rebekah his wife conceived.'"

25:22 "And the children struggled together within her; and she said, 'If it be so, wherefore do I live?' And she went to inquire of the Lord."

The matriarch conceives, but unlike Sarah's pregnancy, Rebekah's is wrought with difficulty.

GENESIS RABBAH 63:6: "Do not think that only after issuing into the light of the world was Esau antagonistic to him [his twin brother Jacob], but even while still in his mother's womb, his fist was stretched out against him."

GENESIS RABBAH 63:6: The Hebrew word for the phrase meaning "and they struggled" is *vayithrozazu.* Analyzing the components of this word, the Rabbis found that it contains within it the root *raz*, meaning "to run" and *razaz*, meaning "to slay" or "to crush." . . . "Rabbi Johanan said: Each ran to slay the other."

And reading the Hebrew phrase "and they struggled"/ "vayithrozazu" as "vither zav," meaning "he annulled the law," "Resh Lakish said: Each annulled the laws of the other." Their convictions were irreconcilable; what was going to be permissible to one would be forbidden to the other.

Again referring to the root *raz*/"to run," contained within the phrase, the rabbis read the verse as follows: "They sought to run within her." Whenever Rebekah passed a school, Jacob struggled to come out of her, and when she passed a temple devoted to idolatrous practices, it was Esau who then expressed his eagerness to get out.

25:22 ". . . If it be so, wherefore do I live?"

RASHI: "If the pain of pregnancy is so great, why did I pray for and aspire to it?"

GENESIS RABBAH 63:6: Rebekah sought out the advice of other women, asking them if pregnancy was as painful for them as for her.

RAMBAN: If this is the way it must be, better that I should die now, or never even have come into existence.

GENESIS RABBAH 63:6: Due to Rebekah's merit as a woman, she deserved to have the twelve tribes spring directly from her, rather than from her future son's wives. But, say the rabbis, because of her complaints and her wishes to not have conceived, the privilege was withdrawn.

ZOHAR II:137b, GENESIS RABBAH 63:6: Scripture states that Rebekah, in her pain, went to "inquire of the Lord," which, the Sages inform us, refers to the Academy of two great men of that generation, Shem and Eber.

25:23 "Two nations are in thy womb, and two peoples shall be separated from thy bowels and the one people shall be stronger than the other."

RASHI: Through Divine Inspiration, Shem perceived and conveyed to Rebekah that she was carrying within her womb two opposing nations. Throughout Scripture, whenever the particular word *li'umim* meaning "peoples" is chosen, as it is here, it always refers to a group of people who embody all the characteristics of a full-fledged kingdom. Examining further the words of the prophecy—"shall be separated from thy bowels," implies that "as soon as they leave thy body, they will each take a different course—one to his wicked ways, the other to his plain life." "The one people shall be stronger than the other people" implies that "they will never be equally great at the same time; when one rises, the other will fall."

25:24 "Behold, there were twins in her womb."

Rebekah, does, indeed, give birth to twins of opposite natures. It is Jacob, the younger son, who is destined to be the one chosen to carry out God's will.

RASHI: In verse 24, the Hebrew word for twins is written in a rather peculiar way. It is written "defectively," it is missing two silent letters, the *aleph* and the *yud*. Later in Genesis when we are presented with the story of a woman named Tamar, who also bears twins, we find the word is written correctly. The reason? Both of Tamar's children will grow up to be righteous individuals, whereas one of Rebekah's children will choose to lead a life of immorality.

25:25–26 "And the first came forth . . . and they called his name Esau. And after that came forth his brother, and his hand had hold on Esau's heel; and his name was called Jacob."

ZOHAR II:138a: The literal translation of the verse regarding Jacob's birth is "and *He* called his name Jacob," that is, it was God who called him so.

RASHI: God spoke to those who named Esau, and said—"You have given your firstborn a name, I, too, will give my son, my firstborn, a name."

GLAZERSON ON IMREI SHEFER: The last line of the prophecy that Rebekah receives regarding her unborn children is "and the older shall serve the younger" (25:23). The word for "will serve"/"ya'avod," if vocalized differently, reads "ye'abod," meaning "will be served," which yields a completely opposite interpretation of the text's prophecy: The older will be served *by* the younger! It is man's actions and deeds that ultimately determine the outcome of even God's decrees.

> *"Night"* is the name given to the angel who is appointed to oversee conception. He takes the seed, brings it before God, and questions the Lord regarding the fate of the unborn speck that would grow to human form. "Will he be rich, or will he be poor, foolish or wise, strong or weak?" And everything concerning a life the angel asks of the Lord. But one question only he never asks, for it's not in Heaven's domain, "Will this grain grow up to be wicked or righteous, a lover of the King?" . . . For all is in the hands of God—except the Fear of Him. (Talmud, Niddah *16b*)

Chapter 25:27. And the boys grew; and Esau was a cunning hunter, a man of the field, and Jacob was a quiet man, dwelling in tents. 28. Now Isaac loved Esau, because he did eat of his venison; and Rebekah loved Jacob. 29. And Jacob cooked pottage, and Esau came in from the field and he was faint. 30. And Esau said to Jacob, "Let me swallow, I pray thee, some of this red, red pottage, for I am faint," therefore was his name called Edom (red). 31. And Jacob said, "Sell me first thy birthright."

25:27 "And Esau was a cunning hunter . . . and Jacob was a quiet man, dwelling in tents."

RASHI: What does the description of Esau as "a cunning hunter" imply? It refers to his ability to verbally entrap and deceive. What of the description of Jacob as "a quiet (or plain) man?" He had no expertise in deception, "his heart was his mouth." And what does "dwelling in tents" refer to?—Dwelling in the tent of Shem and Eber.

Neither were the children equally loved by both their parents. Rebekah's affinity for Jacob intensified, as did Isaac's for Esau.

GENESIS RABBAH 63:10: The more Rebekah heard Jacob's voice engaged in the study of Torah, the stronger her love for him grew.

25:30 "Let me swallow, I pray thee, some of this red, red pottage."

Here we have the episode where, in exchange for a little bit of food, Esau sells Jacob his birthright, which, as the elder son, would have been his privilege and honor.

RASHI ON 25:32: At that time, the sacrificial service was carried out by the firstborn son. When Esau asked Jacob to describe the attendant responsibilities, he replied: "Many prohibitions and punishments and many acts involving even the punishment of death are associated with it." To which Esau answered: "If I am going to die through it, why should I desire it?" Esau "despised" his birthright, that is, he despised the idea of service to God, and Jacob recognizes without doubt his brother's unworthiness.

RASHI: On that very day, Abraham had died, just so that he would be saved from seeing his grandson, Esau, falling into degenerate ways. [Abraham's life was cut short by five years; his son, Jacob, would live to one hundred eighty, his father, Abraham, to only one hundred seventy-five.] Jacob boiled lentils, which is the customary first meal for mourners. Lentils are "round like a wheel, and morning (sorrow) is a wheel that revolves in the world, touching everyone sooner or later, just as a revolving wheel touches every spot, in turn."

ZOHAR II:137b–138a: ". . . Observe that the one was of the side of him who rides the serpent [the forces of 'the other side'], whilst the other was of the side of Him who rides on the sacred and perfect throne; of the side of the sun that illuminates the moon. And observe further that because Esau was drawn after that serpent, Jacob dealt with him crookedly like the serpent who is cunning and goes crookedly . . . in order to draw him further serpentward so that he should separate further from himself and thus not have any share with him either in this world or in the world to come; and our teachers have said, 'When a man comes to kill you, kill him first.'" The rabbis go on to teach that even when in the womb, Jacob's purpose in grabbing the heel of his brother was to force him down to the region that had been assigned to him.

Nonetheless, it will ultimately be Rebekah, his mother, who will see and understand what her son, Jacob, has perhaps forgotten. It is she who will be the key instrument in helping him achieve what needs to be done.

Chapter 26:1. And there was a famine in the land, beside the first famine that was in the days of Abraham. And Isaac went unto Abimelech king of the Philistines unto Gerar. 2. And the Lord appeared unto him, and said, "Go not down into Egypt; dwell in the land which I shall tell thee of. 3. Sojourn in this land, and I will be with thee, and will bless thee; for unto thee, and unto thy seed I will give all these lands, and I will establish the oath which I swore unto Abraham thy father; 4. and I will multiply thy seed as the stars of heaven, and will give unto thy seed all these lands, and by thy seed shall all the nations of the earth bless themselves; 5. because that Abraham hearkened to My voice, and kept My charge, My commandments, My statutes, and My laws." 6. And Isaac dwelt in Gerar. 7. And the men of the place asked him of his wife; and he said, "She is my sister"; for he feared to say, "My wife"; lest the men of the place should kill me for Rebekah, because she is fair to look upon." 8. And it came to pass, when he had been there a long time, that Abimelech king of the Philistines looked out a window and saw and behold Isaac was sporting with Rebekah his wife. 9. And Abimelech called Isaac, and said, "Behold, of a surety she is thy wife; and how saidst thou: She is my sister?" And Isaac said unto him, "Because I said: Lest I die because of her." 10. And Abimelech said, "What is this thou hast done unto us? One of the people might easily have lain with thy wife, and thou wouldest have brought guiltiness upon us." 11.

And Abimelech charged all the people, saying, "He that toucheth this man or his wife shall surely be put to death." 12. And Isaac sowed in that land, and found in the same year a hundredfold; and the Lord blessed him.

26:1 "And there was a famine in the land."

ZOHAR II:140a–140b: ". . . The Almighty does not mete out punishment to a man in strict accordance with the evil deeds to which he is addicted, or else the world could not endure. God is thus long-suffering with the righteous, and even more so with the wicked. . . . But with the righteous, God is strict, as he knows they will turn aside neither to the right nor to the left, and therefore he puts them to the test; not for His own sake, since He knows the firmness of their faith, but so as to glorify them the more." Adam fell, Noah fell, but Abraham and Sarah, when confronted with a time of famine and were forced to seek relief in Egypt, emerged from their potentially dangerous encounter with Pharaoh both physically and spiritually unscathed. Now, their son, Isaac, is put to a similar test with his wife Rebekah, and this couple, too, will emerge unscathed. "Thus God proves the righteous in order to glorify them in this world and in the world to come."

26:7 "And he said: She is my sister."

A famine again accosts Canaan, but God instructs Isaac not to seek respite in Egypt, as his parents did, but rather to remain within the confines of the Promised Land. The couple travels to the city of Gerar, and when they arrive, the Philistines inquire regarding Rebekah. Isaac responds to the strangers of Gerar exactly as his father did to both Pharaoh and to Abimelech—He refers to his wife as his sister.

ZOHAR II:140b: Like Abraham, Isaac is referring to the Shekhinah who is present with both him and Rebekah, just as it was with Sarah.

26:8 "Abimelech, King of the Philistines, looked out a window and saw . . . Isaac was sporting with Rebekah his wife."

Remember now that Abimelech is the same ruler who previously had an encounter with Abraham and Sarah. As a result of his dream-exchange with God at that time, he now modifies his behavior towards Isaac, and does not abduct Rebekah to his palace, even though Isaac claims that they are not husband and wife.

ZOHAR II:140b: Abimelech did not literally see the couple making love; rather, Abimelech was an astrologer, and the window that he looked through was, in fact, the planetary constellation, which instructed him of the truth that contrary to Isaac's assertion, Rebekah was, indeed, his wife.

26:12 "And Isaac sowed in that land and found in the same year a hundredfold."

The rabbis teach that the phrase "in the same year" is meant to convey that this prosperity, which was found in a time of general famine, was therefore a divine blessing, and not at all a natural occurrence.

Chapter 27:1. And it came to pass, that when Isaac was old, and his eyes were dim, so that he could not see, he called Esau his elder son, and said unto him, "My son"; and he said unto him, "Here am I." 2. And he said, "Behold now, I am old. I know not the day of my death.

3. Now therefore take, I pray thee, thy weapons, thy quiver and thy bow, and go out to the field, and take me venison; 4. and make me savoury food, such as I love, and bring it to me, that I may eat; that my soul may bless thee before I die." 5. And Rebekah heard when Isaac spoke to Esau his son. And Esau went to the field to hunt for venison, and to bring it. 6. And Rebekah spoke unto Jacob her son, saying, "Behold, I heard thy father speak unto Esau thy brother, saying, 7. Bring me venison, and make me savoury food, that I may eat, and bless thee before the Lord before my death. 8. Now therefore, my son, listen to my voice according to that which I command thee. 9. Go now to the flock, and fetch me from thence two good kids of the goats, and I will make them savoury food for thy father, such as he loveth; 10. and thou shalt bring it to thy father, that he may eat, so that he may bless thee before his death." 11. And Jacob said to Rebekah his mother, "Behold, Esau my brother is a hairy man, and I am a smooth man. 12. My father peradventure will feel me, and I shall seem to him as a mocker, and I shall bring a curse upon me, and not a blessing." 13. And his mother said unto him, "Upon me be thy curse, my son; only hearken to my voice and go fetch me them." 14. And he went, and fetched and brought them to his mother; and his mother made savoury foods, such as his father loved. 15. And Rebekah took the choicest garments of Esau her elder son, which were with her in the house, and put them upon Jacob her younger son. 16. And she put the skins of the kids of the goats upon his hands, and upon the smooth of his neck. 17. And she gave the savoury food and the bread, which she had prepared, into the

hand of her son Jacob. 18. And he came unto his father, and said, "My father," and he said, "Here am I; who
art thou, my son?" 19. And Jacob said unto his father,
"I am Esau thy firstborn . . . ."

ZOHAR II:137b: Rabbi Judah taught that Isaac had "inspired
knowledge" that his son, Jacob, was destined to be born from
him, and that Jacob was destined to then father the twelve
tribes. Rabbi Judah's young son was puzzled. "'If that is so,
why did not Isaac love Jacob as much as Esau, knowing, as he
did, that the former would rear twelve tribes?' 'That is a good
question,' said his father, 'and the answer is as follows: All
creatures of the same kind love one another and are drawn
to one another. Now we are told that Esau 'came forth ruddy,'
a color emblematic of [the Divine attribute of] severity. There
was thus an affinity between Isaac, the representative of severity
on high, and Esau, the embodiment of severity here below;
and through this affinity, Isaac loved him above Jacob. . . .'"

"And Rebekah loved Jacob . . . ." So the seed is planted for
the climactic event in the life of this family. The father approaches the day of his death and calls his beloved firstborn
to his side to bestow upon him his many blessings. But something is very wrong, and Rebekah takes upon herself the
redirection of the inevitable, manipulating events by what appears to be the fabrication of a supreme deception. How do
the sages view Rebekah's actions? Were they righteous and
wise, or terribly misguided, the product of unequal earthly
affections?

GENESIS RABBAH 65:6: Do not think that Rebekah did this
thing because she loved Jacob more than Esau. Rebekah
merely wished to prevent her elderly husband from being

misled. She wished to prevent a situation wherein the wicked would be rewarded and the righteous condemned, a situation wherein not only Esau, but Isaac, her Godly husband, would be hateful in the eyes of the Lord!

RAMBAN: It seems clear that when Rebekah received God's prophecy, as tradition tells us, from the mouth of Shem—"and the elder shall serve the younger"—she kept it to herself and did not share it with her husband. Perhaps, Rebekah felt that it was unnecessary to relate the prophecy to Isaac, who was an even greater prophet than Shem. Seeing that her husband was, in fact, unaware of the prophecy, she reasoned that if he were now to be informed of it, his probable response would not be to bless Jacob instead of Esau, his more beloved, but rather, to merely leave everything in Heaven's hands. By continuing to keep the prophecy hidden and by going through with the secret arrangement, she felt she'd insure that Jacob would be blessed by Isaac, willingly, and without a heart divided.

ZOHAR II:142a: "Observe that Jacob performed all his actions for the sake of God, and therefore God was always with him and did not ever remove His Presence from him. We know this from the fact that although Jacob was not present when Isaac called Esau his son, the Shekhinah told Rebekah, who in her turn, told Jacob .... Observe that had Esau, God forbid, been blessed there and then, Jacob would never have been able to assert himself; but all was directed by Providence, and everything fell into its right place."

In fact, say the sages, Divine Providence had a hand in everything that had taken place and in everything that was about to.

27:1 "Isaac was old, and his eyes were dim, so that he could not see."

Numerous explanations are offered by the rabbis regarding this aspect of Isaac's aged condition.

GENESIS RABBAH 65:10: At the very moment Abraham was about to slay Isaac, the heavens opened up, and the ministering angels witnessing the impending act began to weep. The tears they shed fell to earth, filling Isaac's eyes, and dimming them.

RASHI: Isaac's eyes became dim only so that Jacob, his second born, could receive the blessings.

27:1 ". . . he called Esau his elder son."

PIRKE DE RABBI ELIEZER, CHAPTER 32: At the nightfall of Passover, Isaac called Esau, his elder son, and said: "O, my son! Tonight the heavenly ones utter songs, on this night the treasuries of dew are opened; on this day the blessing of the dew (is bestowed). Make me savoury meat whilst I am still alive, and I will bless thee." Rebekah called Jacob, Isaac's other son and said: "On this night the treasuries of dew will be opened, and on this night the angels utter a song. Make savoury meat for thy father, that he may eat and whilst he still lives he may bless thee."

27:6–9 "And Rebekah spoke unto Jacob her son . . . 'Listen to my voice . . . Go now to the flocks and fetch from thence two good kids of the goats.' "

GENESIS RABBAH 65:14: In the Book of Ezekiel (34:31), God addresses His chosen people as a flock, and Himself as their faithful shepherd: "For you, My flock that I tend, are men; and I your shepherd, am your God." Rebekah is saying to her son: "Go and anticipate the blessings on behalf of the people that is compared to a flock."

"Good kids?" ask the rabbis. They are good for both Jacob and for his descendants. Good for Jacob because through them, with their aid, he will receive the blessings, and good for his descendants who will, in the future, utilize them in their sin-offerings on the Day of Atonement and thereby seek Divine pardon (Leviticus, chapter 30).

Jacob is afraid to follow his mother's advice, afraid that instead of receiving a blessing, he will be the recipient of his father's curse.

27:13 "And his mother said unto him, 'Upon me be thy curse.'"

GENESIS RABBAH 65:15: "When a man sins, is it not his mother that is cursed?" When Adam, who was taken from the ground, followed Eve's lead and ate the forbidden fruit, it was his mother, the ground, that was cursed: "And unto Adam He said . . . 'Cursed is the ground for thy sake; in toil shalt thou eat of it all the days of thy life'" (Gen. 3:17). It had been Adam's task to care for the garden, to till the ground. Now, the ground would yield its produce only after painstaking labor and prodding, and only weeds, unfit for human consumption, would sprout forth unassisted. "Upon me be thy curse," Rebekah says.

GENESIS RABBAH 65:15: Rebekah is taking upon herself the *duty* of telling her husband that Jacob is the righteous one and that Esau, the one he loves more, is undeserving of his blessing: Upon me be the responsibility for *averting* the curse.

27:15 "And Rebekah took the choicest of garments of Esau . . . and put them upon Jacob."

ZOHAR II:142b: These garments were not ordinary garments; they originally belonged to Adam and later they came into the possession of Nimrod, a mighty hunter. One day out in the field, Esau slayed Nimrod and he took the precious garments for himself, storing them in Rebekah's home, retrieving them and putting them on whenever he went out hunting. But on the day that Isaac wished to bless him, on that particular day ". . . he went out into the field without them, and thus he stayed there longer than usual. Now when Esau put on those garments no aroma whatever was emitted from them, but when Jacob put them on they were restored to their rightful place, and a sweet odor was diffused from them. For Jacob inherited the beauty of Adam; hence those garments found in him their rightful owner, and thus gave off their proper aroma. Said Rabbi Jose: 'Can it really be so, that Jacob's beauty equalled that of Adam, seeing that, according to tradition, the fleshy part of Adam's heel outshone the orb of the sun? Would you then say the same of Jacob' Said Rabbi Eleazar in reply: 'Assuredly Adam's beauty was as tradition says, but only at first before he sinned, when no creature could endure to gaze at his beauty; after he sinned, however, his beauty was diminished and his height was reduced to a hundred cubits. Observe further that Adam's beauty is a symbol with which the true faith is closely bound up . . . . And Jacob assuredly participated of that beauty.'"

Rebekah prepares Isaac's favorite food and hands it to Jacob, her son.

GENESIS RABBAH 65:17: "She accompanied him as far as the door and then said to him: Thus far I owed thee my aid; from here thy Creator will assist thee."

Jacob, with trepidation, follows his mother's instructions, his arms covered with goat skins to mimic the hairy skin of his brother, and enters his father's room.

27:22 "And Jacob went near unto Isaac his father; and he felt him and said, 'The voice is the voice of Jacob, but the hands are the hands of Esau.' 23. And he discerned him not . . . 26. . . . 'Come near now and kiss me, my son.' 27. . . . And he smelled the smell of his raiment and blessed him and said: 'See the smell of my son is as the smell of a field which the Lord hath blessed.'"

GENESIS RABBAH 65:22: "Nothing has a more offensive smell than skins stripped from goats . . . . The fact is, however, that when Jacob went in to his father, the Garden of Eden entered with him."

ZOHAR II:142b: When Jacob enters his father's room, the sweet divine odors emitted by the garments are what encourage Isaac to bless Jacob, for he then felt assured that the son standing before him was indeed deserving of his blessings.

Chapter 27:30. And it came to pass, as soon as Isaac had made an end of blessing Jacob, and Jacob was yet scarce gone out from the presence of Isaac his father, that Esau his brother came in from his hunting . . . 32. And Isaac his father said unto him, "Who art thou?" And he said, "I am thy son, thy firstborn, Esau." 33. And Isaac trembled very exceedingly, and said, "Who then is he that hath taken venison, and brought it me, and I have eaten of all before thou camest, and have blessed him? . . . 34. When Esau heard the words of his father, he cried with an exceeding great and bitter cry, and said unto his father, "Bless me, even me also, O my father."

35. And he said, "Thy brother came with guile, and hath taken away thy blessing." 36. And he said, "Is not he rightly named Jacob? For he hath supplanted me these two times: he took away my birthright; and, behold, now he hath taken away my blessing." And he said, "Hast thou not reserved a blessing for me?" . . . 38. . . . "Hast thou but one blessing, my father? Bless me, even me also, O my father." And Esau lifted up his voice and wept.

27:33: "And Isaac trembled very exceedingly."

ZOHAR II:143a: "At that moment the angel Michael, accompanied by the Shekhinah, appeared before Jacob. Isaac felt all this and he also saw the Garden of Eden beside Jacob, and so he blessed him in the presence of the angel. But when Esau entered, there entered with him the Gehinnom [Hell], and thus we read: 'And Isaac trembled very exceedingly,' as until that time he had not thought that Esau was of that side."

RASHI: Why did Isaac tremble? He thought: Maybe I've erroneously blessed the younger son before the older. When Esau cried out, "He hath supplanted me these two times," Isaac asked him to explain what he meant; what had his brother done to him? When Esau told his father that Jacob had bought his birthright, Isaac's trepidations vanished. "It was on account of this that I was grieved and trembled—perhaps I had overstepped the line of strict justice. Now, however, I have really blessed the firstborn."

Chapter 27:41. And Esau hated Jacob because of the blessing wherewith his father blessed him. And Esau said in his heart, "Let the days of mourning for my father be at hand; then will I slay my brother Jacob." 42. And the words of Esau her elder son were told to Rebekah; and she sent and called Jacob her younger son, and said unto him, "Behold thy brother Esau, as touching thee, doth comfort himself, purposing to kill thee. 43. Now therefore, my son, hearken to my voice; and arise, flee thou to Laban my brother to Haran; 44. and tarry with him a few days. . . 45. until thy brother's anger turn away from thee, and he forget that which thou hast done to him; then I will send, and fetch thee from thence; why should I be bereaved of you both in one day? 46. And Rebekah said to Isaac, "I am weary of my life because of the daughters of Heth. If Jacob take a wife of the daughters of the land, what good shall my life do me?" Chapter 28:1. And Isaac called Jacob, and blessed him, and charged him, and said unto him, "Thou shalt not take a wife of the daughters of Canaan. 2. Arise, go to Paddan-aram, to the house of Bethuel thy mother's father; and take thee a wife from thence of the daughters of Laban thy mother's brother. "7. And Jacob hearkened to his father and his mother . . . . 8. And Esau saw that the daughters of Canaan pleased not Isaac his father; 9. so Esau went unto Ishmael, and took unto the wives that he had Mahalath the daughter of Ishmael Abraham's son, the sister of Nebaioth, to be his wife. 10. And Jacob went out from Beersheba and went toward Haran . . . .

27:42 "And the words of Esau . . . were told to Rebekah."

GENESIS RABBAH 67:9: All the matriarchs were prophetesses, and what Esau thought inside his heart was prophetically revealed to Rebekah by the Holy Spirit. Her job was not over. She saw the probable consequences of her actions and she needed to protect Jacob from Esau's wrath. Again Rebekah beseeches her son to "listen to her voice," her counsel, and to immediately leave Canaan.

27:42 "Esau . . . doth comfort himself."

GENESIS RABBAH 67:9: Esau acts as though Jacob is already dead; he drinks the "cup of consolation" that mourners drink right after a funeral!

27:45 "Why should I be bereaved of you both in one day?"

RASHI: If Esau attacks Jacob, and Jacob in defense kills him, Esau's children would then in turn rise up against Jacob. Rebekah's prophetic visions informed her that if no protective action were now taken, both of her children would be condemned to death in one day!

27:46 "And Rebekah said to Jacob, 'I am weary of my life.'"

To convince her husband of the urgency for their son to depart, Rebekah acts as though she is anguished solely by the possibility that Jacob will take a wife from among the local women, and under this pretense, Jacob is then equally urged by both of his parents to flee to Haran, some five hundred miles away.

28:7–8 "And Jacob hearkened to his father and mother . . . and Esau saw that the daughters of Canaan pleased not Isaac his father."

GENESIS RABBAH 67:12: "The way of a fool is straight in his own eyes" (Proverbs 21:2). Jacob heeds his parents' instruction. Esau, who, to the dismay of his parents, had previously taken wives from among the local idol-worshippers, (ironically marrying at the age of forty, the same age at which his father took the righteous Rebekah, now, after Jacob's departure,) takes wives from among Ishmael's clan to mollify the apparent vexation of his parents over this matter.

In the name of the Good, Rebekah has sent away her beloved son, never to see him again; when Jacob returns to Canaan, some twenty years later, his mother is no longer alive. Unlike Scripture's clear and extensive recounting of the death of Sarah, her predecessor, no explicit mention is made of Rebekah's death. But, why?

PESIKTA RABBATI 12:4: When Rebekah died, everyone asked: Who will walk before her bier? Abraham is dead. Isaac stays at home because his eyes are dim, and Jacob has gone off to Haran. If the wicked Esau walks before her bier, people will curse Rebekah for having borne him. So Rebekah was taken out at night and quietly buried. Our rabbis teach that Rebekah, herself, had asked that this be done.

What of Jacob, the son for whom Rebekah stretched herself to the limits of motherly endurance, all for the sake of Higher Obligation?

Rachel and Leah

The Book of Genesis, Chapter 28.

GENESIS RABBAH 68:4: "A Roman matron asked Rabbi Jose: 'In how many days did the Holy One, blessed be He, create His world?' 'In six days,' he answered. 'Then, what has He been doing since then?' 'He sits and makes matches,' he answered, 'assigning this man to that woman, and this woman to that man.' 'If that is difficult,' she gibed, 'I, too, can do the same.' She went and matched her slaves, giving this man to that woman, and this woman to that man, and so on. Some time after, those who were thus united went and beat one another, this woman saying, 'I do not want this man,' while this man protested, 'I do not want that woman.'. . . Said he [Rabbi Jose] to her [the matron], 'If it is easy in your eyes, it is as difficult before the Holy One, blessed be He, as the dividing of the Red Sea!' "

GENESIS RABBAH 68:3: "Houses and riches are the inheritance of fathers; but a prudent wife is from the Lord (Proverbs 19:14). We find in the Torah, the Prophets, and the Writings, that a man's marriage partner is from the Holy One, blessed be He."

GENESIS RABBAH 68:3: "Sometimes a man goes to his spouse, and sometimes it is the reverse. In the case of Isaac, his spouse came to him.... Jacob, however, went to his spouse, as it is written, 'And Jacob went out.' ..."

> Chapter 28:10. And Jacob went out from Beersheba and went toward Haran. 11. And he lighted upon the place and tarried there all night, because the sun was set; and he took one of the stones of the place and put it under his head and layed down in that place to sleep. 12. And he dreamed, and behold a ladder set up on earth, and the top of it reached to heaven; and behold the angels of God ascending and descending on it. 13. And behold the Lord stood beside him and said, "I am the Lord, the God of Abraham thy Father and the God of Isaac. The land wherein thou liest, to thee will I give it, and to thy seed . . . 16. And Jacob awaked out of his sleep and he said, "Surely the Lord is in this place and I knew it not."

Escaping Esau's wrath, Jacob left his home in Canaan, making his way towards Haran, the home of his mother's brother. His journey, initiated by Rebekah, will provide the means for Destiny to work its hand. Just as Eliezer's journey in search of Rebekah was under the protection and guidance of the Divine, so, too, is Jacob's.

RASHI ON 28:11: Jacob's journey, like Eliezer's, was miraculously shortened, and he arrived quite prematurely at Mount Moriah, the place where his father was bound on the altar. "The sun set unexpectedly—not at its proper time—just in order that he should tarry there overnight" and have his experience of a direct communion with God.

28:11 "And he took one of the stones."

Traditional translations of Scripture indicate that Jacob

placed only one stone beneath his head for a pillow, but the Sages teach that when Jacob lay down to sleep, his head rested upon more stones than were there when he awoke.

TANHUMA, BUBER 7.4: Jacob thought in his heart: My grandfather, Abraham, had two wives and between the two sons they bore, one, Isaac, was righteous, and the other, Ishmael, was wicked. Then my own father, Isaac, from only one woman, my mother Rebekah, also sired one righteous son and one who was wicked. I know that I am destined to take not one wife or even two, but four wives! How many wicked sons will I be responsible for bringing into the world? "The Holy One said to him: 'Heaven forfend! You are beautiful all over, My beloved, there is no blemish in you.' " And when he awoke in the morning, he found that all the stones had merged into one. "The Holy One said to him: 'By your life, just as all these stones have become one, so shall all of your sons be righteous.' "

28:16 "Surely the Lord is in this place and I ["anochi"] knew it not."

ZOHAR II:150a–150b: What Jacob is really saying is that he has never before known the Holy Spirit, the Shekhinah (represented here by this particular form of the word for "I"). When he awakens, he is surprised that he has just been graced with such an amazing Divine revelation even though he had not yet achieved the prophetic level wherein such knowledge could naturally be attained. The mystics teach that the Shekhinah does not rest upon an unmarried man. The rabbis refer back to Genesis 25:22 wherein the pregnant Rebekah, in the midst of a painful pregnancy exclaims, "Then wherefore do I live?" The word for "I" used here is also "anochi";

unlike Jacob, Rebekah saw "the splendor of the Shekhinah" every single day of her life. When "she went to inquire of the Lord" (*Lord* being written here in the form of the four-lettered Tetragrammaton, *Yud-Heh-Vav-Heh*), the sages teach that she proceeded from the prophetic level of the Shekhinah to an even higher level, represented by those deeply mysterious four letters.

According to the sages, Jacob and the two principal wives he will take, are all endowed with prophetic ability. Their dilemmas, decisions, and actions are all influenced not by whim, but by a knowledge and understanding of their earthly purpose, their desire to live in accordance with God's Will, and as our Kabbalists teach, with a wish to have their lives be a perfect reflection of the pattern upon which the heavenly Universes are themselves modeled.

Chapter 29:1. Then Jacob went on his journey, and came to the land of the children of the east. 2. And he looked, and behold a well in the field, and lo three flocks of sheep lying there by it—for out of that well they watered the flocks. And the stone upon the well's mouth was great. 3. And thither were all the flocks gathered; and they rolled the stone from the well's mouth and watered the sheep, and put the stone back upon the well's mouth in its place. 4. And Jacob said unto them, "My brethren, whence are ye?" And they said, "Of Haran are we." 5. And he said unto them, "Know ye Laban the son of Nahor?" And they said, "We know him." 6. And he said unto them, "Is it well with him?" and they said, "It is well; and behold, Rachel his daughter cometh with the sheep." 7. And he said, "Lo, it is yet high day, neither is it time that the cattle should be gathered together;

water ye the sheep, and go and feed them." 8. And they said, "We cannot until all the flocks be gathered together, and they roll the stone from the well's mouth; then we water the sheep." 9. While he was yet speaking with them, Rachel came with her father's sheep; for she tended them. 10. And it came to pass, when Jacob saw Rachel the daughter of Laban his mother's brother, and the sheep of Laban his mother's brother, that Jacob went near, and rolled the stone from the well's mouth, and watered the flock of Laban his mother's brother. 11. And Jacob kissed Rachel, and lifted up his voice, and wept. 12. And Jacob told Rachel that he was her father's brother, and that he was Rebekah's son; and she ran and told her father. 13. And it came to pass, when Laban heard the tidings of Jacob his sister's son, that he ran to meet him and embraced him and kissed him and brought him to his house. And he told Laban all these things. 14. And Laban said to him, "Surely thou art my bone and my flesh." And he abode with him the space of a month. 15. And Laban said unto Jacob, "Because thou art my brother, shouldest thou therefore serve me for nought? Tell me, what shall thy wages be?"

29:1 "Then Jacob went on his journey and came to the land of the children of the east."

ZOHAR II:153a: Jacob's destination is Laban's home in Haran, so why, ask the rabbis, did Jacob travel further on east, past Haran? The Sages refer to the Kabbalist structure of Divine Emanations and their meanings to explain Jacob's motives. They teach that Jacob's aim was to "enter into communion" with the Shekhinah, or in other words, to get married. (Jacob is later taken by the Sages to be a representative or embodiment of the Divine emanation of Tiferet-Beauty. In the system of Kabbalah, when Tiferet is in perfect union or marriage with the final emanation, Malkhut, the Shekhinah, then the supernal universe from whence God's emanations originate, is in perfect harmony and balance, and blessings can freely flow down to the lower levels of creation.) Jacob recalls that when Eliezer went out in search of a wife for Isaac, he found a well of water and subsequently met the woman destined for his father. When Jacob reaches Haran and does not, anywhere, see a well or spring or any body of water, he travels further on, still searching, and it is in "the land of the children of the east" that his search for the well is rewarded.

Is a well merely a hole in the ground, and is water just for drinking? As we've seen, to the Sages dissatisfied with a literal rendering of Scripture, the endeavor to uncover the hidden significance of recurring images is recorded in the Rabbinic midrashim and embedded within the Zohar and other Kabbalistic works. Every miniscule detail of the Scriptural story of the marriage of Jacob to Leah and Rachel and the birth of their children contains a wealth of esoteric meaning. To fully comprehend these secrets, I believe that a full working knowledge is required; one can be no less than a devoted student of Kabbalah. Many of the excerpts that follow, as well as some of the preceding ones, may, in part, be incomprehensible to one not schooled in these mysteries, but my purpose here is to present only the smallest taste, to whet the appetite for further study and investigation. To this author the ideas seem so majestic, that even lacking any true depth of understanding, truths yet somehow seem to be emotionally conveyed.

In previous chapters, Scripture gave lengthy accounts of the efforts of Jacob's father and grandfather to dig and redig wells for water. Besides the obvious necessity for securing physical drinking water, the sages discuss the spiritual implications underlying their efforts. Water, for one, is a symbol of the Divine emanation of Wisdom.

26:18 "And Isaac digged again the wells of water which they had digged in the days of Abraham his father; for the Philistines had stopped them after the death of Abraham."

ZOHAR II:141a: "In digging these wells Isaac acted fittingly, for he discerned from his knowledge of the mysteries of Wisdom that in this way he could attach himself more firmly to his faith. Abraham likewise made a point of digging a well of water. Jacob found the well already prepared for him, and he sat down by it. Thus they all looked for a well and strove, through it, to preserve their faith pure and undiminished. And nowadays, Israel holds fast to the well through the *symbolism* of the precepts of the Torah. . . . Hence our ancestors strengthened themselves in the true faith in digging the well, symbolic of the Supernal Well, which is the abode of the mystery of perfect faith."

ZOHAR II:141a–141b: " 'And thou shalt be like a watered garden' (Isaiah 58:2), that is, like the celestial garden whose supernal waters never fail, but flow on forever and ever; 'and like a spring of water whose waters fail not' alluding to the river that issues from Eden and flows on for all eternity."

26:19 "And Isaac's servants digged in the valley and found there a well of living water."

RAMBAN: The "Well of Living Water" alludes to the Temple in Jerusalem which the children of Israel, Isaac's descendants, will one day build.

Now keeping in mind the dimensions of unspoken symbol, we move on with our story.

29:2 "And he looked and behold a well in the field, and lo three flocks of sheep lying there by it."

GENESIS RABBAH 70:8: The rabbis expound numerous interpretations of the well that Jacob finally comes upon, the stone on its mouth and the three flocks of sheep. All the interpretations have one thing in common—they allude to the future. According to the rabbis, this episode in Scripture is a foreshadowing of Jacob's guaranteed success in his endeavor to father righteous children who will carry forward, to fulfillment, the Divine promise of nationhood. The well is taken by different sages to represent Zion, Sinai, the Sanhedrin, the synagogue, and the Living Waters of the Torah.

RAMBAN: The well alludes to the Sanctuary, and the three flocks of sheep represent the pilgrims who will routinely ascend to the Sanctuary during the three major festivals: Passover, Shavuos, and Succos (as cited in Deuteronomy, chapter 16). "For out of that well they watered the flocks" alludes to the idea that from the sanctuary they will "drink the Holy Spirit."

29:3 "And they rolled the stone from the well's mouth."

ZOHAR II:152a: "They dispelled from it the rigidity of hard judgement, which congeals as it were into stone, from which water cannot flow."

ZOHAR II:153a: "Jacob was at first under sacred jurisdiction, but when he departed from the land [Canaan], he entered into a strange jurisdiction. And before he came under a strange jurisdiction the Holy One, blessed be He, appeared unto him in a dream, and he saw wonderful things, and holy angels accompanied him until he sat down by the well; and when he sat by the well the waters thereof rose toward him, as a portent that he would there meet his wife, and the same thing happened to Moses [also a fugitive]. The inward significance of the matter is that the well only rose when it saw its affinity, to form with him a union."

29:10 "Jacob went near and rolled the stone from the well's mouth."

RASHI, GENESIS RABBAH 70:12: Jacob watches Laban's younger daughter, Rachel, as she approaches with the sheep, and "as easily as one draws the stopper from the mouth of a bottle" he rolls the stone away from the mouth of the well. He kisses the girl, and he weeps. Why the tears? Happiness? No, say the rabbis. Jacob weeps because at the moment of their meeting he perceives, by virtue of the Holy Spirit, that this lovely girl whom he would in time marry and deeply love was not destined to be buried beside him.

In the following chapter, Rachel, barren like her predecessors, will bargain with her sister for possession of some mandrakes (thought to possess fertile powers) that Leah's son found in the field. In exchange for the mysterious plants, Rachel allows Jacob to spend the night with her sister, instead of with her. "Therefore he shall lie with thee tonight," Rachel says to Leah. The rabbis teach that Rachel, too, was exposing her knowledge of the future, her statement referring not only to the situation at hand, to that particular night, but to all eternity. "Jacob will sleep his last sleep with you, Leah, but not with me," she infers.

29:12 "And Jacob told Rachel that he was her father's brother and that he was Rebekah's son."

RASHI: By way of their first introduction, Jacob tells Rachel that he is Rebekah's son *and her father's brother*. Why the falsehood? What do his words actually mean? Jacob is on guard; he refuses to be diverted from his goal of marrying Rachel. "If he (Laban) intends to practice deceit on me, then I am his brother (a match for him) in deception; if however, he is an honest man, then, I, too, am the son of his sister, the pious Rebekah."

29:13 "When Laban heard the tidings of Jacob, his sister's son . . . he ran to meet him and embraced him and kissed him."

GENESIS RABBAH 70:13, 70:14: The rabbis paint Laban as a true rogue, none of his motives or actions having merit. Tradition has it that when Laban ran out to greet Jacob, embracing and kissing him, it was solely to discover the money and gems he felt certain that this beloved member of Abraham's household would come bearing as gifts—just as Eliezer, a mere servant, had. He finds nothing. "I have come laden with naught but words."

One month later, when Laban questions Jacob's willingness to work for him, to serve him without receiving wages, the rabbis put words to Jacob's attitude, "Thinkest thou that I have come to demand money? I have come only for the sake of thy two daughters."

So the intricate story begins to play itself out, step by step by step, moving relentlessly toward the fulfillment of a Divine predestination.

Chapter 29:16. Now Laban had two daughters: the name of the elder was Leah, and the name of the younger was Rachel. 17. And Leah's eyes were weak, but Rachel was of beautiful form and fair to look upon. 18. And Jacob loved Rachel, and he said, "I will serve thee seven years for Rachel thy younger daughter." 19. And Laban said, "It is better that I give her to thee, than that I should give her to another man; abide with me." 20. And Jacob served seven years for Rachel; and they seemed unto to him but a few days, for the love he had for her. 21. And Jacob said unto Laban, "Give me my wife, for my days are fulfilled, that I may go in unto her." 22. And Laban gathered together all the men of the place, and made a feast. 23. And it came to pass in the evening, that he took Leah his daughter, and brought her to him; and he went in unto her. 24. And Laban gave Zilpah his handmaid unto his daughter Leah for a handmaid. 25. And it came to pass in the morning that, behold, it was Leah; and he said to Laban, "What is this thou hast done unto me? Did not I serve with thee for Rachel? Wherefore then hast thou beguiled me?" 26. And Laban said, "It is not so done in our place to give the younger before the first born. 27. Fulfill the week of this one, and we will give thee the other also for the service which thou shalt serve with me yet seven other years." 28. And Jacob did so, and fulfilled her week; and he gave him Rachel his daughter to wife. 29. And Laban gave to Rachel his daughter Bilhah his handmaid to be her handmaid. 30. And he went in also unto Rachel, and he loved Rachel more than Leah, and served with him yet seven other years.

29:16 "Now Laban had two daughters."

GENESIS RABBAH 70:15: ". . . like two beams running from end to end of the world. Each produced captains, each produced kings, from each arose slayers of lions, from each arose conquerors of countries."

The rabbis read the word for *daughter*/"banoth" as *bonoth*/"builders." Why? From Rachel and Leah the whole of Israel was built up: From Leah will come the first six of the twelve tribes; from her handmaid, two more. From Rachel will sprout two tribes; from her handmaid, the two remaining (the children of the handmaids being regarded as direct descendants of the women they serve).

Leah will be the first to conceive, giving birth to four sons in succession—Reuben, Simeon, Levi, and Judah. From the tribe of Levi will come four illustrious individuals, Jochebed, Miriam, Aaron, and Moses. From Judah will descend Bezalel, the Tabernacle's artist; Boaz, Ruth's second husband; King David; and King Solomon. Rachel's handmaid Bilhah will be the next to conceive, bearing Dan and Naphtali. From the tribe of Dan we will receive Samson; from Naphtali will come the beloved judge, Deborah and her general, Barak. Leah's handmaid, Zilpah, will then bear Gad and Asher. From Asher will descend a woman who figures throughout Rabbinic lore, Serach. Leah will give birth to two more sons, Issachar and Zebulun, and one daughter, Dinah. (Dinah's daughter is said to have become Joseph's wife in Egypt.) And then Rachel, herself, will finally bear two sons, Joseph and Benjamin, Joseph's sons being Ephraim and Menasseh. From the tribe of Ephraim will come Moses' successor, Joshua. From Menasseh will come Gideon and the wise daughters of Zelophehad. From the tribe of Benjamin we will be given Saul, Mordecai, and the brave and beautiful Esther.

29:17 "And Leah's eyes were weak, but Rachel was of beautiful form."

Scripture has already introduced us to the stunning Rachel, but just as the first thing we are told about the righteous Sarah is the sad fact that she is barren, the first thing we are told about the future progenitor of six tribes, the matriarch Leah, is the seemingly unflattering fact that her eyes are weak. But, say the rabbis, despite its surface appearance, this description means no disgrace to Leah, but, in fact, relays exactly the opposite: Her weak eyes are cause for praise.

TANHUMA, BUBER 7.12: "When Rebekah bore Esau and Jacob, there were born to Laban two daughters, Leah and Rachel. They sent letters to each other and agreed among themselves that Esau would take Leah, and Jacob Rachel. Now Leah would ask about the conduct of Esau and would hear that his conduct is bad. So she would cry all the time and say: Thus my lot has fallen to this wicked man. And for this reason her eyes became weak."

GENESIS RABBAH 70:16: She would cry and pray to God that somehow she would be kept from falling into Esau's possession. So "great is prayer, that it annulled the decree [her destiny], and she even took precedence of her sister."

TANHUMA, BUBER 7.12: Leah is not to be thought of as ugly in any way. "In fact, she was as beautiful as Rachel. . . . They were equal in beauty, in loveliness, and in stature."

It is, nonetheless, Rachel whom Jacob meets at the well, and Rachel whom he asks Laban for permission to marry.

29:18 "I will serve thee seven years for Rachel thy younger daughter."

GENESIS RABBAH 70:17: Jacob said to Laban: "Knowing that the people of your town are deceivers, I make my demands absolutely clear . . . 'For Rachel,' not for Leah; 'Thy daughter'—Thou art not to bring some other woman from the marketplace named Rachel; 'Younger'—Thou art not to exchange their names. But even if you fix a wicked man in a carpenter's vice, it will avail you naught."

29:20 "And Jacob served seven years for Rachel, and they seemed unto him but a few days."

"But a few days?" How can this be? Wouldn't we expect the very opposite—that because of his extraordinary love for her, each day seemed to prolong itself into an interminable eon? The Chasidic Rabbi of Apt explained to his disciples that there are two very different types of love. In the first type, the love felt by the lover "attaches" itself to his beloved one, and then, to the lover, returns. In the second type, the kind felt by Jacob for Rachel, the love remains attached to the beloved, and in not returning to the lover, relieves him of any desperate longing, all self-centered involvement and need. His is the purest love that can be, the love shared by those unquestionably ordained to be mated.[31]

When the agreed upon seven years of service had ended, Jacob demands his due.

29:21 "Give me my wife, for my days are fulfilled."

GENESIS RABBAH 70:18: Why does Jacob speak to Laban

---

31. Martin Buber, *Tales of the Hasidim. Later Masters* (New York: Schocken Books, 1975), 116–117.

so curtly, so roughly, disregarding common courtesy? The rabbis explain that Jacob, aware of the Divine decree that he was
to father twelve tribes, is beginning to grow anxious in his
urgency, given that he is already eighty-four years old!

(Talmud, *Megillah* 17a: Jacob was sixty-three years old when
he received his father's blessings. He is said to have spent the
next fourteen in seclusion, studying at the academy of Shem
and Eber. Adding on another seven years of service to Laban,
we find that Jacob is eighty-four when he takes his first wife;
Esau, his brother, was only forty when he married.)

29:22 "And Laban gathered together all the men of the place and made a feast."

GENESIS RABBAH 70:19: Laban was convinced that it was
the righteous Jacob's presence in his town that caused their
supply of water to become suddenly abundant, and not want-
ing to relinquish this boon, he gathered the townsmen together and conspired with them to plan a deception. He
would secretly give Leah to Jacob in marriage knowing that
out of love for Rachel, he would agree to remain in the town
and work for another seven years. Laban demanded that the
men all give him pledges as an assurance that none of them
would disclose his plan, and they agreed. With their pledges,
however, Laban went and bought wine, oil, and meat for the
feast. This is why he is called Laban the Arami; because he
deceived ("rimmah") even his own townspeople. All day long,
the men sang Laban's praises, but when evening fell, still they
did not stop. "Hi leah, hi leah," they sang, which is an excla-
mation of joy, but without Laban's knowledge it was actually
meant to be a subtle hint for the innocent Jacob, who, unfortunately, did not comprehend their meaning. Later that
evening, they led Leah to the bridal chamber and extinguished

the light. The entire night, Jacob called his new bride "Rachel," and all night, Leah answered him. In the morning, however, Jacob saw that he had been tricked. "Said he to her, 'You are a deceiver and the daughter of a deceiver!' 'Is there a teacher without pupils?' she retorted. 'Did not your father call you "Esau," and you answered him? So did you, too, call me, and I answered you!' "

TALMUD, *MEGILLAH* 13b, RASHI: When Jacob first asked Rachel if she would marry him, she warned him of her father's deceptive nature, how he would use any means in an attempt to trick him. "In trickery," Jacob answered, "I am your father's brother." (The rabbis derive this midrash from verse 29:12 wherein Jacob falsely introduces himself to Rachel as her father's brother!) "But is it permissable for a man like you to indulge in trickery?" she asked. "Yes," he replied. "With the pure you act in purity, and with the perverse and crooked you are wiley" (from II Samuel 22:27). So Jacob gave Rachel certain secret signs by which they could always recognize one another. When night came and Rachel saw Leah about to be brought to Jacob for the marriage ceremony, she transmitted the signs to her sister, not wishing to put her to shame. In reward for this act of kindness, Rachel would be restored to her destined role as Jacob's principal wife.

29:30 "And he loved Rachel more than Leah, and served with him yet seven other years."

GENESIS RABBAH 70:20: "When a laborer works for an employer, he generally works zealously for two or three hours, but eventually becomes indolent in his work. Here, however, as the former years were complete, so were the latter [seven years]; as he worked faithfully in the former, so did he in the latter"—despite Laban's deception.

ZOHAR II:153a, 158a: "Since Jacob had to find his wife by the well, why did he not meet there Leah, who was to be the mother of so many tribes? The answer is that it was not the will of God that Leah should be espoused to Jacob openly, and, in fact, he married her without his knowledge."

"All that concerned Leah is kept under a veil, as she typified the upper world, which is veiled and undisclosed [to man].... She symbolizes the world that is absolutely concealed." Rachel, however, symbolizes the world that is disclosed, our manifest world, the created world, the lower world.

> *"Noah, who lived blamelessly, was called righteous. Likewise, we find that because Abraham lived blamelessly ... he earned the merit of acquiring both heaven and earth.... He merited heaven in that his offspring deserved to inherit the Torah, which was given from heaven. And he merited the earth in that they deserved to be fruitful and multiply like the dust of the earth. Why all this? Because of the blamelessness that he exhibited.*
>
> *And so you find in every case where one had perfected his heart in blamelessness that God paired him off with an equally good counterpart. Thus we find in the case of Abraham that because he lived blamelessly, Sarah was paired off with him; and so we also find in the case of Isaac that because he lived blamelessly, Rebekah was paired off with him; and likewise in the case of Jacob we find that because he lived blamelessly, Rachel and Leah were paired off with him.... It is of them that Solomon spoke explicitly in his Wisdom, saying, 'Property and riches are bequeathed by fathers, but an efficient wife*

comes from the Lord'" (Proverbs 19:14). Midrash on
Proverbs, chapter 19

The Zohar tells us that Jacob had a knowledge of mystic
symbolism, and that all his actions were guided by this awareness. In fact, the rabbis view the marriage of Jacob to Rachel
and Leah and the subsequent birth of all their children, as
having meanings far beyond the literal; each event, both those
directed by man and those ordained by God, is the expression of an effort to reproduce the heavenly supernal pattern
in the world of man.

Chapter 29:31. And the Lord saw that Leah was hated,
and He opened her womb; but Rachel was barren. 32.
And Leah conceived and bore a son, and she called his
name Reuben; for she said, "Because the Lord hath
looked upon my affliction; for now my husband will love
me." 33. And she conceived again and bore a son and
said, "Because the Lord hath heard that I am hated, He
hath therefore given me this son also." And she called
his name Simeon. 34. And she conceived again and bore
a son and said, "Now this time will my husband be
joined unto me, because I have borne him three sons."
Therefore was his name called Levi. 35. And she conceived again and bore a son and she said, "This time
will I praise the Lord." Therefore she called his name
Judah; and she left off bearing.

29:31 "Leah was hated."

TANHUMA, BUBER 7.11: Leah was not hated because she
was repugnant to Jacob, but because of her chastisement of
him. When he discovered that he'd been wed to the wrong
woman, Jacob called her a swindler, and Leah callously re-

minded him of his own deception of his father. Because of these scalding remarks, Jacob began to hate her.

GENESIS RABBAH 71:2: The rabbis teach that the hatred for Leah was not limited to Jacob—the townspeople, even visiting travellers condemned her. She pretends to be a good woman, they'd all say, but how can this possibly be true? She deceived her own sister! Jacob was determined to divorce her.

TANHUMA, BUBER 7.10: "The behavior of the Holy One is not like the behavior of one who is flesh and blood. According to flesh and blood behavior, if one has a wealthy friend, he clings to him and pines for him; but as soon as his power declines and he becomes poor, he laughs at him. With the Holy One, however, things are not like that. As soon as he sees someone whose power is down, He gives him a hand and raises him up. . . . Would you say that He also raises the wicked, if they come to a fall? No, for it is stated: There the evildoers have fallen; they are thrust down and cannot rise (Psalm 36:13). They have fallen; there is no standing for them. Why? Because it is stated: They shall be like chaff before the wind with the angel of the Lord overthrowing them (Psalm 35:5). But those who are righteous the Lord upholds. As soon as the Holy One saw that Leah was hated, He said: How am I to make her dear to her husband? Just look, I am raising her up and giving her children first so that she will become loved by her husband."

GENESIS RABBAH 71:2: As soon as she bore, Jacob no longer wished to divorce her—she was the mother of his children. And eventually, he gave thanks for her.

29:31 ". . . but Rachel was barren."

Prior to telling us about the children that Leah was granted,

Scripture very simply informs us that Rachel, like both her forebears, is barren. It is not until chapter 30 that any focus will be placed on Rachel's predicament. So why this textual interruption just now?

TANHUMA, BUBER 7.15, GENESIS RABBAH 71:2: It was only because of Rachel that Jacob willingly subjugated himself to Laban, and so it was Rachel who was, in fact, ultimately responsible for Jacob's marriage to Leah. Do not read it "barren"/"akarah," but "ikarah"/"the chief one"; Rachel is the true chief of this household, the chief wife of Jacob. Even in the Book of Ruth (4:11), when the elders pronounce a blessing upon Boaz on the occasion of his marriage to Ruth—"The Lord make the woman that is come into thy house like Rachel and Leah"—they place Rachel first, despite the fact that most of those present were descendants of the tribe of Judah, *Leah's* son!

GENESIS RABBAH 71:2: In connection with Leah and the handmaids, Scripture writes: "and the children of so and so were...." But only in the case of Rachel is it written, "The sons of Rachel, Jacob's wife...." She, alone, is designated as Jacob's spouse, she is the House of Jacob, she is the House of Israel. [In a subsequent episode, Jacob's name will be changed by an angel, to Israel.]

Despite Leah's tremendous contribution, all Jacob's descendants are ascribed (in the Book of Jeremiah, chapter 31) to her younger sister, with the image of Rachel weeping for her exiled children, all of Israel. In this midrash, which takes place after the destruction of the Temple and the forcible and cruel exile of the Israelites from their home, she alone, not Abraham, not Isaac, not Jacob, not Moses is able to awaken mercy within the Creator.

LAMENTATIONS RABBAH, PROEM 24: " 'Sovereign of the Universe, it is revealed before You that Your servant Jacob loved me exceedingly and toiled for my father on my behalf seven years. When those seven years were completed and the time arrived for my marriage with my husband, my father planned to substitute another for me to wed my husband for the sake of my sister. It was very hard for me, because the plot was known to me and I disclosed it to my husband; and I gave him a sign whereby he could distinguish between me and my sister, so that my father should not be able to make the substitution. After that I relented, suppressed my desire, and had pity on my sister so that she should not be exposed to shame. In the evening they substituted my sister for me with my husband, and I delivered over to my sister all the signs which I had arranged with my husband so that he should think that she was Rachel. More than that, I went beneath the bed upon which he lay with my sister, and when he spoke to her she remained silent and I made all the replies in order that he should not recognize my sister's voice. I did her a kindness, was not jealous of her, and did not expose her to shame. And if I, a creature of flesh and blood, formed of dust and ashes, was not envious of my rival and did not expose her to shame and contempt, why should You, a merciful King Who lives eternally, be jealous of idolatry in which there is no reality, and exile my children and let them be slain by the sword . . .?' Forthwith the mercy of the Holy One, Blessed be He, was stirred, and He said, 'For thy sake, Rachel, I will restore Israel to their place.' "

And so it is written, "Thus said the Lord: A voice is heard in Ramah, lamentation and bitter weeping; Rachel weeping for her children; she refuses to be comforted for her children who are gone. Thus said the Lord: Restrain your voice from weeping, and your eyes from tears, for your work shall be rewarded. . . . There is hope for your future; said the Lord; your children shall return to their own border" (Jeremiah 31:15).

29:32 "And Leah conceived."

At this time, Leah bears four sons, Reuben, Simeon, Levi, and Judah. The rabbis tell us that under the inspiration of the Holy Spirit, she called all her children by names that contained symbolic and prophetic meanings.

29:32 "And she called his name Reuben" [Riuvane].

In Hebrew, this name bears a resemblance to a phrase meaning "He has seen my misery." Literally, the name means, "See, a son!" To Leah, the name acknowledges that God has seen her affliction and as a result of His blessing, her husband will now love her.

RASHI: The Rabbis explain that the name points to a future event in the child's adult life: " 'See'/'riuh' the difference 'between'/'bayne' my son and my father-in-law's son [Esau]." Esau willingly sold his birthright to Jacob, but nonetheless he sought to kill him afterwards: My son, Reuben, technically the first born, will not relinquish his birthright to Joseph (who will later be regarded as Jacob's firstborn), and yet my son will raise no protest, but will even seek to rescue him from death when his other brothers throw him into a pit!

29:33 "And she called his name Simeon" [Shimeon].

This name is based upon the word for "hear"/"shama"; "the Lord hath heard that I am hated."

29:34 "This time will my husband be joined [yillaveh] unto me. . . . Therefore was his name called Levi."

RASHI, TALMUD, *BERAKHOT* 60a: Since the matriarchs were prophetesses and knew that twelve tribes would issue from Jacob and that he would take four wives, Leah felt that after the birth of her third son she had assumed her full share of the responsibility. Jacob, as a result, could no longer find fault with her.

RASHI: Of all the other sons it is written, "And *she* called," but of Levi it is written, "And *he* called." The verse regarding Levi therefore translates literally as, "He called his name. . . ." God sent the angel Gabriel to bring Levi up to His Presence, wherein He gave him the "twenty-four prerequisites with which the priesthood was favored, and because he gave him these prerequisites as an accompaniment, He called him Levi [accompanied]."

29:35 "This time will I praise [odeh] the Lord; therefore she called his name Judah [Yehudah]."

TALMUD, *BERAKHOT* 7b: Upon the birth of her fourth son, Leah became the first person to ever praise the Lord.

Three Partners

"When God created man, He made him in the likeness of God; Male and female he created them. And when they were created, he blessed them and called them Man." (Genesis 5:1)

"Man"/"adam"—aleph, daled, mem. Can the word, itself, shed light on our human origins? The sages say yes.

In the Kabbalist system, the first letter of the Hebrew alphabet, aleph, is taken to denote God, the Divine. The first letter of the word for "man," the aleph, thus represents, for the Sages, the sacred element present within the human being. The last two letters of the word, the daled and the mem, when taken together, spell the word for "blood"/"dam," the essential physical substance bestowed by virtue of the child's earthly parents. Using gematria, we find that "blood"/"dam" is equivalent to forty-four, the daled being equal to four and the mem to forty. The word for "father"/"av" aleph, vav, is equivalent to three— aleph, one plus vav, two. The word for "mother"/"em" aleph, mem, is equivalent to forty-one aleph, one plus mem, forty. The mother and father taken together, three plus forty-one, add up to forty-four, the same value that is represented by the blood.

The word for "mother" itself contains a hint of our makeup and the mystery of conception and birth. The second letter, mem, equivalent to forty, represents the forty days that the sages teach are required for the formation of the embryo inside the womb; the first letter, aleph, again denotes the embedded spark of the Divine.

Our Talmudic sages teach that three partners, not two, take part in the creation of a human being: the father, the mother and the Holy One, blessed be He. (Talmud, Niddah 31a)

Chapter 30:1. And when Rachel saw that she bore Jacob no children, Rachel envied her sister; and she said unto Jacob, "Give me children, or else I die." 2. And Jacob's anger was kindled against Rachel and he said, "Am I in God's stead, who hath withheld from thee the fruit of the womb?" 3. And she said, "Behold my maid Bilhah, go in unto her that she may bear upon my knees, and I also may be builded up through her." 4. And she gave him Bilhah her handmaid to wife; and Jacob went in unto her. 5. And Bilhah conceived and bore Jacob a son. 6. And Rachel said, "God hath judged me, and hath also heard my voice and hath given me a son." Therefore called she his name Dan. 7. And Bilhah Rachel's handmaid conceived again and bore Jacob a second son. 8. And Rachel said, "With wrestlings of God have I wrestled with my sister and have prevailed." And she called his name Naphtali. 9. When Leah saw that she had left off bearing, she took Zilpah her handmaid and gave her to Jacob to wife. 10. And Zilpah Leah's handmaid bore Jacob a son. 11. And Leah said, "Fortune has come!" And she called his name Gad. 12. And Zilpah Leah's handmaid bore Jacob a second son. 13. And Leah said, "Happy am I, for the daughters will call me happy." And she called his name Asher.

30:1 "Rachel envied her sister."

Was Rachel's nature so coarse that she was capable of unbridled envy? This would seem to dispute everything we've thus far said about her.

RASHI: In truth, Rachel believed that perhaps Leah was more deserving than she was. Rachel was envious of Leah only because of her sister's good deeds. . . . "Unless she [Leah] were more righteous than I am," thought Rachel, "she would not have been privileged to bear children."

GENESIS RABBAH 71:8: "I should have been a bride before my sister. Now, had I sent a warning to Jacob: 'Beware, you are being deceived,' would he not have refrained? But I thought, if I am not worthy that the world should be built up through me, let it be built up through my sister."

30:1 "... And she said unto Jacob, 'Give me children or else I die.' "

RAMBAN: Rachel seems to be holding Jacob personally accountable for her failure to conceive, but in actuality, behind the literal words, she is beseeching her husband to pray earnestly on her behalf.

30:2 "And Jacob's anger was kindled against Rachel, and he said, 'Am I in God's stead, who hath withheld from thee the fruit of the womb?' "

GENESIS RABBAH 71:7, TANHUMA, BUBER 7.19: God confronted Jacob, "Is that any way to speak to a woman in distress? By your life, your own children will one day stand in supplication before Rachel's son Joseph, who will rise up and say these very same chastising words to them, 'Am I in the place of God?' " (50:19, Out of envy, Jacob's sons will set the stage for Joseph's sale into slavery. After Jacob's death, the brothers fear that Joseph, now in a position of power, will exact revenge upon them. Joseph allays their fears, pointing out that their evil actions led in the end to a positive outcome. "I am not in the place of God." I am not God; no man can counter the Divine Plan.)

In the Scriptural text Jacob now chastises his wife, implying that it is from *her* that God withheld the fruit of the womb, not from *him*; their childlessness is her fault, not his. Our rabbis allow Rachel to respond, "Did your father act this way towards your mother?" "Didn't he pray with all his heart and soul so that she'd be blessed with a child?" "My father, Isaac, had no children, whereas I already do," Jacob retorts.

"And didn't your grandfather, Abraham, have a child from Hagar," she went on, "yet he also actively interceded for Sarah, your grandmother, who was then granted a child of her own?" "Are you able to do what my grandmother did?" he asked her. "And what did she do?" "She brought another woman [Hagar] into her home!" he replied. "If that is the only obstacle," Rachel returned, "Behold my maid Bilhah, go in unto her . . . and I also may be builded up through her."

30:5–6 "And Bilhah, Rachel's handmaid conceived . . . and Rachel said, 'God hath judged me. . . .' Therefore she called his name Dan."

TANHUMA, BUBER 7.19: The Hebrew word *dan* has two meanings: "to find guilty" as well as "to champion one's cause." God "has judged me and found me guilty by not giving me a son; He has judged me and found me innocent by giving my bondmaid a son."

30:7–8 "And Bilhah conceived again. . . . And Rachel said, 'With wrestlings of God' [naftulay elohim] have I wrestled [niftali] with my sister, and have prevailed.' And she called his name Naphtali."

RASHI: Rachel is expressing: I offered prayers that were pleasing to God and they were accepted and answered like my sister's; I have been persistent in my urgent solicitations of God. Rachel "wrestled" with God, not once or twice, but again and again.

30:10–11 "And Zilpah, Leah's handmaid bore Jacob a son. And Leah said, 'Fortune [gad] is come.' "

Following Rachel's lead, Leah now sends her own

handmaid unto Jacob, and she, too, bears a son. Unlike the previous cases, Scripture here makes reference only to the birth and not to the conception.

RASHI, GENESIS RABBAH 71:9: When Laban deceived Jacob by giving him Leah instead of Rachel, he also sent along with her the younger of the two handmaids, for the younger maid traditionally attended the younger daughter. The rabbis say that because Zilpah was so young, her pregnancy was not noticeable until the very end.

GENESIS RABBAH 71:9: Upon his birth, Leah cries, "The fortune of the house has come; the fortune of the world has come; he [Elijah] has come who will overthrow ["gadad"] the foundations of the heathen." But from which tribe did the great prophet Elijah actually descend—from the tribe of Gad, Leah's son, or from Benjamin, the second son that Rachel will be granted? One night, while the rabbis debated this question, it is said that Elijah himself appeared before the sages; He told them to quit their debating—he is a descendant of Rachel!

30:12–13 "And Zilpah, Leah's handmaid bore Jacob a second son. And Leah said, 'Happy am I!' "

Thus far, eight of the twelve preordained births have come to be. Still, Rachel, herself, is not to be counted among the mothers.

Chapter 30:14. And Reuben went in the days of wheat harvest, and found mandrakes in the field and brought them unto his mother Leah. Then Rachel said to Leah, "Give me I pray thee of thy son's mandrakes." 15. And she said unto her, "Is it a small matter that thou hast taken away my husband, and wouldest thou take away my son's mandrakes also?" and Rachel said, "therefore he shall lie with thee tonight for thy son's mandrakes." 16. And Jacob came from the field in the evening, and Leah went out to meet him and said, "Thou must come in unto me; for I have surely hired thee with my son's mandrakes." And he lay with her that night. 17. And God hearkened unto Leah and she conceived and bore Jacob a fifth son. 18. And Leah said, "God hath given me my hire, because I gave my handmaid to my husband." And she called his name Issachar. 19. And Leah conceived again and bore a sixth son to Jacob. 20. And Leah said, "God hath endowed me with a good dowry; now will my husband dwell with me, because I have borne him six sons." And she called his name Zebulun. 21. And afterwards she bore a daughter and called her name Dinah. 22. And God remembered Rachel, and God hearkened to her, and opened her womb. 23. And she conceived and bore a son and said, "God hath taken away my reproach." 24. And she called his name Joseph saying, "The Lord add to me another son." 25. And it came to pass, when Rachel had born Joseph, that Jacob said unto Laban, "Send me away that I may go unto my own place and to my country. 26. Give me my wives and my children for whom I have served thee and let me go."

30:14 "And Reuben went . . . and found mandrakes in the field."

In desperation, Rachel begs her sister for the strange love charms that Reuben has found in the field, but Leah refuses her request until Rachel agrees to relinquish her conjugal rights to Jacob for the night. "Therefore shall he lie with thee tonight," Rachel says.

RASHI ON 30:15: "Because Rachel thought lightly of companionship with so righteous a man, she was not privileged to be buried together with him."

GENESIS RABBAH 72:3: "Each lost by the transaction and each gained. . . . The one lost mandrakes and gained two tribes and the privilege of burial with him, while Rachel gained mandrakes and lost the tribes and burial with him."

30:16 "And Jacob came from the field in the evening, and Leah went out to meet him and said, 'Thou must come in unto me.' "

ZOHAR II:157a: The rabbis advise: Do not be put off by Leah's apparently immodest, blunt language. Rather, it is, in fact, *proof* of her modesty. Why? Leah went to great lengths to avoid conveying to Jacob, in the presence of her sister, her right and desire to spend the night with him. She hurredly intercepted him outside the tent to spare Rachel from having to witness the proposal, and likewise, to spare Jacob the difficulty of having to leave Rachel once he set eyes on her. "Leah went to all this trouble because the Holy Spirit stirred within her, and she knew that all those holy tribes would issue from her; and she thus hastened the hour of union in her long devotion to God, and under the same inspiration she called them by names with deep symbolical meanings."

GENESIS RABBAH 72:5: Leah's motive was none other than to produce tribes; her intentions were honorable, and so God blessed her with additional sons. "Come and see how acceptable was the mediation of the mandrakes, for through these mandrakes there arose two great tribes in Israel. . . . Issachar studied the Torah while Zebulun went out to sea [engaging in trade] and provided Issachar with sustenance, and so the Torah spread in Israel."

Do the Sages *really* attribute the birth of Leah's sons to the supernatural power of the mandrakes? Where does God figure into the equation? The Kabbalists explain the way it is, the hidden reality underlying and directing the mundane.

ZOHAR II:156a–156b: ". . . Just as the one hammer-blow causes sparks to fly off in all directions, so God brought into being simultaneously manifold species and hosts, each differing from the other, without number. The world was brought into being by a word and a breath together. . . . Now when God was about to create the world, He produced a secret spark from which there issued and radiated all the lights which are disclosed. First there spread from it those lights which constitute the upper world. Then it continued its radiation, and the Artificer made it into a light without brightness, and thus He made the lower world. And by reason of its being a light, but without illumination, it feels itself attracted towards the upper world. Now it is that light without illumination which through its attachment to the upper world brought into being all those legions and hosts of existences, all the multitudinous species. . . . And whatever is on earth has its counterpart on high, there being no object, however small, in this world but what is subordinate to its counterpart above which has charge over it; and so whenever the thing below bestirs itself, there is a simultaneous stimulation of its counterpart above, as the two realms form one interconnected whole. . . . It was not the mandrakes that made Rachel bear children, but God used them as an instrument for procuring the birth of a child, Issachar, who should hold fast to the Torah more than all the other tribes." Rachel relinquished her hold on Jacob only for the promise of receiving Leah's mandrakes. "Thus the mandrakes were responsible for the birth of Issachar, through whom the fragrance of the Torah ascended to the presence of the Almighty."

Leah bears two more sons. The first she names Issachar, from the root *sachar*, meaning "hire" or "reward," "God hath given me my hire," and the second son, Zebulun, from *yizbelani*, meaning "will dwell with me."

RASHI: Leah believed that because she had borne more sons than all the other women together, Jacob would now feel that his real home was with her.

30:21–22 "And afterwards she bore a daughter and called her name Dinah. And God remembered Rachel."

Leah bears one more child, a girl, and immediately Scripture informs us that Rachel, too, was finally remembered by God. The rabbis comment that these two verses are intentionally juxtaposed, the two events being seen as interdependent.

RASHI: Remember that Leah, thus far, has borne six sons, and each of the handmaids, two, yielding a total of ten. Leah knew by prophetic insight that Jacob was destined to have twelve sons. If this last child she was now pregnant with, her seventh, turned out to be a boy, that would leave only one more son remaining to be born before the total of twelve would be achieved. Rachel could, therefore, at the very most, become the mother of only one son and would be, in terms of her contribution to the tribes, inferior to even the handmaids.

TANHUMA, BUBER 7.19: What did Leah do? She prayed to God that the child inside her become female and that Rachel be blessed with a son. "The Holy One said to her: By your life, you have had mercy on your sister. See, I am making that which is in your belly female, and I am remembering her in this regard." When Leah gave birth to a girl, she named her Dinah. Why? Because she "argued"/"dynh," against giving birth to a boy.

RASHI: *Dinah* also means judgment. "Leah set herself up as judge against herself saying, 'If this be a son, then my sister Rachel cannot be even the equal of any of the handmaids.' "

30:22 "And God remembered Rachel."

GENESIS RABBAH 73:1: It was on New Year's Day that Sarah, Rachel, and Hannah (Samuel's mother) were each remembered by God; at that time He decreed that each of them should conceive.

GENESIS RABBAH 73:4: "What did He remember in her favor? Her silence on her sister's behalf. When Leah was being given to Jacob, she knew it, yet was silent."

RASHI: God remembered her for her meritorious decision to transmit the secret signs to Leah. God remembered her because she was terribly concerned that, due to her barrenness, Jacob might divorce her and that she might then fall to Esau.

30:22 "And God hearkened to her."

RAMBAN: When Rachel saw that she could not rely upon her husband to pray for her, she went and prayed on her own behalf.

30:22 "And opened her womb."

ZOHAR II:156b: Despite the power that the mandrakes are endowed with, it was not they that actually opened Rachel's womb. God, Himself, God alone, is responsible for this. The birth of children is dependent solely on fate ("mazal").

GENESIS RABBAH 73:4, TANHUMA 7.16: There are four keys in the hands of the Holy One—the key of rain, the key of sustenance, the key of resurrection, and the key of barren women.

> *Upon the birth of Cain, her first child, Eve exclaimed, "With the Lord's help I brought a man into being" (Genesis 4:1); prior to this, Adam had been created out of the earth and Eve, out of Adam. But from now on, it would be "in our (joint) image, after our (joint) likeness" (Genesis 1:26)—henceforth no man would come into being without a woman and no woman without a man, and neither of them without the Divine Presence. (Genesis Rabbah 8:9)*

ZOHAR II:159b: Unlike Sarah's pregnancy, which was due to a process taking place above the level of luck or "mazal," Rachel was still dependent upon mazal. Scripture tells us that God "visited"/"pakad" Sarah, whereas He "remembered"/ "yizkor" Rachel. Visitation takes place after remembrance, the key to childbirth in Sarah's case, having already been handed over to the lower world when Abraham was directly promised by God that his wife would bear.

30:23 "And she conceived and bore a son."

TANHUMA, BUBER 7.19: "Just as her conception was painless, so was her giving birth painless." As with Sarah, Rachel becomes exempt from the Divine decree issued against women since the time of Eve.

30:24 "And she called his name Joseph [Yosef], saying, 'The Lord add to me another son.' "

GENESIS RABBAH 73:6: Translate *another* as "different," "the Lord add to me a *different* son." In future times, after the reign of King Solomon, the tribe of Benjamin (sprouting from Rachel's second son) would be the only tribe choosing not to separate itself from the tribe of Judah. All the remaining ten tribes would revolt against the Davidic Dynasty, thus breaking Palestine up into two independent kingdoms. Due to Rachel's prayer, Judah and Benjamin remained united.

RASHI: Being a prophetess like her sister, Rachel also knew that Jacob was destined to rear twelve tribes. "She therefore prayed: May it be God's will that the tribes which he is yet destined to rear may issue from me." Joseph was Jacob's eleventh son; the son Rachel now prayed for would be the twelfth and last.

30:25 "And it came to pass, when Rachel had borne Joseph that Jacob said unto Laban, 'Send me away. . . .' "

As soon as Joseph is born, and before anything is even said about Benjamin's conception or birth, Scripture informs us that Jacob has asked Laban for permission to leave Haran and to return with his wives and children to his home in Canaan.

ZOHAR II:158a: "With the birth of Joseph, Jacob saw that the adversary of Esau had appeared, and he therefore made ready to depart."

TANHUMA, BUBER 7.15, GENESIS RABBAH 73:7:
"There is a tradition handed down through the children of
Esau that they will fall only at the hands of the children of
Rachel." If any of the other tribes should approach Esau in
judgment and ask him why he persecuted his brother, Esau
would turn the question back upon them and ask, "Why did
you persecute *your* own brother?" (referring to the time they
threw him into a pit); "You are no better than I!" If Esau
should then approach Joseph, seeking empathy, Joseph would
ask him the very same question, "Why did you persecute your
brother?" When Esau defends himself by saying it was because
his brother did him evil, Joseph would render Esau silent by
responding, "My brothers also did evil unto me, but unlike
you, I requited and awarded them with Good" (referring to
their reconciliation in Egypt).

ZOHAR II:158b: Jacob's straightforward character would
seem to indicate that he would not even think of leaving without Laban's knowledge and permission. The fact is, he *did* depart without telling him. Why? Jacob was afraid that if Laban
did not honor his request and tried to detain him, the last of
the prophesied tribes would be born in an "alien" land. When
Jacob saw that the time had come for Benjamin's birth, he
fled, and "as soon as Benjamin was born, the Shekhinah attached herself to the company of the tribes and made her
home with them."

Chapter 31:2. And Jacob beheld the countenance of
Laban and behold, it was not toward him as beforetime.
3. And the Lord said unto Jacob, "Return unto the land
of thy father's and to thy kindred, and I will be there
with thee." 4. And Jacob sent and called Rachel and
Leah to the field unto his flock 5. and said unto them,
"I see your father's countenance, that it is not toward

me as beforetime. . . . 6. And ye know that with all my power I have served your father. 7. And your father hath mocked me and changed my wages ten times. . . ." 14. And Rachel and Leah answered and said unto him, "Is there yet any portion or inheritance for us in our father's house? 15. Are we not thought strangers by him, for he hath sold us and hath also quite devoured our price. 16. . . . now then, whatsoever God hath said unto thee, do." 17. Then Jacob rose up and set his sons and his wives upon the camels; 18. And he carried away all his cattle and all his substance which he had gathered . . . to go to Isaac his father unto the land of Canaan. 19. Now Laban was gone to shear his sheep. And Rachel stole the teraphim (idols) that were her father's. 20. And Jacob outwitted Laban the Aramean, and that he told him not that he fled. 21. So he fled with all that he had. . . .

31:15 "Are we not accounted strangers by him?"

RASHI: It was customary for fathers to present their daughters with a dowry upon marriage, but Laban not only withheld a dowry from both Leah and Rachel, but he, in effect, *sold* them in return for fourteen years worth of labor provided by their husband! He treated them unlike daughters, so now they have no objection to Jacob's wish to take them away and return to his own homeland and parents in Canaan.

31:19 "And Rachel stole the teraphim."

GENESIS RABBAH 74:5: It is the opinion of the rabbis that Rachel's theft had a noble purpose; before leaving, she took her father's household idols in an attempt to turn the misguided Laban away from idolatry.

When Laban discovers the flight of his daughters, he pursues them and finally overtakes them.

Chapter 31:26. And Laban said to Jacob, "What hast thou done that thou has outwitted me and carried away my daughters as though captives of the sword? . . . 29. It is in the power of my hand to do you hurt, but the God of your father spoke unto me yesternight saying, "Take heed to thyself that thou speak not to Jacob either good or bad." 30. And now that thou art surely gone because thou sore longest after thy father's house, wherefore hast thou stolen my gods? 31. And Jacob answered and said to Laban, "Because I was afraid; for I said: lest thou shouldest take thy daughters from me by force. 32. With whomsoever thou findest thy gods, he shall not live; before our brethren discern thou what is thine with me, and take it to thee"—for Jacob knew not that Rachel had stolen them. 33. And Laban went into Jacob's tent and into Leah's tent and into the tent of the two maidservants, but he found them not. 34. Now Rachel had taken the Teraphim, and put them in the saddle of the camel and sat upon them. And Laban felt about all the tent but found them not.

31:32 "With whomsoever thou findest thy gods, he shall not live."

As we will later see, this vow and curse pronounced by Jacob, who does not realize that he is waging it against the love of his life, will be blamed by the rabbis as one of the hidden causes of Rachel's seemingly premature and untimely death.

Chapter 32:1. And early in the morning Laban rose up and kissed his sons and his daughters, and blessed them.

And Laban departed, and returned unto his place. 2. And Jacob went on his way, and the angels of God met him. 3. And Jacob said when he saw them, "This is God's camp."

ZOHAR II:165a–165b: "Male and female He created them" (Gen. 5:2). . . . "Adam and Eve were created as a united pair; and since they were coupled together, God blessed them. For blessing does not reside save in a spot where there are male and female." When Jacob left his parent's home and traveled by himself, a single man, towards Haran, Scripture says of the spot where he stopped to rest and dreamed his prophetic dream of deliverance: "And he lighted upon [*vayifga*/entreated] the place." When Jacob again approaches the same spot on his return journey to his birthplace, he is no longer alone; he is now a married man, he is accompanied by his wives and children. Scripture now describes Jacob's arrival differently: "And the angels of God met [*vaifge'u*/entreated] him. "Before, *Jacob* entreated the *place*; now, the angels entreated *him*. Why did the angels come out to meet him and greet him—and not in a dream, as before, but in broad daylight? Now, as a married man, the Shekhinah, the Holy Spirit, the representative of the female forces of Providence, accompanied him.

The journey may be a perilous one. In approaching his home in Haran, Jacob is bound to put his family at risk by meeting up with Esau, his brother, who, years prior, vowed to kill him.

ZOHAR II:167b: ". . . God always delights in the prayer of the righteous, and He crowns Himself, as it were, with their supplications. So we affirm that the angel in charge of the prayers of Israel, Sandalphon by name, takes up all those prayers and weaves out of them a crown for the Living One of the Worlds. . . . Seeing that Jacob had with him legions of holy angels, it may be asked why he was afraid. The truth is that the righteous rely not on their merits but on their prayers and supplications to their Master."

Jacob sends messengers ahead to meet up with Esau, who lives in Seir of the country of Edom. Meanwhile, camping alone at the River Jabbok, Jacob has an encounter with an angel who changes his name to Israel. "And he said, 'Thy name shall be called no more Jacob, but Israel ("He who struggles with God"), for thou hast struggled with God and with men and hast prevailed' " (32:29).

Chapter 33:1. And Jacob lifted up his eyes and looked and behold, Esau came, and with him four hundred men. And he divided the children unto Leah and unto Rachel and unto the two handmaids. 2. And he put the handmaids and their children foremost, and Leah and her children after and Rachel and Joseph hindermost. 3. And he himself passed over before them and bowed himself to the ground seven times, until he came near to his brother. 4. And Esau ran to meet him and embraced him and fell on his neck and kissed him; and they wept. . . . 18. And Jacob came in peace to the city of Shechem, which is in the land of Canaan . . . and encamped before the city.

33:1–2 ". . . And he divided the children . . . and he put . . . Rachel and Joseph hindermost."

ZOHAR II:175a, GENESIS RABBAH 78:10: Why did Jacob place Rachel all the way behind in the ranks? Jacob feared that Esau might assail her because of her great beauty. The rabbis also teach that the children of Leah and the handmaids stood *behind* their mothers, but Rachel's son, Joseph, stood in *front* of his mother, to protect her. To shield Rachel from the eye of Esau, Joseph drew himself up to his full greatness (or height), and he would, in turn, be blessed with greatness in Egypt.

The Israelites do not receive the Torah until after they leave Egypt, but prior to this event, the Sages often speak of the Patriarchs and of their children engaging in the study of the Torah—which had not yet been received! It is the opinion of our Rabbis that the entire Torah was conveyed to Abraham by virtue of the Holy Spirit, and Abraham thereby studied it and lived by it, even though he had not been commanded to. Wishing to counter the influence of the idolatrous Egyptians, the Sages also teach that Joseph, for the sake of his children, observed the Sabbath while in Egypt, it, alone, being equal in importance to all the commandments, a testimony to the One God who created a world out of nothingness. (Ramban on Genesis 26:5)

After the worrisome encounter with Esau, which proves to be a peaceful reconciliation, Jacob camps with his family in Shechem. Despite his new found ease, Jacob's troubles are far from over, as Shechem will prove to be a place of recurrent misfortune.

RASHI: The sons of Jacob will sin there by selling Joseph, there the kingdom of David will be divided, and there, Jacob's only daughter will be maltreated.

We come now upon the story of Dinah's "violation" and the revenge taken on her behalf by her brothers, Simeon and

Levi. It is a tale of malevolence and ruthless bloodshed perpetrated by the fathers of two of the tribes of Israel.

GENESIS RABBAH 73:9: In contracting with Laban regarding what possessions he will take with him when he leaves, Jacob boasts of his honesty and promises that he will take only that which is duly his. "So shall my righteousness witness against me tomorrow," Jacob says. But, warn the rabbis, "Boast not thyself of tomorrow. Tomorrow thy only daughter will go out and be violated. . . ."

Chapter 34:1 And Dinah the daughter of Leah, whom she had borne unto Jacob, went out to see the daughters of the land. 2. And Shechem, the son of Hamor the Hivite, the prince of the land, saw her, and he took her, and lay with her and humbled her. 3. And his soul did cleave unto Dinah, the daughter of Jacob, and he loved the damsel. . . . 5. Now Jacob heard that he had defiled Dinah his daughter; and his sons were with his cattle in the field, and Jacob held his peace until they came. . . . 7. And the sons of Jacob came in from the field when they heard it, and the men were grieved . . . because he had wrought a vile deed in Israel in lying with Jacob's daughter, which thing ought not to be done. 8. And Hamor spoke with them, saying, "The soul of my son longeth for your daughter; I pray you give her unto him to wife. 9. And make ye marriages with us; give your daughters unto us and take our daughters unto you. . . ." 13. And the sons of Jacob answered Shechem and Hamor his father with guile. . . . 15. "Only on this condition will we consent unto you: if ye will be as we are, that every male of you be circumcised, 16. then we will give our daughters unto you, and we will become one people." 20. And Hamor and his son came unto the gate of their city and spoke with the men of their city. . . . 24. And unto Hamor and unto Shechem his son hearkened all that went out of the gate of his city. 25. And it came to pass on the third day, when they were in pain, that two of the sons of Jacob, Simeon and Levi, Dinah's brothers, took each man his sword and came upon the city unawares and slew all the males. . . . 27. The sons of Jacob came upon the slain and spoiled the city. . . . 30. And Jacob said to Simeon and Levi, "Ye have troubled me, to make me odious unto the inhabitants of the land . . . and I being few in number, they will gather themselves against me and smite me, and I shall be destroyed, I and my house."

RAMBAN: Now, if Dinah was so very beautiful, why doesn't Scripture narrate her beauty as it does for Sarah and Rachel? It is because Scripture does not want to mention that which was to her "a stumbling block of iniquity" (Ezekiel 18:30).

After the event, Jacob curses his sons for doing violence to the men and women of the city. Judging from the words of Shechem and Hamor, Jacob felt that they might have returned to God, they might have chosen to believe. Simeon and Levi, from Jacob's perspective, killed without due cause.

Is Jacob, himself, blameless? No, say the rabbis. Back in chapter 32 when Jacob is preparing his family for their encounter with Esau, Scripture yields a subtle clue. "And he rose up that night and took his two wives and his two handmaids and his eleven children, and passed over the ford of Jabbok." His *eleven* children? Where was Dinah?

RASHI, TANHUMA, BUBER 8.19: Jacob took Dinah and put her in a chest so that Esau would not see her and want her for his wife. "The Holy One said to him: You have with-held her from him. . . . If she had been married to Esau, per-haps she would have converted him"; Dinah may have been able to guide him back to the right path. Jacob is thus ad-monished for the same crime he curses his sons for having committed. Jacob is, likewise, punished. All his family is placed in jeopardy.

Chapter 35:1. And God said unto Jacob, "Arise, go up to Bethel and dwell there; and make there an altar unto God who appeared unto thee when thou didst flee from the face of Esau, thy brother." 5. And they journeyed. . . . 8. And Deborah, Rebekah's nurse died, and she was buried below Bethel, under the oak; and the name of it was called Allon-bacuth. 16. And they journeyed from Bethel, and there was still some way to come to Ephrath; and Rachel travailed, and she had hard labor. 17. And it came to pass when she was in hard labor that the midwife said unto her, "Fear not, for this also is a son for thee." 18. And it came to pass as her soul was in departing, for she died, that she called his name Ben-oni; but his father called him Benjamin. 19. And Rachel died and was buried in the way to Ephrath—the same is Bethlehem. 20. And Jacob set up a pillar upon her grave; the same is the pillar of Rachel's grave unto this day.

35:8 "And Deborah, Rebekah's nurse died."

After the encounter with Esau, and after leaving Shechem due to the violence committed on Dinah's behalf, Scripture informs us that, on the road, *Rebekah's* nurse has died. How did Rebekah's nurse come to be in Jacob's household in Haran?

RASHI, GENESIS RABBAH 81:5: Prior to sending away her favored son, Rebekah promised to fetch him home as soon as Esau's anger was assuaged. True to her word, she sends her nurse, Deborah, to Laban's home to inform Jacob that it is safe to return to her in Canaan. It is on this return journey that Deborah dies. Rabbinic aggadah tells us that at that same time, Jacob receives news of yet another death, his mother's. Rebekah's death is not explicitly mentioned in Scripture, but the Rabbis find an oblique reference to it within the words used here in verse 8, "*allon bacuth*," the name of the nurse's burial place. *Allon* in Greek, means "another"; *baccuth* in Hebrew, means "weeping." The hybrid phrase literally translates as "weeping for another"; while burying Deborah, Jacob mourns the death of his mother.

35:16 "And Rachel travailed and she had hard labor."

Soon after the death of Rebekah's nurse and the death of Rebekah, herself, Jacob suffered a blow that he felt more acutely than all the other sufferings that befell him—the death of the love of his life. When on his own deathbed, Jacob will say to his son Joseph, "Rachel died upon me" (48:7), which the rabbis teach could also be translated as "on account of me," indicating Jacob's feelings of guilt and responsibility in the matter of her death. Unbeknownst to Jacob, Rachel had stolen her father's idols, and when Laban questioned the innocent Jacob regarding the theft, Jacob denounced the thief with a potent vow, "With whomsoever thou findest the gods, he shall not live!"

ZOHAR II:174b–175a: ". . . The curse of a righteous man, even if pronounced under a misapprehension, once uttered, is caught up by the evil prompter to be used at a moment of danger. . . . And Satan (adversary), who perpetually dogs the footsteps of the sons of men, seized upon that utterance."

". . . And so it was on account of Jacob having delayed to fulfill his vows which he had made to God that the accuser came forward against him, selecting the moment when Rachel's life was in danger [when Jacob set his family up in ranks, anticipating a confrontation with Esau]. 'Behold,' he said, 'Jacob has made vows and has not paid them; he has wealth and children and is short of nothing, yet he has not paid his vow that he made before Thee; and Thou hast not punished him.' Then straightway, 'Rachel travailed and she had hard labor,' the term 'hard' indicating that a severe doom was issued on high at the instigation of the angel of death."

The curse would not take effect until after the birth of the son she was destined to bear. Just before she dies, Rachel names her new born infant Ben-oni, meaning "Son of My Sorrow," but Jacob calls him Benjamin, "Son of the Right Hand."

> The world is darkened for him whose wife has died in his lifetime. (Talmud, Sanhedrin 22a)

For the Kabbalists, embedded within the Scriptural rendering of the story of the birth of Jacob's twelve sons and the subsequent death and burial of Rachel is a hidden world of mystical meaning. Every event, both those which appear to be motivated by human desire or choice and those dictated by some preordained fate, are in actuality directed by a cause not evident to the senses and certainly not available to anyone reading Scripture on its most literal level. Herein lies a living manifestation of the entire system of Kabbalah.

The Sefirot

1. Keter-Crown

3. Binah-Understanding   2. Chakhmah-Wisdom
Supernal Mother (Leah)   Father

5. Gevurah-Strength   4. Chesed-Love

6. Tiferet-Beauty

(Jacob)

8. Hod-Splendor   7. Netzach-Victory

9. Yesod-Foundation

10. Malkhut-Kingship

The Shekhinah, Sister, Queen, Bride

(Rachel)

Leah is the earthly representation of the third sefirah, Binah-Understanding. This emanation, which belongs to the upper hidden world, is personified as the Supernal Mother. The Kabbalists teach that she gave birth to six sons and one daughter, the seven sefirot beneath her. The six sefirot from Chesed-Love kindness to Yesod-Foundation represent the male forces of Providence. The last emanation, Malkhut-Kingship, represents the female, the final receptive vessel who is then responsible for transmitting her collected influences to the worlds beneath her. Like Binah, Leah gives birth to exactly six sons and one daughter. The tenth supernal emanation, Malkhut, the Shekhinah, is likened to Rachel. In contrast to Leah, she represents, for the Kabbalists, our manifest disclosed world, the "lower" one.

ZOHAR II:153b, 155a, 155b: "All the worlds are built on the same pattern, and through this relation, the lower world was completed on the pattern of the upper world."

"Observe that Leah bore six sons and one daughter. That was in the order of things, since six world directions were stationed above her, and so the six sons and one daughter formed a symbol of the grades [sefirot]. . . . Then again, the four sons of the handmaids were associated with them, they being, as it were, the four joints that were linked with them."

What about the sons of Rachel, Joseph and Benjamin? It seems that since they come from Rachel, symbolic of the "lower" world, they are not in the same category as the other sons who sprouted from the "upper" world, from Leah. The rabbis teach that both Joseph and Benjamin are represented by the sefirah Yesod-Foundation, personified as "The Righteous One," and "The Righteous One is both in and out of this lower world." When she was dying, Rachel called the child Son of My Sorrow, "thinking that what she bore belonged to the lower world, the world of separation, thus leaving only eleven as belonging to the upper world. His father, however, called him Benjamin, Son of the Right Hand, implying that he ascended on high to the upper world; for when Joseph disappeared [sold into slavery], Benjamin took his place [with Jacob and his other sons]. Thus did the Righteous One both enter the lower world and leave it. Hence Joseph and Benjamin and all the others completed the number of twelve, who formed a unity after the supernal pattern."

The Zohar expresses that Jacob had knowledge of the mystical, and that all his choices stemmed from his understanding of his earthly purpose and his desire to have his life be a reflection of the pattern upon which the supernal universe itself is modeled. The Kabbalists teach that Jacob knew beforehand that Rachel would *have* to die, that it was inevitable. Her young death would be in accordance with Divine predestination and would further serve to complete and perfect the emulation of this "supernal pattern."

ZOHAR II:158b: "As soon as Benjamin was born, the Shekhinah attached herself to the company of the tribes and made her home with them. And Jacob, through his knowledge of the mystic symbolism, was aware that as soon as the twelve tribes should be complete, the Shekhinah would make them her adornment and attach herself to them, and that Rachel would die and the Shekhinah would take possession of the House."

Each of the Universes described by the Kabbalists is equated with one of the four letters of the Divine Name—the Tetragrammaton—*yud, heh, vav, heh.* These letters are also equated with the different emanations within the Universe of the Sefirot itself. The apex of the *yud* is applied to the first emanation, Keter-Crown; the *yud*, to Chakhmah-Wisdom; the first *heh* to Binah-understanding. The *vav* represents the level of the six sefirot that follow, the male forces, the power of giving. The final *heh* applies to the last emanation, Malkhut-Kingship, the Shekhinah, the female force of receptivity.

So great was Jacob's love for Rachel that Scripture recounts that the seven long years he worked for Laban with the expectation of receiving her, "seemed unto him but a few days." Jacob lived his life as an embodiment of the male aspect of the Divine emanations, the vav, and Rachel as the female, the final heh. Their earthly love, their union, became a reflection of the unification of the male and female forces on the level of the Divine.

Most surprisingly, the beloved Rachel is not transported to the Cave of Machpeleh. Her sister, Leah, is subsequently granted eternal rest in the sacred burial site beside Jacob and the other matriarchs and patriarchs! Rachel's adoring husband gives her, instead, a plain, road-side burial. Why? What could possibly be the explanation? There are many.

35:19 "And Rachel died and was buried in the way to Ephrath."

RAMBAN: Although Jacob married Rachel for love and wished to keep the vow he had made to her, the Torah, had it been received at that time, would have forbidden Jacob to have her. The Torah specifically prohibits a man from marrying two sisters (Leviticus 18:18). Leah, being the woman that Jacob married first, became the only one permitted to him.

The Sages teach that Abraham learned the precepts of the not-yet-received Torah by means of the Holy Spirit, and pondered its meanings and observed its contents even though he was not commanded to do so. The Sages go on to teach that at that time this strict adherence to the whole of the Divine Law, passed down from father to son, took place only in the Land of Israel, not outside of it. Although Jacob married his wives outside of the Land of Israel, in light of the future prohibition that his descendants would abide by, Jacob buries the sisters separately.

ZOHAR II:223a: The power of prayer . . . "Leah used to go out everyday to the highway to weep for Jacob when she learnt that he was righteous, and prayed on his behalf, but Rachel never did so. Hence Leah was privileged to be buried with him, while Rachel's grave was set by the highway. . . . Hence we have learnt that whoever prays with tears before the Almighty can procure the cancellation of any chastisement that has been decreed against him; for so Leah, though she had been assigned by Divine decree to Esau, yet by her prayer succeeded in procuring the preference for Jacob and saved herself from being given to Esau."

Prayerful tears ascend before the King, no gate can with-

stand them and they are never turned away empty.
(Zohar II:132b)

Despite the roadside burial he gave his wife, Jacob, in his old age, seventeen years after entering Egypt, will deliver explicit instructions to his sons regarding his own burial, insisting that his body must be laid to rest nowhere save Canaan, the Promised land (chapter 48).

RASHI ON 48:7: Jacob's apology to Joseph, his son: ". . . Although I trouble you to take me for burial in the Land of Canaan and I did not do this for your mother (I did not take the trouble to bury her in a place other than that in which she died, which was by the roadside), which I might easily have done since she died quite close to Bethlehem. . . . Do not imagine that it was the rains which prevented me from bringing her to Hebron for burial. It was the dry season when the ground is riddled and full of holes like a sieve. . . . [I] did not carry her even the short distance to Bethlehem to bring her into a city. I know that in your heart you feel some resentment against me. Know, however, that I buried her there by the command of God."

What command is Rashi referring to? Rachel was buried north of Jerusalem; the Cave of Machpeleh in Hebron is south of Jerusalem. In the future, when the Israelites are exiled from their homeland and led northeast into Babylonian captivity, they would pass en route by Rachel's grave.

GENESIS RABBAH 97: Jacob saw prophetically that the exiles would one day pass by that very spot. He buried Rachel there so that she could pray for them, could beg for mercy on their behalf. "A voice is heard in Ramah . . . Rachel weeping for her children" (Jeremiah 31:15).

RAMBAN: Is there a flaw in the text? Rachel's grave, claims Ramban, is not in Ramah, not even near it! What is even more peculiar is that a distance of less than a mile exists between her roadside grave site and the major city of Bethlehem. It is Ramban's contention that Jacob buried her where he did because he prophetically saw that Bethlehem would one day belong to the tribe of Judah, whereas the spot he chose for Rachel's burial would lie within the territory of her own son, Benjamin. Rachel's voice is heard in Ramah because she is weeping that loudly. Ramban also takes note of an interpretation given in the Targum of Jonathan ben Uziel, wherein the word *Ramah* is not interpreted as a place at all, but rather is interpreted on the basis of its root, *ram*, which means "high." "A voice is heard high in the world." The verse is taken to apply not to Rachel, alone, but to the "Congregation of Israel," yet another appellation for, or representative of, the Shekhinah.

35:20 "And Jacob set up a pillar on her grave."

ZOHAR II:175a–175b: "Rabbi Jose said: He did this in order that her burial place should never be forgotten until the day when God shall raise the dead to life. . . . Rabbi Judah said: It means until the day when the Shekhinah will return with the exiles of Israel to that spot. . . . Israel are destined when they return from exile to stop at Rachel's grave and weep there, as she wept over Israel's exile. . . . At that time, Rachel, who lies on the way will rejoice with Israel and the Shekhinah."

Scripture speaks vividly of Rachel's death and burial, but no mention is made of Leah's. Again, the Kabbalists find this differential treatment of the two sisters completely consistent with their esoteric understanding.

ZOHAR II:158a–158b: ". . . All that concerned Leah is kept under a veil, as she typified the upper world, which is veiled and undisclosed; and this is another reason why Leah's death is not divulged like that of Rachel. It is in accordance, too, with this difference between the upper and the lower worlds that Leah was buried away from sight in the Cave of Machpeleh, whereas Rachel was buried by the open road. Hence it is that all blessings are from two worlds, the disclosed and the undisclosed, though the whole originates from the upper world. . . . The one world and the other form together an absolute unity."

GENESIS RABBAH 82:10: "Tombstones [mausoleums] are not erected for the righteous, as their words [teachings] are their memorials."

After Benjamin is born and Rachel dies, Jacob and his remaining family travel on toward his father's home in Hebron. Isaac, Jacob's father, dies and is buried by both his sons.

> Chapter 37:1 And Jacob dwelt in the land of his father's sojournings, in the land of Canaan. 2. These are the generations of Jacob. Joseph . . .

The rabbis find it interesting that verse 37:2 does not read "These are the generations of Jacob. Reuben . . .", that is, going on to speak about Jacob's actual firstborn son, rather than Joseph, his eleventh. All the events to follow, say the rabbis, the entire history of the Israelites, was precipitated by the birth of Rachel's first child, Joseph.

GENESIS RABBAH 84:5: "These generations came only for Joseph's sake. 'And it came to pass when Rachel had borne Joseph, that Jacob said to Laban: send me away' (30:25). Who brought them down to Egypt? Joseph. Who sustained them in Egypt? Joseph. The sea was divided for Joseph's sake alone. . . ."

GENESIS RABBAH 84:6: "These are the generations of Jacob. Joseph. . . ." The Rabbis observe that Jacob's deep connection with this child transcends the obvious. Jacob's mother Rebekah and Joseph's mother Rachel remained childless for a very long time, and after conception, both suffered a difficult labor. Rebekah bore two children, Rachel bore two. Both Isaac and Jacob found their wives outside of the homeland, and both women also gave birth outside of the Promised Land. Both men had brothers who sought to kill them, both were escorted by angels, both went down to Egypt, both died in Egypt, but the bones of neither man remained there.

Chapter 37 recounts the story of the coat of many colors and Joseph's prophetic dreams. Out of envy and disdain, Joseph's brothers throw him into a waterless pit. While debating whether to kill him or to sell him into slavery, a passing band of Midianite merchants hear Joseph's cries, pull him out of the pit, and sell him themselves to an Ishmaelite caravan heading for Egypt. Jacob, led to believe that his favorite son was killed by a wild beast, goes into mourning, a grief from which he refuses to be comforted.

Chapter 38:1. And it came to pass at that time, that Judah went down from his brethren and turned in to a certain Adullamite, whose name was Hirah. 2. And Judah saw there a daughter of a certain Canaanite whose name was Shua; and he took her and went in unto her. 3. And she conceived and bore a son; and he called his name Er. 4. And she conceived again and bore a son; and she called his name Onan. 5. And she yet again bore a son and called his name Shelah. . . . 6. And Judah took a wife for Er, his firstborn.

Scripture abruptly turns aside from its main focus, the story of Joseph's bondage in Egypt, and inserts the story of Judah and his Canaanite daughter-in-law—a heathen woman for whom no genealogy is given.

The rabbis teach that two passages of moral descent are being intentionally brought together. Joseph has been enslaved, and Judah, the most distinguished in his father's house has married a woman who worships an alien god. Although Judah was the one who stood up against his brothers and suggested that it was unnecessary to actually kill Joseph, the rabbis condemn him for not going further.

RASHI ON 38:1: "You told us to sell him: If you had told us to send him back to his father, we would have obeyed you."

TALMUD, *SOTAH* 13b: R. Hana said: "Whoever performs a task without finishing it and another comes and completes it, Scripture ascribes it to the one who completed it as though he'd performed it." And R. Eleazar adds that the one who neglects completion is then deposed from his greatness, as it is written, "And it came to pass that Judah went down."

GENESIS RABBAH 85:1: "Judah dealt treacherously" (Malachi 2:11) when he showed Joseph's coat, dipped in blood, to Jacob and asked, "Discern now whether this is thy son's coat or not"; "An abomination was committed in Israel" (Malachi 2:11) when Joseph was sold.

Nevertheless, from the ashes of apparent immorality, Divine Providence will procure the birth of the Highest Good.

Tamar

The Book of Genesis, Chapter 38.

"The tribal ancestors were engaged in selling Joseph, Jacob was taken up with his sackcloth and fasting, and Judah was busy taking a wife, while the Holy One, blessed be He, was creating the light of the Messiah" (Genesis Rabbah 85:1). For from the union of Judah and Tamar, an impossibly improbable union which will, nonetheless, come to pass, King David, and then Solomon, and in time, say our Rabbis, the Messiah, himself, will sprout . . .

Chapter 38:6. And Judah took a wife for Er, his firstborn, and her name was Tamar. 7. And Er, Judah's firstborn was wicked in the sight of the Lord, and the Lord slew him. 8. And Judah said unto Onan, "Go into thy brother's wife and perform the duty of a husband's brother unto her, and raise up seed to thy brother." 9. And Onan knew that the seed would not be his; and it came to pass, when he went in unto his brother's wife, that he spilled it on the ground, lest he should give seed to his brother. 10. And the thing which he did was evil in the sight of the Lord, and He slew him also. 11. Then said Judah to Tamar his daughter-in-law, "Remain a widow in thy father's house til Shelah my son be grown up," for he said: lest he also die like his brethren. And Tamar went and dwelt in her father's house. 12. And in the process of time Shelah's daughter, the wife of Judah, died; and Judah was comforted and went up unto his sheep shearer's to Timnah, he and his friend Herah the Adullamite.

38:7–10 "And Er, Judah's firstborn was wicked . . . and the Lord slew him . . . and Onan . . . was evil . . . and He slew him also."

GENESIS RABBAH 85:4: Er was so-named "because he was destroyed (or 'emptied out'/'hu'arah') from the world." Onan, his second son, was so-named "because he brought grief ('aninah') upon himself."

The wickedness that Scripture speaks of is thought to mean the engagement in "unnatural intercourse," specifically with the intent of preventing the woman from conceiving. When Er is slain by God, Judah urges Onan, Er's brother, to take part in a practice which will come to be called "levirate marriage" (described in Deuteronomy, chapter 25). The scenario would be as follows: *A* and *B* are brothers. *A* marries a woman, *C*, but before they have any children, *A* dies. Brother *B* becomes permitted to *C*, but with some restrictions. He may not marry her because she is beautiful or even because he loves her, but solely to fulfill his religious duty. The eldest son resulting from this new union would then inherit both the name and property of the deceased first husband, *A*. If *B* marries the woman for any other reason except duty, he transgresses the general prohibition against marrying a widowed sister-in-law! It is for this reason that the practice of levirate marriage was in time abolished and replaced by the symbolic ceremony of "drawing off the shoe," "halizah."

Despite his duty, Onan commits the same sin as did his brother Er, and he is likewise slain.

RASHI ON 38:11: Fearing a similar outcome for his youngest son, Shelah, Judah withholds him from Tamar with a rather lame excuse, never really intending, at all, to give him to her in marriage.

Chapter 38:13. And it was told to Tamar saying, "Behold, thy father-in-law goeth up to Timnah to shear his sheep." 14. And she put off from her the garments of her widowhood and covered herself with her veil, and wrapped herself and sat in the entrance of Enaim, which is by the way to Timnah; for she saw that Shelah was grown up and she was not given unto him to wife. 15. When Judah saw her, he thought her to be a harlot, for she had covered her face. 16. And he turned unto her by the way and said, "Come I pray thee, let me come in unto thee," for he knew not that she was his daughter-in-law. And she said, "what wilt thou give me that thou mayest come in unto me?" 17. And he said, "I will give thee a kid of the goats from the flock." And she said, "Wilt thou give me a pledge til thou send it?" 18. And he said, "What pledge should I give thee?" And she said, "Thy signet and thy cord and thy staff that is in thy hand." And he gave them to her and came in unto her, and she conceived by him. 19. And she arose and went away and put off her veil from her and put on the garments of her widowhood. 20. And Judah sent the kid of the goats by the hand of his friend the Adullamite, to receive the pledge from the woman's hand; but he found her not. 21. Then he asked the men of her place saying, "Where is the harlot that was at Enaim by the wayside?" And they said, "There hath been no harlot here." 22. And he returned to Judah and said, "I have not found her"; and also the men of the place said: there hath been no harlot here! 23. And Judah said, "Let her take it, lest we be put to shame; behold, I sent this kid, and thou hast not found her."

38:14 "And she put off from her the garments of her widowhood and covered herself with her veil."

This action was an unconscious prophecy, say the Rabbis.

GENESIS RABBAH 85:7: "Two covered themselves with a veil and gave birth to twins, Rebekah and Tamar."

38:14 "... and (she) sat in the entrance of Enaim."

GENESIS RABBAH 85:7: "We have searched through the whole of Scripture and found no place called Petach Enaim ['the entrance of Enaim']. What then is the purport of Petach Enaim? It teaches that she lifted up her eyes to the gate ('petach') to which all eyes ('enaim') are directed ['to God, the recipient of our prayers], and prayed, 'May it be Thy will that I do not leave this house with nought.' "

RASHI: The Hebrew phrase meaning, "at the entrance of Enaim" translates literally as "the opening of the eyes." Tamar sat "at the place where the eyes become opened," where people open up their eyes so that they may carefully examine, and thereby know, which road to take.

RASHI: Tamar, perceiving that Shelah was being intentionally withheld from her, resolves to offer herself to Judah, his father, to satisfy her desire to bear children from that family, to have Judah as an ancestor in any way that she could.

GENESIS RABBAH 85:8, TALMUD, *SOTAH* 10b: While sitting at the crossroads, Tamar's face was covered, preventing Judah from recognizing her. Because of her extreme sense of modesty and propriety, Tamar had covered her face even when she had stayed, as a married woman, at her father-in-law's home. For this reason, Judah did not recognize her now and did not suspect her.

The Rabbinic interpretation of the encounter between Tamar and Judah at the crossroads is infused with the sense that their actions and decisions were guided not by lust or anger or any other emotion to which ordinary human beings are subject, but rather by some higher obligation, and they were, likewise, visited with Divine Aid.

38:16 "And he turned unto her . . . and said, 'Come, I pray thee.' "

GENESIS RABBAH 85:8: Judah "wished to go on, but the Holy One, blessed be He, made the angel who is in charge of desire appear before him, and he said to him: 'Whither thou goest, Judah? Whence then are kings to arise, whence are redeemers to arise?' Thereupon, 'And he turned unto her'—in spite of himself and against his wish."

TANHUMA, BUBER 9.17: "Judah said: 'This is a harlot. What concern do I have about her?' He went on. When he had gone on, Tamar raised her eyes to the Holy One. She said to Him: 'Sovereign of the World, am I to go away empty from the body of this righteous man?' Immediately the Holy One sent Michael and brought him back."

RASHI: "And he turned unto her by the way"—"From the road he was following, he turned to the road where she was"; "Come, I pray thee"—"Prepare yourself and your mind for this."

To ensure payment for her services, she asks Judah for a pledge, three specific items that the rabbis view as symbolically significant—silent references to Judah and Tamar's future descendants.

GENESIS RABBAH 85:9: It was due to the Holy Spirit, alive within her, that she requested these particular items. The signet alludes to royalty, the future kingdom of Judah; the cord refers to the blue thread that will hang from the garments (tefillin) to be worn by the members of the Sanhedrin; the staff refers to the royal Messiah.

38:20 "And Judah sent the kid of the goats by the hand of his friend . . . but he found her not."

Judah decides to redeem the pledge items with the gift of a kid goat, and he sends a friend out in search of the unknown harlot, who, of course, cannot be found.

GENESIS RABBAH 85:9: "The Torah laughs at men. The Holy One, blessed be He, said to Judah, 'Thou didst deceive thy father with a kid of goats; by thy life, Tamar will deceive thee with a kid of goats!' " [The brothers dipped Joseph's coat of many colors in the blood of a kid to make their story about Joseph's death seem plausible to their father.]

Judah forfeits the items he gave her and calls off the search for fear that the disgraceful matter, if pursued further, might, in time, become public.

Chapter 38:24. And it came to pass about three months after that it was told Judah saying, "Tamar thy daughter-in-law hath played the harlot; and moreover behold, she is with child by harlotry." And Judah said, "Bring her forth, and let her be burnt." 25. When she was brought forth, she sent to her father-in-law saying, "By the man whose these are, am I with child"; and she said, "Discern, I pray thee, whose are these, the signet and the cord and the staff." 26. And Judah acknowledged them and said, "She is more righteous than I, forasmuch as I gave her not to Shelah my son." And he knew her again no more. 27. And it came to pass in the time of her travail, that behold, twins were in her womb. 28. And it came to pass, when she travailed, that one put out a hand; and the midwife took and bound upon his hand a scarlet thread saying, "This came out first." 29. And it came to pass, as he drew back his hand, that behold, his brother came out; and she said, "Wherefore hast thou made a breach for thyself?" Therefore his name was called Perez (a breach). 30. And afterward came out his brother that had the scarlet thread upon his hand, and his name was called Zerah.

38:24 "Let her be burnt."

Judah, not yet suspecting that he, himself, is the cause of Tamar's pregnancy, calls for corporal punishment when he is told that his daughter-in-law has become pregnant via harlotry.

GENESIS RABBAH 85:10: Judah does not say, "Let her be killed," but rather, he specifically decrees that Tamar should be burned! Why? The rabbis believe that Tamar was the daughter of Shem, a priest. When the written Torah is subsequently revealed to Moses and to the children of Israel, the Book of Leviticus (21:9) will declare: "And the daughter of any priest, if she profane herself by playing the harlot . . . she shall be burnt with fire."

38:25 "By the man whose these are, I am with child."

Out in public, and face to face with Judah, Tamar does not, in anger and self-defense blurt out, "It is by you that I am pregnant!" Rather, she publicly displays the items that Judah gave her as a pledge and says, "By the man whose these are, am I with child."

RASHI, TALMUD, *SOTAH* 10b: Tamar hopes that Judah will voluntarily acknowledge his guilt, once it becomes clear to him, even if it means being condemned to death if he proved himself unwilling to confess. Based on Tamar's handling of the situation, our Talmudic rabbis derive the teaching—"Better for a man to submit to being cast into a fiery furnace than to shame his fellow in public!"

38:25 "Discern, I pray thee, whose these are."

GENESIS RABBAH 85:11: God said to Judah: "You, yourself, once said to your father, 'Discern, I pray thee' [whether this is thy son's coat or not]; And now, this woman, Tamar, will likewise corner you with these very same words, 'Discern, I pray thee!' "

GENESIS RABBAH 97: "Discern, I pray thee." What do these words mean? "Lift up thine eyes and acknowledge thy Creator, and be not ashamed of flesh and blood. He immediately mastered his evil inclination (to keep silent) and confessed his deeds."

38:26 "And Judah acknowledged them and said, 'She is more righteous than I.' "

TANHUMA, BUBER 9.17, GENESIS RABBAH 97: "In that hour a heavenly voice (bat kol) came forth and said to him [Judah], 'You are to say—She is pregnant from me!' And afterwards he confessed, 'The affair stemmed from me.' The Holy One said to him 'Judah, for Me you have saved three lives from the fire [Tamar and her two unborn twins] and one from the pit [Joseph]. By your life, I will save four lives for you, just as you have saved them for me.' " Four righteous men will descend from the tribe of Judah, four men on whose behalf "wonders and miracles" will be wrought in Babylon: Daniel, Hananiah, Mishael, and Azariah. As a reward for saving Tamar and her sons, the latter three will be saved from death in a furnace, and it is as a reward for protecting Joseph that Daniel will emerge alive from the lion's den.

GENESIS RABBAH 85:12: The phrase meaning, "than I"/ "mimmeni" in Hebrew, can also be translated into English as "through me." It was the Holy Spirit who spoke the word "mimmeni"—"Through Me (mimmeni) did these things occur!" Tamar's condemnation and acquittal took place at the court of Shem, and it was God Himself who brought the trial to its rightful conclusion. The rabbis teach that God revealed Himself in this manner in two other places in Scripture; in the Court of Samuel (Samuel I 12:5) and in the court of Solomon (Kings I, chapter 3).

The True Mother

In a dream, God appeared to King Solomon. "Ask," spoke God, "What shall I grant you?" And Solomon requested that God grant him Understanding, the ability to distinguish between good and bad. "The Lord was pleased that Solomon has asked for this. And God said to him, "Because you asked for this—you did not ask for long life, you did not ask for riches, you did not ask for the life of your enemies, but you asked for discernment in dispensing justice. I now do as you have spoken."

Soon after, two prostitutes came to the king with a problem. "We live in the same house," the first woman began to explain, "and I gave birth to a son while she was in the house; we were alone. Three days later, she, also, gave birth to a boy. But during the night, her child died, and while I was fast asleep, she took my child from my arms, placed her dead one in its place, and took my live one for her own. When I awoke in the morning, I saw that he wasn't the child I had borne!" At this point, the other woman cried out, "No! The live one is mine and the dead one is yours!" And the first woman retorted, "You're lying! The live one is mine and the dead one is yours!" And so they went on arguing in the presence of the king.

Suddenly the king ordered, "Fetch me a sword!" And when it was brought to him he decreed that the only fair solution to this problem would be to cut the live child in two, and to give half to one and half to the other. But the true mother, overcome with compassion for her son cried, "Please, my lord, give her the live child, only, please, do not kill it," while the other woman insisted, "No! Cut it in two!" The king pointed to the first woman and decreed, "Give the live child to her. Do not put it to death; she is its mother." And our Rabbis teach that it was the Holy Spirit who spoke these final words. (From Kings I, chapter 3)

RASHI: Translate "mimmeni" as "from me." The Heavenly voice was expressing that all these events were Divinely directed, they came about "from Me and My agency." God ordained that kings would descend from Tamar and that kings would be raised up in Israel from the tribe of Judah. Therefore, the two persons from whom kings would arise were brought together so that His purpose might be accomplished.

38:27 "Behold, twins were in her womb."

RASHI, GENESIS RABBAH 85:13: The rabbis note that the

word for "twins"/"te'omim," is written here with an *aleph* and a *yud*, whereas in regard to Rebekah's twins it was written "defectively," it lacked these two letters, a mystical indication that one of Rebekah's children would be wicked (Esau) and that one would be righteous (Jacob). Here, in the case of Tamar, both of her children will grow up to be righteous men.

Zerah pushes out his hand first, and a scarlet thread, marking him, is tied around it. Suddenly, in the midst of labor, his brother, Perez, pokes out his head, bursting from the womb.

RASHI: "What a strong effort thou hast made!"

In truth, it is from the line of Perez that the great King David will ultimately arise.

GENESIS RABBAH 97: From the unlikely and deceptively arranged union of Judah and Tamar we will receive Elisheba, Aaron's wife, the mother of the priesthood; Bezalel, the creator of the Tabernacle, a man filled with "the spirit of God, with Wisdom, Understanding and Knowledge"; Othniel, Israel's first Judge; Boaz, the man Ruth will marry; King David and his son King Solomon, the builder of the first holy Temple; and Zerubbabel, the builder of the second.

From the tribe of Judah will come a whole litany of individuals referred to by Scripture as righteous and wise men, individuals who, when faced with difficult decisions, did "that which was right in the eyes of the Lord."

A Match Made in Heaven

One particularly cold winter day, a certain Rabbi Tsevi Hirsh ha-Cohen of Romanov, approached one of the young attendants living with him in his home and, without reason, asked him to leave. The distressed boy, along with the other attendants, begged the Rabbi to change his mind, but the Rabbi remained indifferent to their pleas.

Traveling alone, the boy came upon a village inn in a neighboring city. The innkeeper was away, but the innkeeper's wife kindly allowed the displaced boy to take refuge there for the night. A few hours later, a group of traveling merchants came to the inn, woke up the innkeeper's wife, and asked her to prepare food and drink for them. When they were filled with wine and feeling jovial, they searched the house for others to help them celebrate, and upon finding the boy, they entreated him to join them in their revelries. The merchants then asked the innkeeper's wife if she had any children. She told them that she had a daughter, and upon being introduced to her, the revelers asked the girl if she'd like to have the young boy for a bridegroom, and if she did, said the revelers, they'd make her a feast in celebration. The girl was confused, but her mother, seeing an opportunity to bring in more money, coerced her to participate in the mock marriage. The merchants conducted a ritually correct Jewish wedding, but of course, the woman regarded it as nothing more than a joke. As they had promised, the men ordered a great quantity of food and drink, and when the festivities were over, they paid their bill and left.

When the girl's father returned a few hours later, he was extremely agitated and disturbed about their tale of the strange boy and the marriage, and he feared the possibility that their game was, in fact, a profanation of · the sacred. He asked the boy where he came from, and when he told his sad story, how he was suddenly expelled from the Rabbi's home, the innkeeper harnessed his wagon and rode off with the boy to the neighboring city.

When they entered the Rabbi's home, they were unexpectedly greeted with felicitations; the Rabbi sat them down and explained: Sometime back, he had perceived that this man's daughter was the Divinely appointed companion and mate for the expelled boy. He also knew that this wealthy gentleman, the father of the young girl, would not have willingly consented to her betrothal to such a poor boy. The solution? Send the boy out into the world and allow Fate to work its hand. The Rabbi consoled the father of the bride, encouraging him not to feel that an iniquity had been committed, for all had come to its Divinely ordained conclusion. "My friend," said the Rabbi, "I submit to you a question—Is it possible that those merchants were not actually merchants, at all?"[32]

Scripture now resumes the story of Joseph in Egypt, his rise to prominence, the descent into Egypt of Jacob's remaining sons in response to a famine that accosts Canaan, and the union of and reconciliation between Joseph and his brothers. Jacob learns that his son, Joseph, is still alive. "I must go and see him before I die"—and the text recounts Jacob's decision, Divinely approved, to uproot himself and his family and to temporarily relocate in Egypt. The patriarch lives for seventeen more years, dies at the age of one hundred forty-seven, and is buried beside Leah in the Cave of Machpeleh. In chapter 50—the final chapter of the Book of Genesis—Rachel's firstborn, Joseph, before dying at the age of one hundred ten, asks his brothers to swear that when they leave Egypt, whenever that may be, that his remains will be brought out of Egypt

---

32. Adapted from: Micha Joseph Bin Gorion, "Intermediaries from Heaven," *Mimekor Yisrael* (Bloomington and Indianapolis: Indiana University Press, 1990), 1024–1026.

and buried in Canaan, the land promised to Abraham, Isaac and Jacob.

Serach, Daughter of Asher

After Jacob's sons discover that their brother, Joseph, is alive and well, they feared that they would send their despondent father into shock if they suddenly told him that his favorite was not dead, but prospering in Pharaoh's court. The rabbis teach that it was a young woman named Serach who was responsible for gradually breaking the overwhelming news to him with a gentle song. It is said that in times of sorrow, the Holy Spirit does not rest upon a man, and that it was Serach who helped revive Jacob's spirit by bringing back to him the presence of the Shekhinah. In his happiness, Jacob gave the young Serach a blessing of long life . . . .

In the Book of Genesis, Serach is listed among those who journey to Egypt with Jacob. Three hundred years later, after fleeing Egyptian bondage, a new census is taken by Moses in the wilderness, and again, a woman named Serach is mentioned. Our rabbis say that the Serach mentioned in both places is the very same woman, an extraordinary individual who was granted a life long enough to witness both the fall into bondage and the rise to freedom of her people.

It is taught that there was a mystery pertaining to the redemption from Egypt which involved the letters of the Hebrew alphabet. Among all the twenty-two letters, there are five which are given a different shape when they occur as the final letter of a word. These five letters concern a secret tradition which was communicated first, to Abraham, from Abraham to Isaac, from Isaac to Jacob, from Jacob to Joseph, from Joseph to his brothers, and

Asher, one of Joseph's brothers, entrusted the mystery to Serach, his daughter. "Any redeemer that comes forth and says: 'God will surely visit you' (a phrase involving the letter peh, one of those five letters) should be regarded as the true deliverer." When Moses appeared before the elders of Israel performing signs and wonders, they did not believe in him or in his proclaimed mission until Serach came forth and confirmed that the words he spoke to them were, indeed, the divinely ordained message.

When the Israelites prepared themselves to finally leave behind their bondage in Egypt, and Moses occupied himself with finding Joseph's buried coffin (his deathbed request), it was Serach, alive in Joseph's generation, who is said to have directed Moses to the spot, deep in the Nile, where it lay. "Joseph, Joseph," Moses called out at the bank of the river, "the time has come in which the Holy One, blessed be He, swore, 'I will deliver you.' Surface now, or we will be released from our promise." And Joseph's metal coffin floated up to the surface of the Nile . . . .

Serach continues to figure in Rabbinic lore. The rabbis name her as the "wise woman" in the second Book of Samuel (chapter 20) who intervenes in a battle against the House of David. In the later Talmudic times, Serach herself is reported to have appeared outside a house of study. . . . When R. Yohanan was teaching that the parted walls of the Red Sea looked like sprouting bushes, a little voice interrupted his discourse, saying, "No, you are not correct; they looked like reflecting mirrors!" The voice belonged to an old woman who, when asked her name, said that she was none other than Serach, the daughter of Asher.

When her time to die had finally come, our rabbis teach that Serach, like other righteous individuals before her, was permitted to avoid the taste of Death and to enter Paradise, the Garden of Eden, alive. (Pirke de Rabbi Eliezer, chapter 48, Exodus Rabbah 5:13, Zohar III:46a, Talmud, Sotah 13a)

Jochebed

The Book of Exodus, Chapter 1.

Exodus, Shemoth is the second of the Five Books of Moses, its Hebrew name taken from the first line of the text, "And these are the names," a census of all those who descended with Jacob into Egypt. Prosperity will, however, give way to humiliation, and time will turn the growing family of Jacob into a bitter, enslaved people. But, say the rabbis (Genesis Rabbah 44:9, Talmud, Sotah 12a), after Jacob's family left behind the Promised Land, and just as the caravans entered into the border city of Egypt, a baby girl was born to Levi and his wife . . . . She was named Jochebed and would, in time, give birth to three children—the eldest destined to become one of Israel's seven prophetesses, the second destined to become Israel's first High Priest, and the youngest to be chosen by God to fill the role of Israel's leader and savior. Jochebed herself, teach the Talmudic sages, will survive all three of her illustrious children, entering the promised land of Israel along with Joshua, her righteous son's successor, at the age of two hundred and fifty.

Chapter 1:6. And Joseph died and all his brethren and all that generation. 7. And the children of Israel were fruitful and increased abundantly, and multiplied, and waxed exceeding mighty; and the land was filled with them. 8. Now there arose a new king over Egypt, who knew not Joseph. 9. And he said unto his people, "Behold, the people of the children of Israel are too many and too mighty for us. 10. Come let us deal wisely with them, lest they multiply, and it come to pass that when there befalleth us any war, they also join themselves unto our enemies, and fight against us . . . . 11. Therefore they did set over them taskmasters to afflict them with their burdens . . . . 12. But the more they afflicted them, the more they multiplied . . . . 13. And the Egyptians made the children of Israel to serve with rigor. 14. And they made their lives bitter with hard service, in mortar and in brick, and in all manner of service in the field . . . . 15. And the King of Egypt spoke to the Hebrew midwives, of whom the name of the one was Shiphrah, and the name of the other Puah. 16. And he said, "When ye do the office of the midwife to the Hebrew women, ye shall look upon the birthstool; if it be a son, then ye shall kill him; but if it be a daughter, then she shall live." 17. But the midwives feared God, and did not as the King of Egypt commanded them, but saved the men-children alive. 18. And the King of Egypt called for the midwives and said unto them, "Why have ye done this thing and have saved the men-children alive?" 19. And the midwives said unto Pharaoh, "Because the Hebrew women are not as the Egyptian women; for they are lively, and are delivered ere the midwife come unto them." 20. And God dealt well with the midwives, and the people multiplied and waxed very mighty. 21. And it came to pass, because the midwives feared God, that He made them houses. 22. And Pharaoh charged all his people saying, "Every son that is born ye shall cast into the river, and every daughter ye shall save alive."

Joseph died, as well as his brothers and their children and all the families of his generation. The Pharaoh who knew and favored Joseph was also dead and gone, and the new Pharaoh who came to power in Egypt, knowing nothing of Joseph, feared the swelling multitudes of Israelites in his kingdom.

1:13 "And the Egyptians made the children of Israel to serve with rigor."

EXODUS RABBAH 1:12: The Pharaoh decreed that a set daily quota of bricks must be met by the Israelites. He then forbade the workers to sleep in their homes at night, thinking that this would prevent them private access to their spouses and thus limit the number of Hebrew births. The taskmasters slyly told the Hebrew slaves that if they were to go home at night, they would lose hours every morning from their work and would thereby not be able to complete their allotted number of bricks. "Whereupon God said to the Egyptians: 'I promised Abraham, their father, that I would multiply his children like the stars . . . and now you are cunningly planning that they do not increase. Well, we will see whose word will prevail, yours or Mine,' At once, we are told: 'But the more they afflicted them, the more they multiplied.' "

EXODUS RABBAH 1:12, TALMUD, *SOTAH* 11b: On whose merit did God see fit to save this enslaved people, to Divinely intervene? On the past merits of the Patriarchs and Matriarchs? No, say the rabbis. "Israel was redeemed from Egypt on account of the righteous women of that generation." The rabbis wax poetic, drawing on verses from the Psalms and Song of Songs to envision and describe the many unheralded Divine miracles that occurred on behalf of the enslaved Israelites . . . . When the women drew water, they found their pitchers always half-filled with fish. Out in the fields, they fed their husbands cooked fish and made love to them between the mounds. (The rabbis teach that the taskmasters gave the women tasks that were suited to men and to the men tasks usually performed by women.) When their time to give birth arrived, they did so away from home, under the apple trees in the fields, out of the sight of the Egyptians. An angel from heaven cleansed the newborns and fed them cakes of oil and honey. As soon as the Egyptians noticed them, yet another miracle occurred. The ground opened up and swallowed the infants, releasing them again when the taskmasters departed. When the babies grew up, they returned, in flocks, to their homes. It is said that when God revealed Himself to the Israelites at the Red Sea, these children were the first to recognize Him, and it is they who declared, "This is my God and I will praise Him" (Ex. 15:2).

1:15 "And the King of Egypt spoke to the Hebrew midwives . . . Shiphrah and Puah."

When Pharaoh saw that despite his decrees, the Israelites multiplied, he issued an edict specifically concerning the male children yet to be born. Who exactly were these midwives?

EXODUS RABBAH 1:13: There is a teaching that the midwives specifically referred to here were none other than Jochebed and her five-year-old, Miriam. The word for "bitterness" is *mar*, and Miriam was so named from this root because she was born in the year the decrees were issued. One of Solomon's proverbs states, "Even a child is known by his doings"—one's character is recognizable even when very young. The sages say that Miriam, who always accompanied Jochebed, earnestly and eagerly tended to all the needs of both mother and child.

EXODUS RABBAH 1:13, TALMUD, *SOTAH* 11b: Shiphrah refers to Jochebed, and Puah to Miriam, the names being based on the roots of numerous words illustrative of the character of these two individuals. Shiphrah is based upon "she-paru"/"multiplied," because Israel multiplied greatly on account of her. Shiphrah is based also upon "shafrah"/"pleasing," because her acts were all pleasing in the eyes of God. Puah means "to open the mouth," and Miriam was so named because through her cooing, the children opened their mouths and could thus be fed. Puah comes also from "hofi'ah"/"lifted," because she dared to lift her face up against Pharaoh and voice her warnings to him of Divine retribution. When Pharaoh became so enraged that he wished to have her killed, Jochebed "smoothed over"/"meshapereth," Miriam's words, explaining that her daughter was only an ignorant child and wasn't worth his anger. Miriam was called Puah because this "ignorant child" would one day "lift"/"hoi'ah" Israel up towards God; Puah, because under the influence of the Holy Spirit, she would "cry out"/"puah" the prophecy that her own mother would soon bear the child destined to be Israel's savor!

> *R. Jose was expounding upon Scripture when his congregation became drowsy. To awaken them, he suddenly said, "A certain woman in Egypt brought forth 600,000 in one birth!" Perking up, one of his disciples asked, "Who could that have been?" And R. Jose replied, "It was Jochebed, who bore Moses—counted as equal to 600,000 of Israel" (Song of Songs Rabbah 1:15)*

Pharaoh outrightly directs all the midwives to kill any boys subsequently born to the Hebrews; the girls, on the other hand, may be left alive.

EXODUS RABBAH 1:14: The midwives asked: How can we immediately know if the emerging child is a boy or a girl? Rabbi Hanina said that Pharaoh instructed them of a sign: If its face is turned downward, it is a male, because he is looking down to his true mother, the earth, from which he was created. If the face is turned upward, it is female, because she too is looking at the source of her creation, the rib.

1:17 "But the midwives feared God and did not as the King of Egypt commanded them, but saved the men-children alive."

EXODUS RABBAH 1:15, TALMUD, *SOTAH* 11b: This verse is redundant—we are told that the midwives, as a group, did not fulfill the King's command, and then we are told that they saved the boys. What is Scripture's underlying intention?

"Only to add praise to praise." The midwives not only disregarded the royal command, but went even further. They collected water and food from rich families and brought it to the poor ones so that even these poor children could remain alive and healthy. Because of the great lengths they went to, they prayed earnestly to God asking that all the infants emerge safely, not crippled. They prayed also that their mothers survive the danger of childbirth so instead of blessing them for their efforts, all Israel does not turn on them with a curse. God granted their prayers.

EXODUS RABBAH 1:15: "The midwives feared God." They modeled their behavior upon that of Abraham, a man who, according to tradition, allowed himself to be thrown into a fiery furnace and as Scripture recounts, was willing to sacrifice his own son, Isaac. "For now I know that thou art a God-fearing man," God declares. Likewise, the midwives endangered their own lives by disobeying Pharaoh's edict. The midwives said: Abraham, out of loving kindness, fed all passersby, regardless of their faith, and we are not only unable to provide the babies with food, but we've been ordered to murder them! No. We will keep them alive in any way that we can.

1:20–21 "And God dealt well with the midwives... He made them houses."

EXODUS RABBAH 1:17: "Houses" refers to the priestly, levitical and royal families which will descend from Jochebed and Miriam—the priestly and levitical ones from Jochebed's sons, Moses and Aaron; the royal family from Jochebed's daughter, Miriam, a direct ancestress of King David.

Then Pharaoh goes one step further in his obsessive need

to obliterate the body and soul of the community in his midst. (1:22) "Every son that is born ye shall cast into the river."

SONG OF SONGS RABBAH 2:15, TALMUD, *SOTAH* 12a, EXODUS RABBAH 1:20: What did the Israelite women do? They hid their infants in holes in the walls of their homes. When the Egyptian women were informed that a Hebrew child had been born, they would bring their own children to the Hebrew's home and pinch them to make them cry, hoping that the Hebrew children in their hiding places would hear them and begin to cry along with them. The disclosed infants were seized and thrown into the Nile.

When boys were born, the Israelites continued to circumcise them, despite Pharaoh's decree. Neighboring Egyptians would ask, "Why do you bother circumcising them? Won't they, in time, just be thrown into the Nile?" To which the Israelites replied, "You can do with them as you see fit. But we will continue to circumcise them, and whoever dies will die, and whoever is destined to live, he will live."

Chapter 2:1. And there went a man of the house of Levi and took to wife a daughter of Levi. 2. And the woman conceived and bore a son, and when she saw him that he was a goodly child, she hid him three months. 3. And when she could no longer hide him, she took for him an ark of bulrushes, and daubed it with slime and with pitch; and she put the child therein and laid it in the flags by the river's brink. 4. And his sister stood afar off, to know what would be done to him. 5. And the daughter of Pharaoh came down to bathe in the river; and her maidens walked along by the riverside and she saw the ark among the flags and sent her handmaid to fetch it. 6. And she opened it, and saw it, even the child; and behold a boy that wept. And she had compassion on him and said, "This is one of the Hebrew's children." 7. Then said his sister to Pharaoh's daughter, "Shall I go and call thee a nurse of the Hebrew women, that she may nurse the child for thee?" 8. And Pharaoh's daughter said to her, "Go." And the maiden went and called the child's mother. 9. And Pharaoh's daughter said unto her, "Take this child away and nurse it for me, and I will give thee thy wages." And the woman took the child and nursed it. 10. And the child grew, and she brought him unto Pharaoh's daughter, and he became her son. And she called his name Moses and said, "Because I drew him out of the water."

2:1 "And there went a man of the house of Levi, and took to wife a daughter of Levi."

ZOHAR III:11b: The man is Amram and the woman, Jochebed. "A heavenly voice bade him unite himself with her, as through the son which should be born of them the time of the redemption of Israel would be brought near. And the Holy One came to his aid . . . . The Shekhinah reposed upon the nuptial bed and the will of the two in their union was one with the will of the Shekhinah."

TALMUD, *SOTAH* 12a: "And there went a man . . ." Went? Where did he go? The rabbis note that this moment did not mark the beginning of the couple's marriage! Miriam was already six years old, her younger brother Aaron, almost three. Amram, the rabbis teach, "went" in the direction his little daughter advised, he acted upon her guidance. In response to Pharaoh's decree that all boys must be thrown into the Nile, Amram divorced Jochebed, feeling that his marriage had been rendered pointless. Amram, it is taught, was the greatest man of his generation, and all the Israelite men followed his example, also divorcing their wives to avoid procreation. "His daughter said to him: Father, thy decree is more severe than Pharaoh's because Pharaoh decreed only against the males, whereas thou hast decreed against the males and females. In the case of the wicked Pharaoh there is a doubt whether his decree will be fulfilled or not, whereas in thy case, though thou art righteous it is certain that thy decree will be fulfilled!" At his daughter's admonishment, Amram remarried his wife, and all of Israel likewise took back their wives. Scripture does not say here that he "took back" his wife, merely that "he took." Our rabbis teach that he responded to Jochebed as though it was their very first marriage. They publicly went through a full marriage ceremony; Jochebed was carried on a bridal palanquin, and their children, Aaron and Miriam, played castanets and danced before their mother.

When Lamech, Noah's father, summoned his wives to their marital duties, they said to him, "Do you expect us to bring children into a cursed world? Tomorrow a flood is coming!" Lamech then suggested that they all pay a visit to Adam for consultation in the matter. Adam said to them, "Your obligation is to procreate. Do your duty while God does His!" "Physician, heal your own limp!" retorted Lamech. "You've kept apart from Eve, your wife, for one hundred thirty years! Was it for any reason except to avoid bearing children?" Upon being chastised in this manner, Adam returned to Eve and he "knew his wife again, and she bore a son and named him Seth, meaning God has 'provided me with' another offspring in place of Abel, for Cain had killed him" (Genesis 4:2). (Genesis Rabbah 23:4)

2:2 "And the woman conceived and bore a son."

TALMUD, *SOTAH* 12a: Just as Sarah was blessed with a renewal of her youthfulness, "the signs of maidenhood were reborn" in Jochebed. Just as it was for Sarah and Rachel, when Jochebed gave birth it was as painless as her conception. "Righteous women were not included in the decree [pronounced] upon Eve."

The Hidden Miracle

The Israelites remained in Egypt for two hundred and ten years. The Sages teach that Jochebed was born just as the Israelites entered into its border city and that Moses, Jochebed's son, was eighty years old when he stands before Pharaoh, negotiating for their release. Based on these numbers, the rabbis calculate that Jochebed, when she gave birth to Moses, was one hundred and thirty years old! So why doesn't Scripture explicitly mention this miracle that befell Jochebed, whereas it speaks fully about the case of Sarah who gave birth at the much "younger" age of ninety?

RAMBAN (ON GENESIS 46:15 AND EXODUS 6:2): *"I will tell you a principle, the truth of which is clearly indicated in the Torah, namely, that Scripture records only those miracles which were foretold and performed by a prophet, or an angel who revealed himself as a messenger of God especially for that purpose. All other miraculous events, involving either the salvation of the righteous or the punishment of the wicked, are not mentioned in the Torah and Prophets. Indeed, why should Scripture mention them altogether? The very foundation of the Torah rests upon (a belief in) invisible miracles ... by what law of nature does man's ob-*

servance of the Divine Law cause the rains to come in their seasons (Leviticus 26:4)? And how does it bring peace in the land (ibid. 6)? . . . It is obvious that all these blessings are founded upon Nisim Nistarim—the constant invisible interposition of God in the world."[33]

God wished to have Moses and Aaron be the ones to fulfill the function of leading Israel to redemption. He therefore delayed their births until the proper time for the Redemption had arrived. And at that proper time, Jochebed, their mother, was very old . . .

2:2 "He was a goodly child."

EXODUS RABBAH 1:20, TALMUD, SOTAH 12a: When Moses was born, Jochebed saw the Shekhinah hovering about him, and the whole house became flooded with light. (When the rabbis see the same phrase or word used in two different places, they take it to have a similar meaning in both verses. "And God saw the light that it was good" (Genesis 1:4); Moses is described here as a "goodly child.")

2:3 "And when she could no longer hide him, she took for him an ark of bulrushes."

EXODUS RABBAH 1:21, TALMUD, SOTAH 12a: Jochebed constructed an ark out of pliable materials that could withstand the pressure of the river, putting the waterproofing slime on the inside and the ill-smelling pitch on the outside, its odor far away from the righteous child.

Why did Jochebed put her child into the dangerous river,

---

33. R. Charles B. Chavel, *Ramban, His Life and Teachings* (New York: Philipp Feldheim, Inc., 1960), 84–85.

unlike the other mothers who were choosing to hide their infants in the fields?

EXODUS RABBAH 1:21, 24, TALMUD, *SOTAH* 12b: Before Moses was born, the Egyptian magicians had predicted his birth, a child who would grow up to be the Hebrew's saviour and lead them out of the Pharaoh's kingdom. They also foresaw that this leader would be punished by water. To bypass their prophecy, Pharaoh decreed that all newborn boys be condemned to death in the river. Three years later, Moses was born to Jochebed, and when the magicians perceived that somewhere, hidden in Egypt, the prophesied birth had taken place, Jochebed set her infant afloat in an ark. The magicians wrongly perceived that their prophecy had been averted, and Pharaoh rescinded his decree. Little did these seers know that the punishing waters they foresaw referred to the waters of Meribeh, the site of a later transgression by Moses, and had nothing at all to do with the waters of the Nile.

2:4 "And his sister stood afar off."

TALMUD, *SOTAH* 12b–13a, EXODUS RABBAH 1:22: Miriam's urgency to reunite her parents stemmed from her prophetic abilities. And when Moses was born, "the whole house was filled with light, and her father arose and kissed her upon the head, saying, 'My daughter, thy prophecy has been fulfilled'; but when they cast him into the river, her father arose and smacked her upon her head saying, 'My daughter, where now is they prophecy?'" And Miriam "stood afar off" to see what would become of her oracle.

2:5 "And the daughter of Pharaoh came down to bathe."

The daughter of the oppressor of the Hebrew nation, this

anonymous Egyptian princess, only later called by the name of Bathya, is the subject of numerous commentaries and legends. Counted among the "good" women of the Bible, tradition has it that she was even among those privileged to enter Paradise without tasting Death. Who was this daughter of Pharaoh and why does she merit such praise?

TALMUD, *SOTAH* 12b: As part of the religious ceremony of conversion, the initiate immerses himself in water. Some of our rabbis teach that Pharaoh's daughter had come down to the river as an act signifying her resolve to cleanse herself of her father's idolatry.

EXODUS RABBAH 1:23: Others teach that Pharaoh's daughter came down to the river to bathe because she had been smitten with leprosy. All is ordained from above: It is at this moment that she sees the ark of the infant Moses, reaches out to him, touches him, and her leprosy is instantly healed. It is for this reason that she takes pity on the child, believes that he is worthy of being saved.

2:6 "And she opened it and saw it, the child, and behold a boy that wept."

EXODUS RABBAH 1:24: Why, ask the rabbis, is Moses first referred to as a child, and then immediately after, as a boy? Although Moses was a child, he behaved like a grown up boy in that he didn't cry. To move along His Divine plan, God instructed the angel, Gabriel, to hit the infant and to make him cry so that the princess would be filled with pity.

EXODUS RABBAH 1:23, TALMUD, *SOTAH* 12b: Her handmaids tried to discourage her from preserving the child, pointing out to her that although it is customary to find that not everybody obeys a human king's decree, at the very least his own children and household *must* obey it! Having thus spoken, the angel "Gabriel came down and beat them to the ground."

PIRKE DE RABBI ELIEZER, CHAPTER 48: In the face of her own father's decree, and in the face of contrary advice from her fellows, the daughter of Pharaoh chooses her own path and decides to save the child. The familiar teaching, "Whosoever preserves a life it is as though he had kept alive the entire world," is quoted by our Sages in reference to this act of compassion.

EXODUS RABBAH 1:24, TALMUD, *SOTAH* 12b: Scripture does not say "and she saw the child," but "and she saw it, the child." The princess saw not only the child in that instant, but also the Shekhinah by his side. The word *et*, a nontranslatable Hebrew particle which appears before *child* in this verse, is often taken by the rabbis to refer to the presence of the Holy Spirit.

ZOHAR III:12b: It was the Shekhinah, always hovering over Israel like a mother over her child, and always pleading to God in Israel's defense, who saw the crying infant. It was the Shekhinah who had compassion for "the child," the people of Israel, crying out to their Creator.

2:7 "Then said his sister to Pharaoh's daughter, 'Shall I go and call thee a nurse of the Hebrew women?' "

EXODUS RABBAH 1:25, TALMUD, *SOTAH* 12b: Moses was passed around to all the Egyptian women, but he refused to suck. God said: "Shall a mouth which will speak with the Shekhinah suck what is unclean?" (idolatrous)

2:8 "And the maiden went and called the child's mother."

EXODUS RABBAH 1:25, TALMUD, *SOTAH* 12b: Scripture here refers to Jochebed's daughter as "the maiden," and the rabbis teach that this particular word serves to further reveal the young Miriam's traits. "Maiden"/"almah" comes from a root word meaning "strong"; although Miriam was only six years old, she performed her mission with great strength or speed. *Almah* also bears resemblance to *he'elimah,* meaning "she concealed," coming from the root word *alam/*"to hide"; the young Miriam was capable of concealing her identity as the infant's sister.

2:9 "And I will give thee thy wages; and the woman took the child and nursed it."

EXODUS RABBAH 1:25: Jochebed had made it her business to help save and keep alive the children of *other* mothers, and as a reward, God not only restored her own child to her, but she received monetary compensation as well.

2:10 "And the child grew and she brought him unto Pharaoh's daughter and he became her son."

After suckling him for twenty-four months, Jochebed brings Moses to the princess, who will continue the process of raising him.

EXODUS RABBAH 1:26: "Pharaoh's daughter used to kiss and hug him, loved him as if he were her own son . . . . Because he was so handsome, everyone was eager to see him, and whoever saw him could not tear himself away from him. Pharaoh also used to kiss and hug him, and Moses use to take the crown of Pharaoh and place it upon his own head, as he was destined to do when he became great . . . and even so did the daughter of Pharaoh bring him up who was destined to exact retribution from her father."

TALMUD, *MEGILLAH* 13a: In the Book of Chronicles, Pharaoh's daughter is spoken of as actually having "borne" Moses. "This tells us that if anyone brings up an orphan boy or girl in his house, the Scripture accounts it as if he had begotten him!"

LEVITICUS RABBAH 1:3: "The Holy One, blessed be He said to Bathya, the daughter of Pharaoh: Moses was not your son, yet you called him your son; you, too, though you are not My daughter, yet I will call you My Daughter."—*Bath Yah*, meaning "daughter of God" . . . and thus the Hebrew name that Scripture anoints her with.

2:10 "And she called his name Moses."

The Hebrew form of Moses is "Moshe," from "*mashah*"/ "to draw out."

EXODUS RABBAH 1:26: "From here you can infer how great is the reward of those who perform kind acts. Although Moses had many names [Book of Chronicles], the name by which he is known throughout the Torah is the one which Bathya the daughter of Pharaoh called him, and even God called him by no other name."

Moses grows into a man. One day, while still living within Pharaoh's domain, he sees an Egyptian taskmaster beating a Hebrew slave. In response, he slays the taskmaster. When it becomes clear to Moses that his deed has become known, he flees from the kingdom, fearing for his life. Traveling into the southeastern part of the Sinai peninsula, an area beyond Egyptian jurisdiction, he encounters seven sheperdesses who are being harassed by a group of shepherds. Moses' sense of justice is again aroused, and he comes to the aid of the women, one of whom would in time become the prophet's wife. Interesting to note that, once again, it is at a well of water that the encounter between the man and his destined wife takes place.

2:17–19 Moses stood up and helped them and watered their flock. And when they came to Reuel their father, he said, "How is it that ye are come so soon today?" And they said, "An Egyptian delivered us out of the hand of the shepherds."

EXODUS RABBAH 1:32: Was Moses actually an Egyptian now? No, of course not, say the rabbis, who offer an allegory: A man was once bitten in the foot by a lizard. To soothe the sting, he ran to the river to immerse his foot, but when he got there, he saw a drowning child, and he immediately stretched out his hand to rescue him. The child said, "If it weren't for you, I'd be dead." The man replied, "It wasn't I who save you; it was the lizard who bit me and from whose bite I was running—it was he who saved you." Likewise, when the women thanked Moses for saving them from the shepherds, he replied, "It was the Egyptian who I killed—he is the one who saved you." That is why the women, in recounting the event to their father mentioned an Egyptian, meaning, that the true cause of the aid they received was the Egyptian whom Moses had slain.

2:21 And Moses was content to dwell with the man; and he gave Moses Zipporah, his daughter.

PIRKE DE RABBI ELIEZER, CHAPTER 40: On the eve of the sixth day of creation, a rather special rod was created. It was presented to Adam in the Garden of Eden. Adam then passed it onto Enoch, Enoch gave it to Shem, Shem gave it to Abraham, Abraham gave it to Isaac and Isaac gave it to Jacob. Jacob brought it with him to Egypt, and he gave it to Joseph, his son. After Joseph's death, all his belongings were brought to the Pharaoh's palace. Zipporah's father was, at that time, one of the Pharaoh's magicians. When he first laid eyes upon that rod, he recognized its value. His wish to possess the rod was so great that he took it from the palace, brought it to his home, and planted it outside in his garden. No man was ever able to even approach that rod, no one, that is, until Moses arrived. Moses deciphered the strange signs written upon it. He stretched out his hand and effortlessly removed the rod from the ground. When Zipporah's father witnessed this act he knew that this was the man destined to redeem Israel from Egypt! For that reason, he gave his daughter to Moses, for a wife. Rabbinic lore has it that when Moses stands before Pharaoh beseeching him to release the Israelites from bondage, it is this rod that God instructs him to bring along, this Divine rod with which miracles can be wrought.

Zipporah and Moses bear two children, Gershom and Eliezer. Gershom: *Ger* meaning "stranger," and "*sham*" meaning "there"—"A stranger, there, in a strange land." Eliezer: *El* referring to God, and *ezer* meaning "help"—"For the God of my father was my help and delivered me from the sword of Pharaoh."

After her marriage to Moses, nothing more will be said of Zipporah until we reach chapter 4. By performing the ritual circumcision on Gershom, she wards off a Divine attack which appears to occur as she and her son return to Egypt from Midian with Moses. In chapter 18, Scripture suggests that while the events of the Exodus were taking place, Zipporah remained in Midian with her father and was reunited with Moses when the Israelites approached the Sinai wilderness. Zipporah will never again be mentioned in Scripture, although according to our Sages, an indirect reference to her is made in the Book of Numbers, an event in which the grown up Miriam is a key player.

The contented and quiet life that Moses had chosen for himself was soon to end. One day, while tending his father-in-law's flock, grazing them in the western part of the desert near Mount Horeb (Sinai), Moses comes upon a burning bush that appears to remain unconsumed by the flames. It is here that God speaks to Moses and tells him of his purpose on the planet, his task of a lifetime—to free His people from slavery and to lead them to the Promised Land.

MEKILTA: Why did God choose a thornbush as the site of the revelation? It is characteristic of a thornbush that if a man sticks his hand into it, he'll be harmed only when trying to withdraw it. The thorns are pointed downward; upon entering the bush, no injury is inflicted. Likewise, upon entering Egypt, the Israelites were warmly received, but when they tried to leave, the Egyptians fastened onto them, like thorns, and refused to let them go. So too, it is said, that the task of aiding anyone to emerge from slavery in Egypt was more difficult and intricate, even for God, than out of any other bondage in the world. In fact, Sarah's handmaid, Hagar, was the only servant to ever emerge from Egypt free and unscathed.

Which Name?

A great kabbalistic mystery is contained within the meanings of the Divine Names used in Scripture. It is said that God first created the letters of the Hebrew alphabet and then He began the act of Creation by engraving with these letters the Divine Names. The names pertain to the different ways through which God manifests Himself; they

---

are symbols of His attributes. None of the names actually refer to God Himself.

When God appears to Moses through the burning bush and tells him of his mission, Moses asks, "And they shall say unto me"—what is His name? What shall I say unto them?" (Exodus 3:13) What does Moses mean?

Moses knew that in time of need his ancestors had been assisted by God Who had acted through the attribute represented by the Divine Name, El-Shaddai. The plagues that descended upon Pharaoh's house on Sarah's behalf, Abraham's ability to miraculously subdue the powerful kings—these miracles were performed with El-Shaddai. Moses now inquired regarding the nature of the mission he was being sent on. Would he be assisted with the attribute that was sufficient for the purposes and needs of the patriarchs and matriarchs, or would he be accompanied, as he wished to be, by the Great Name of God, the attribute through which the very laws of Nature may, themselves, be visibly overturned . . . ? (Ramban on Exodus 3:13)

Chapters 5 through 12 relay the sequence of ten plagues that descend upon Egypt and the subsequent dispelling of the Hebrew slaves.

13:21 "And the Lord went before them by day in a pillar of cloud, to lead them the way, and by night in a pillar of fire, to give them light."

ZOHAR III:51b: "What was this pillar of cloud? . . . It was the cloud which is always seen with the Shekhinah . . . . The pillar of cloud by day represented Abraham (the attribute of Mercy) and the pillar of fire by night, Isaac (the attribute of Severity), both attributes being united in the Shekhinah."

ZOHAR III:45a: "When the children of Israel went out of Egypt, their spirits were broken because of their past sufferings, and there was no energy left in them and no will to participate in the joy, singing, and exultation of Moses and Miriam. But when all those celestial hosts and chariots who accompanied the Shekhinah on the way from Egypt began to sing and praise the Lord for His glorious deeds, the Holy One awakened the spirits of the Israelites, putting new life into them, and they who had tasted death were healed by His touch . . . . Pharaoh, however, and his hosts and all the celestial principalities of Egypt and the other heathen nations, followed them from behind, until they reached Etham, on the edge of the Wilderness."

The Israelites follow a route that leads them in the direction of the Sinai desert and heading straight for the Red Sea. No sooner had they been released from bondage that Pharaoh regrets his decision and sends the Egyptian cavalry out in hot pursuit of his former slaves. Caught between certain death by drowning or death at the hands of their captors, the Hebrews turn upon their leader in terror and revolt.

Chapter 14:11. "Because there were no graves in Egypt, hast thou taken us away to die in the wilderness?" . . . 14:13. And Moses said unto the people, "Fear ye not, stand still, and see the salvation of the Lord, which He will work for you today; for whereas ye have seen the Egyptians today, ye shall see them again no more forever." 14:15. And the Lord said unto Moses, "Wherefore criest thou unto Me?"

EXODUS RABBAH 21:8: "The Holy One, blessed be He, said to Moses: There is a time to pray briefly and a time to pray at length. My children are in dire distress, the sea shuts them in and the enemy is pursuing, and you stand here adding prayer on prayer!"

14:15. Speak unto the children of Israel, that they go forward. 14:16. And lift up thy rod and stretch out thy hand over the sea, and divide it.

Thus ensues the climactic salvation of the Israelites who cross over on dry land, while behind them, their enemies are swallowed by the collapsing walls of the sea.

> *"The same power which exercised Judgement on the Egyptians was the agent of mercy to Israel." Zohar III:36a*

Chapter 15:20. And Miriam the prophetess, the sister of Aaron, took a timbrel in her hand; and all the women went out after her with timbrels and with dances. 15:21. And Miriam sang unto them: "Sing ye to the Lord, for He is highly exalted; the horse and his rider hath He thrown into the sea."

Here on the far side of the Red Sea, the woman, who as a child prophesied the birth of her bother, is called by name for the very first time in Scripture. Our exceptional Miriam is here also for the first time explicitly called a prophetess, and her exalted response to their triumph is most definitely highlighted in the text. What could be the special significance of a song and a dance?

Our Talmudic Sages teach that whoever sings a song of praise to God merits to sing it in the Messianic future, the world to come . . . his sins have been forgiven (Talmud, *Sanhedrin* 91b). One explanation given by our Sages is that

Shirah, the word for "song" in its feminine form is related to the word *shurah*, which means "a straight line." In joyfully singing, a person's soul and heart become "straightened," aligned with and directly connected to God.

> *Whenever the Israelites recite a song, Scripture records the word for "song" in its Hebrew feminine form, "shirah"—a symbolic reference to the woman's experience of the process of labor and birth . . . . Just as the pains of labor ultimately give way and result in a birth, the recurrent pangs of trouble falling upon the Israelites will always, in time, give birth to salvation. (Exodus Rabbah 23:11)*

Shir, song in its masculine form, has been shown by our Sages to be related to the word *shur*, meaning "to see," and is interpreted as the ability to see far, to see the Hidden, the Divine, via song.

ZOHAR III:60a: "When the Israelites stood at the Red Sea and sang, the Holy One, blessed be He, revealed Himself to them with all His hosts and chariots, in order that they should know their king who had wrought all those signs and mighty works for them, and that each of them should perceive of the Divine more than was vouchsafed to any prophet. Should anyone say that they did not know and did not cleave to the Supernal Wisdom, this song that they sang in perfect unison is a proof to the contrary; for how could they, without the inspiration of the Holy Spirit, have sung together as if through one mouth? Yea, even the embryos in their mother's wombs sang it in unison and beheld things that the prophet Ezekiel could not see.

They all beheld the Divine glory eye to eye, and when their

singing was ended their souls were so filled with joy and ec-
stasy that they refused to continue on their journey, desiring
yet more perfect revelations of that glorious mystery . . . . "What
did the Holy One do? He hid His glory and transferred it from
there to the wilderness, half disclosing it to them there. Moses
bade them many times to proceed, but they refused, until he
took hold of them and showed them the light of the glory of
the Holy One in the wilderness." Exodus 15:22—"The Israelites then went out into the wilderness of Shur," the wilderness of "Beholding," the literal meaning of *shur* being "to look
around."

So the Israelites do, indeed, go on. On the morning of
their third day in the desert, standing at the foot of Mount
Sinai, they receive the Torah.

ZOHAR III:93b–94a: "At that hour all the mysteries of the
Torah, all the hidden things of heaven and earth, were un-
folded before them and revealed to their eyes, for they saw
eye to eye the splendour of the glory of their Lord. Never
before, since the Holy One created the world, had such a
revelation of the Divine Glory taken place. Even the crossing
of the Red Sea, where, as has been said, even a simple maidservant saw more of the Divine than the prophet Ezekiel, was
not so wonderful as this. For on this day all the earthly dross
was removed from them and purged away, and their bodies
became as lucent as the angles above when they are clothed
in radiant garments for the accomplishment of their Master's
errands . . . . There, at Mount Sinai, even the embryos in their
mothers' wombs had some perception of the Lord's glory, and
everyone received according to his grade of perception."

Just forty days later in the temporary absence of Moses who
is communing with the Lord on the mountain, the Israelites
lose faith in their leader, forget God, and beg Aaron to cre-

ate for them a visible god, a god like those of the Egyptians ... a golden calf. Aaron yields to the demands of the rebels: "Break off the golden earrings that are on the ears of your wives, of your sons and of your daughters and bring them unto me" (32:2).

ZOHAR IV:192a, PIRKE DE RABBI ELIEZER, CHAPTER 45: Aaron thought to himself: If I merely ask them to bring gold, any gold, they will immediately comply. If I instruct them to bring the gold of their family's earrings, they may fail in their attempts, or at any rate, while they are arguing, I may gain some time and Moses might return before any wrong is actually done.

Now as it turned out, the women refused to yield up their earrings and chastised their husbands for wishing to create a powerless molten image. Not heeding their wives, the men removed the earrings from their own ears and gave them to Aaron; and before Moses returned, a golden calf was molded.

While up on the mountain, God informs Moses of the behavior of the people below, and Moses on their behalf beseeches Mercy. In response to his wish, God will destroy by sword and plague, only the sinners. When Moses himself witnesses the idol-worshipping masses, his human fury is aroused, and he smashes the tablets. Moses again ascends the mountain. When he returns with the new tablets, he conveys to the survivors, those on the side of God, the Divine instructions for the construction of a Sanctuary and Tabernacle, the edifice which will contain the Ark.

EXODUS RABBAH 33:1: "It can be compared to the only daughter of a king whom another king married. When he wished to return to his country and take his wife with him, he (the father) said to him: 'My daughter, whose hand I have given thee, is my only child. I cannot part with her, neither can I say to thee: "Do not take her," for she is now thy wife. This favor, however, I would request of thee; wherever thou goest to live, have a chamber ready for me that I may dwell with you, for I cannot leave my daughter.' Thus God said to Israel: 'I have given you a Torah from which I cannot part, and I also cannot tell you not to take it; but this I would request—wherever you go, make for Me a house wherein I may sojourn,' as it says, 'And let them make for Me a sanctuary, that I may dwell among them' (25:8)."

Chapter 35:1. And Moses assembled all the congregation of the children of Israel and said unto them, "these are the words which the Lord hath commanded, that ye should do them . . . . 5. Take ye from among you an offering unto the Lord, whosoever is of a willing heart, let him bring it, the Lord's offering, gold and silver and brass . . . . 20. And all the congregation of the children of Israel departed from the presence of Moses. 21. And they came, everyone whose heart stirred him up, and everyone whom his spirit made willing, and brought the Lord's offering, for the work of the tent of meeting, and for all the service thereof, and for the holy garments. 22. And they came, both men and women, as many as were willing-hearted, and brought nose-rings and ear-rings and signet rings . . . . all jewels of gold . . . . 25. And all the women that were wise-hearted did spin with their hands and brought that which they had spun, the blue and the purple, the scarlet and the fine linen. 26. And all the women whose heart stirred them up in wisdom spun the goats hair . . . . 29. The children of Israel brought a free-will offering unto the Lord; every man and woman, whose heart made them willing to bring for all the work, which the Lord had commanded by the hand of Moses to be made. 30. And Moses said unto the children of Israel, 'See, the Lord hath called by name Bezalel the son of Uri, the son of Hur, of the tribe of Judah. 31. And He hath filled him with the Spirit of God, in wisdom, in understanding, and in knowledge, and in all manner of workmanship.'

35:22 "And they came . . . and brought . . . ear-rings."

EXODUS RABBAH 48:6: "It was with ear-rings that they sinned, and with ear-rings that they became reconciled to God."

35:30 "The Lord hath called by name Bezalel."

Who was Bezalel, this man whose name translates literally as Bezel-El, "in the shadow of God"? The rabbis teach that Miriam was not childless.

EXODUS RABBAH 48:3–4, PIRKE DE RABBI ELIEZER, CHAPTER 45: From an analysis of Scriptural names and titles in the Book of Chronicles, the rabbis have derived that Miriam had a son named Hur. It was Hur who stood in opposition to the masses as they demanded a golden god, jeopardizing his life on God's behalf, and who, in turn, was slain by his former neighbors. At the moment of Hur's death, God spoke to him: "I assure thee that I will repay thee for this . . . . By thy life, I shall give all thy children that will descend from thee a great name in the world." As promised, Hur's grandson is Bezalel, and it is this individual who is chosen by God to build the Tabernacle, a man whom God endows with wisdom, understanding, and knowledge.

PROVERBS 3:19 "The Lord by Wisdom founded the earth, by Understanding He established the heavens, by His Knowledge the depths were broken up and the skies distilled dew."

ZOHAR IV:234b: "The letters of the Divine Name embrace the mystery of the Torah, and all the worlds are a projection of the mystery of those letters . . . . Now the same letters were the instruments used in the building of the Tabernacle. This work was carried on by Bezalel for the reason that, as his very name implies, he had a knowledge of the various permutations of the letters, by the power of which, heaven and earth were created."

EXODUS RABBAH 48:4: Why did Bezalel merit all this wisdom? It is because of the merit of Miriam. "And He (God) made them houses" (1:21). From Jochebed came the priestly and royal houses, Aaron and Moses. From Miriam came the wise Bezalel, and from the line of Bezalel came David, the King.

Chapter 40:33. So Moses finished the work. 34. Then the cloud covered the Tent of Meeting and the Presence of the Lord filled the Tabernacle. . . . 38. For the cloud of the Lord was upon the Tabernacle by day, and there was a fire therein by night, in the sight of all the house of Israel throughout all their journeys.

RAMBAN ON EXODUS (INTRODUCTION): Why doesn't the Book of Exodus end with the telling of the miraculous escape from Bondage? Even after leaving Egypt, Scripture continues to view the Israelites as exiles. It is not until they reach Mount Sinai, receive the instructions for the building of the Tabernacle, complete its construction, and enable God's presence to permanently dwell among them—just as it once did in the tents of their fathers and mothers—that they are finally considered redeemed. The Book of Exodus concludes with the building of the Tabernacle which was permeated with God's glory, His light.

All was not destined to remain to temperate, so ordered. The episode of the golden calf was not the last of the internal rebellions. Rumbling just beneath the deceptively tranquil surface, veiled upheavals brewed. "Oh, why did we ever leave Egypt?" (Numbers 11:20).

Miriam

"Remember what the Lord, thy God, did unto Miriam" (Deuteronomy 24:9).

Vayikra is the third of the Five Books of Moses, its Hebrew name derived from its opening phrase, "And the Lord called unto Moses."

Its English title, Leviticus, is derived from the Septaguint. This book deals mostly with the functions and duties of the priesthood.

Bamidbar is the fourth of the Five Books of Moses, its Hebrew name derived from the fourth word in its opening phrase, "in the wilderness," and likewise, records everything that happens to the Israelites from the time they leave Mount Sinai until they reach the border of Canaan.

This book opens with the census taken of the Israelites as they begin their journey to the Promised Land, and hence, its English title, the Book of Numbers.

For the purpose of our specific inquiry into the lives of our foremothers, we move directly to the Book of Num bers and focus upon an event with severe repercussions for the sister of Aaron and Moses, our beloved prophetess.

T he Book of Numbers, Chapter 11—The Israelites again complain about their difficult plight in the desert, and Moses, in his distress, calls upon God.

Chapter 11:11. Wherefore hast Thou dealt ill with Thy servant . . . that Thou layest the burden of all this people upon me? 12. Have I conceived all this people? Have I brought them forth that Thou should say onto me, "Carry them in thy bosom as a nursing father carryeth the sucking child, unto the land which Thou did swear unto their fathers? 13. Whence should I have meat to give unto all this people, for they trouble me with their weeping . . . . 14. I am not able to bear all this people myself, alone, because it is too heavy for me . . . . 16. And the Lord said onto Moses, "Gather unto me seventy men of the elders of Israel . . . and bring them unto the tent of meeting, that they may stand there with thee. 17. And I will come down and speak with thee there, and I will take of the spirit which is upon thee, and will put it upon them; and they shall bear the burden of the people with thee, that thou bear it not thyself, alone.

The discontent, the criticisms waged at Moses, did not come solely from the multitudes; it also struck at him from the most unlikely of sources.

> 12:1. And Miriam and Aaron spoke against Moses because of the Cushite woman he had married . . . . 2. And they said, "Hath the Lord indeed only spoken with Moses? Hath He not spoken also with us?" And the Lord heard it.

Miriam, as we know, is portrayed by the rabbis as an individual who was never afraid to deliver a severe rebuke when necessary—to her father, even to the Pharaoh. As an adult, Miriam now harshly condemns her brother, Moses. This time, she will not come out unscathed.

The text seems to suggest that the cause of the rebuke was the marriage of Moses to a Cushite (Ethiopian) woman, but many scholars believe that this particular line was added by a later editor of Scripture. Our rabbis also offer quite a different explanation for Miriam's and Aaron's bitterness. Moses is Divinely directed to gather together seventy elders at the Tent of Meeting, and the spirit of prophecy is said to have rested upon all of them. It is later reported to Moses that Eldad and Medad, two men not chosen by Moses, were going about the camp engaging in the mystery of prophecy and ecstatic communion with the Divine. Moses, unlike his informants, did not become riled up when advised of their actions. "Are you wrought up on my account? Would that ALL the Lord's people were prophets!" he responds (11:29).

RASHI: When the report of the two men was brought to Moses, Zipporah, standing within earshot, spontaneously exclaimed, "Woe to the wives of these (two men) if they have anything to do with prophecy, for they will separate from their wives, just as my husband has separated from me!" Miriam, who witnessed Zipporah's reaction, reported it to her brother, Aaron. Miriam, at that moment, realized that Moses had separated himself from his wife, and she believed that Zipporah had been wronged, deprived of the possibility of and obligation to procreate. Miriam brags that even though she and Aaron *also* receive Divine revelations, they, unlike Moses, chose not to halt their conjugal life. Miriam falsely accuses Moses of unwarranted pride, of falsely displaying the appearances of a Holy Man. Rashi further teaches that the specific word chosen in verse 12:1 for "spoke," is used throughout Scripture whenever the use of harsh language is implied. The verb appears here in its feminine form, further implying that it was Miriam who opened the conversation, that it was Miriam, not Aaron, who led the revolt.

Chapter 12:3. Now the man Moses was very meek . . . . 4. And the Lord spoke suddenly unto Moses, and unto Aaron, and unto Miriam, "Come out ye three unto the tent of meeting." And they three came out. 5. And the Lord came down in a pillar of cloud, and stood at the door of the tent, and called Aaron and Miriam; and they both came forth. 6. And He said, "Hear now My Words: If there be a prophet among you, I, the Lord do make Myself known unto him in a vision, I do speak with him in a dream. 7. My servant Moses is not so; he is trusted in all My house. 8. With him do I speak mouth to mouth, even manifestly, and not in dark speeches; and the similitude of the Lord doth he behold; wherefore, then were ye not afraid to speak against My servant, against Moses?" 9. And the anger of the Lord was kindled against them; and He departed. 10. And when the cloud was removed from over the tent, behold, Miriam was leprous and white as snow; and Aaron looked upon Miriam, and behold, she was leprous. 11. And Aaron said unto Moses, "Oh, My Lord, lay not I pray thee, sin upon us, for that we have done foolishly, and for that we have sinned. 12. Let her not I pray, be as one dead, of whom the flesh is half consumed . . . . 13. And Moses cried unto the Lord saying, "Heal her now Oh God, I beseech Thee." 14. And the Lord said unto Moses, "If her father had but spit in her face, should she not hide in shame seven days? Let her be shut up without the camp seven days, and after that she shall be brought in again." 15. And Miriam was shut up without the camp seven days; and the people journeyed not till Miriam was brought in again. 16. And afterward the people journeyed from Hazeroth, and pitched in the wilderness of Paran.

12:3 "Now the man Moses was very meek."

All the Sages portray Moses as a man who overlooked injustices that were perpetrated against him, taking no steps to vindicate himself.

RAMBAN ON R. IBN EZRA: Moses and Aaron spoke against their brother for no good reason. His character was such that he never flaunted his position or privilege. Scripture mentions Moses' meekness to reveal that he endured their insults and accusations without responding or defending himself. This is the reason why God Himself stepped in on his behalf.

12:4 "And the Lord spoke suddenly unto Moses, unto Aaron and unto Miriam."

RAMBAN: Our Talmudic rabbis have taught that Moses was required to abstain from relations with his wife so that his mind and heart could receive Divine communications at any moment. Moses did not need any preparation—his customary state was one of receptivity and preparedness for Divine Revelation. Ramban teaches that the word *suddenly* in this verse refers to the idea that here, the Divine words came to Moses, Aaron, and Miriam simultaneously. In honor of their brother, Aaron and Miriam received the communication without their customary time of mental preparation.

ZOHAR III:82b: Some of our Sages compare the vision of Moses to the reflection given off by a bright mirror, as opposed to the visions of the other prophets which were akin to blurred images reflecting off a dim one.

RAMBAN ON ONKELOS: "Suddenly" infers "in a hurry." Before they had even finished speaking their words, God ordered them outside to receive His rebuke.

12:4 "Come out ye three."

RAMBAN: God wanted Moses to be present in the Tent of Meeting, to witness His ardent passion to defend his honor. In addition, God would not forgive Miriam and Aaron unless Moses forgave them first and unless it was also his wish that they be forgiven by Him, as well.

12:8 "With him do I speak mouth to mouth."

RASHI: God tells Miriam and Aaron that it was He Himself who had instructed Moses at Mount Sinai to separate from his wife, unlike all the others who were instructed to rejoin their partners (see Deuteronomy 5:27–28).

12:8 "Wherefore then were ye not afraid to speak against My servant, against Moses?"

RASHI: "It does not state, 'against my servant Moses' but 'against my servant, against Moses,' which suggests: Why were ye not afraid to speak against my servant—even though he were not a Moses, and why were ye not afraid to speak against a Moses—even though he were not my servant—in either of these cases, you ought to have feared him! How much more ought you to be afraid to speak against him, he being also my servant—and the servant of a king is a king himself! You should have said: the king doesn't love him without reason! But if you reply that I am not cognizant of his doings (that is, that I love him though he does not deserve it, since I am not aware of his treatment of his wife), then *this* statement is even *worse* than your previous one."

When God's presence had departed, Miriam was covered with leprosy. Apparently, say the rabbis, Aaron was excluded from this punishment because he was merely drawn into the attack on his brother. Why leprosy? Because leprosy is the symbolic Divine punishment for the crime of slander.

DEUTERONOMY RABBAH 6:8, SIFRE DEUTERONOMY: Miriam spoke only with her brother's interest in mind, wishing that he would take back his life and father more children. If she was punished so severely, how much more will he who publicly disparages his neighbor be punished for his actions!

Likewise, the story of Miriam's punishment is juxtaposed with the story of the twelve spies sent into the Promised Land and who bring back disheartening reports. Miriam had just been punished for slander and yet these unrighteous men did not learn a lesson from her. All except Joshua and Caleb, who refute the faithlessness of the other spies and the picture of impossibility of victory that they paint and spread throughout the community, are consumed by plague.

Over and over again, we find evidence of the Rabbinic teaching that the greater the man or woman, the stricter and higher the standard he is held to, and the more extreme the punishment or loss suffered if and when the individual falls short of that mark.

Aaron speaks up on his sister's behalf. Moses, likewise, beseeches God to show compassion. God, in turn, decrees a seven-day quarantine for Miriam, outside the camp, after which time she is to rejoin her people, fully healed.

12:15 "And the people journeyed not till Miriam was brought in again."

RASHI: The tribes waited for Miriam's period of confinement to end before resuming their travels, a Divine reward for the single hour she waited for her infant brother when he was cast into the Nile.

In response to the faithless report of the twelve spies and the recurrent rantings of the people against Moses and Aaron, and therefore, against God Himself, Divine Fury is released upon the Israelites. The fate of the generation who escaped enslavement in Egypt is now sealed.

Chapter 14:23. Surely thy seed shall not see the land which I swore unto their fathers . . . . 31. But your little ones . . . them will I bring in . . . . 32. But as for you, your carcasses shall fall in the wilderness. 33. And your children shall be wanderers in the wilderness forty years, and shall bear your strayings, until your carcasses be consumed in the wilderness.

Nothing more is said of the following years, the lifetime of the generation condemned to extinction. The chronological sequel to this section is chapter 20 of the Book of Numbers, which brings us to the very last of the forty years spent wandering in the Sinai, the year, too, in which the prophetess, Miriam, dies.

> Chapter 20:1. And the Children of Israel, even the whole congregation, came into the wilderness of Zin in the first month, and the people abode in Kadesh; and Miriam died and was buried there.

"For I brought thee up out of the Land of Egypt and redeemed thee out of the House of Bondage, and I sent before thee Moses, Aaron and Miriam" (Book of Micah, the Prophet 6:4).

TARGUM: "Moses to instruct you in the Divine Law of righteousness and mercy; Aaron to show the way to atonement; Miriam to teach and guide the women."

TALMUD, *BABA BATHRA* 17a: Our rabbis taught that there were six individuals over whom the Angel of Death had no power, six individuals who died by "a kiss"—Abraham, Isaac, Jacob, Moses, Aaron, and Miriam.

None of the three illustrious siblings will reach the Promised Land, not Miriam, nor Aaron, nor Moses. Like her brothers, Miriam is granted immunity from the powers of the Angel of Death and is removed from among the living by "the kiss of God."

Immediately after recording Miriam's death, Scripture tells

us that "the community was without water, and they assembled themselves together against Moses and Aaron" (20:2). A recurrent difficulty for the journeying Israelites is the lack of drinking water in the desert. Scripture records nothing about the thirty-nine intervening years between God's decree against the travelers and Miriam's death. Is there some significance to the juxtaposition of her departure and the sudden need for water? The rabbis unanimously say, "Yes."

Let's trace the water problem as described in the text. After crossing the Red Sea, the Israelites first find themselves without water just three days into their desert journey. "And when they came to Marah, they could not drink of the waters of Marah, for they were bitter . . . . And the people grumbled against Moses saying, 'What shall we drink? And he cried out to the Lord, and the Lord showed him a piece of wood and he cast it into the waters, and the waters were made sweet" (Exodus 15:23–25).

Upon leaving Marah, "They came to Elim, where there were twelve springs of water and seventy palm trees; and they encamped there by the waters" (Exodus 15:27).

From there, the Israelites continued on to Rephidim, where, again, there is no drinking water, and they cry out at Moses for having brought them out of Egypt, only to die of thirst in the desert.

Moses cried out to the Lord, saying, 'What shall I do with this people? Before long they will be stoning me!' Then the Lord said to Moses, 'Pass before the people . . . and take along with thee the rod with which thou struck the Nile . . . . I will stand then before thee on the rock at Horeb. Strike the rock and water will issue from it, and the people will drink.' And Moses did so in the sight of the elders of Israel. The place was

named Massah (trial) and Meribah (quarrel), because
the Israelites quarrelled and because they tried the Lord,
saying, "Is the Lord present among us or not?" (Exodus
17:4–7)

This last incident marks the appearance of what tradition
has come to call "Miriam's Well," divinely ordained sustenance
which is said to have supplied the rebellious and often faithless Israelites with a constant source of water for the next
thirty-nine years.

NUMBERS RABBAH 1:2: "Did I not assign to you three special tutors, Moses, Aaron, and Miriam? It was due to the merit
of Moses that you ate the 'manna.' . . . It was due to the merit
of Aaron that I set clouds of glory about you . . . . And again,
the well was due to the merit of Miriam who sang by the
waters of the Red Sea."

PIRKE DE RABBI ELIEZER, CHAPTER 18: Ten things
were created in the twilight of the eve of the first Sabbath,
among them "the mouth of the well."

RAMBAN: And it was this well which appeared whenever God
willed it . . . . When Ishmael, as a child, lay in the wilderness
of Beersheba, dying of thirst, it was this well which appeared
to his mother, Hagar.

ZOHAR II:132a: When Rebekah met Eliezer at the well, "this
fountain was none other than the well of Miriam."

ZOHAR V:181a: "When Miriam departed, the well which accompanied Israel in the wilderness also departed."

*A tale is told by the descendants of Rabbi Jacob, how one
year, on the Eve of Yom Kippur, the zaddik, the Rabbi*

of Kalev, intercepted him on his way to the synagogue, asked him to harness his horse and carriage and to accompany him on a short drive. Rabbi Jacob did not ask any questions. They drove across Rabbi Jacob's fields, and when they came upon a small body of water in their midst, the zaddik stopped the carriage, took off his clothes and submerged himself in the water. Rabbi Jacob just stood and watched, somewhat bewildered. Not only did the zaddik's unpredictable behavior take him aback, but he had never before seen any water at that location· on his property (nor did he ever again)!

At the conclusion of the holiday, Rabbi Jacob approached the zaddik and asked him if he would favor him with an explanation of the prior day's events. The zaddik looked at Rabbi Jacob, and with a mixture of confusion and harshness, he berated him: Miriam's Well, the extraordinary well that followed the Israelites through the desert, providing Divine sustenance, just happened to pass through their part of town. In God's name, why didn't he bathe himself in its waters instead of just blankly standing there on the sidelines? [34]

After Miriam's death, God instructs Moses to speak to the rock, which, throughout their travels yields up water, but he defies the direct instruction and instead strikes the rock with the rod. Due to the merit of Moses, water again flows, but for his lack of trust in the word of God, his seemingly small violation in the face of all that he has done, the great prophet Moses will be denied entrance into the Promised Land, the possession of which has been the sole directive of his life.

34. Martin Buber, *Tales of the Hasidim, The Later Masters* (New York: Schocken Books, 1975), 101–102.

Is there a hidden dimension to the scriptural anecdotes? Do they contain veiled meanings, couched within a symbolism of water itself?

In the system of Kabbalah, "water" is associated with the Divine emanation of Chesed-Love. Chesed also parallels the first day of creation, and it is in this respect that the idea of water is expressed in Scripture's description of the very First Day. It is through the Divine emanation of Chesed-Love that man finds a portal into the mysteries of the Torah.[35]

ZOHAR III:60a: Throughout Scripture, water is a symbol for the Torah.

BOOK OF JEREMIAH 2:1: "For My people have done a two-fold wrong: They have forsaken Me, the fountain of living waters, and hewed them out cisterns, broken cisterns, which cannot hold water."

BOOK OF ISAIAH 55:1: "Ho, let all who are thirsty come for water, let him without silver, come, stock and eat."

---

35. Aryeh Kaplan, *The Bahir* (York Beach, ME: Samuel Weiser, 1979), 121.

The Daughters of Zelophehad

The Book of Numbers, Chapter 27.

In anticipation of entering and taking possession of Canaan, a new census is taken to fairly divide the land among the tribes. The Israelites considered it unlawful to take property away from the family or tribe to which it belonged. In cases where there were no male heirs, only daughters, the family line risked loss of that property when the daughter, herself, married. Scripture, here, recounts the story of five sisters who challenge the status quo.

After the Hebrew spies met with their Divinely ordained demise, Moses and the community of Israel endure yet another upheaval. Korah, a man of the tribe of Levi, questions Moses' leadership. He and his band of followers are consequently destroyed for this insurgence, a battle which, in the words of the Sages was "not waged in the name of Heaven." On the other hand, the challenge here posed by these five women is not only tolerated, but is ultimately praised by God Himself.

Chapter 27:1. Then drew near the daughters of Zelophehad of the families of Menassah, the son of Joseph . . . 2. And they stood before Moses and Eliezer the priest . . . 3. "Our father died in the wilderness and he was not among the company of them that gathered themselves together against the Lord in the company of Korah, but died in his own sin; and he had no sons. 4. Why should the name of our father be done away from among his family, because he had no son? Give unto us a possession among the brethren of our father." 5. And Moses brought their cause before the Lord. 6. And the Lord spoke unto Moses saying, 7. "The daughters of Zelophehad speak right. Thou shalt surely give them a possession of an inheritance among their father's brethren."

27:1 ". . . the daughters of Zelophehad, of the families of Menasseh, the son of Joseph."

Prior to their mention here in connection with a legal matter, nothing at all is recorded in the text regarding the deeds or the merit of these five women. However in every case, when Scripture makes a point of recording an individual's ancestry, tracing his genealogy back to someone who merits praise, the rabbis take this as clear evidence of the righteousness of the person in question. Likewise, if the genealogy connects him with someone disreputable, it is assumed that all who are mentioned in connection with him are also dishonorable (Talmud, *Megillah* 15a).

NUMBERS RABBAH 21:11: "They were righteous [women] in as much as they married none but such as were worthy of them. Why did the Holy One, blessed be He, introduce them to Moses at the end of his career? In order that Moses might not plume himself on having departed from his wife for forty years." Moses was *required* to stay away from his wife, due to his constant communication with God, but these five women who were not commanded to abstain, freely chose to do so until they could find men worthy of them.

NUMBERS RABBAH 21:11: "They were wise and righteous women. What shows their wisdom? They spoke at the appropriate moment." Moses had been speaking to the Israelites on the subject of inheritances (Numbers 26:53), and it was at this moment that the women aired their grievance. They did not merely launch a resentful gripe. They spoke cleverly, so cleverly, in fact, that their logic stumped Moses. The five sisters based their argument on the law of Levirite marriage wherein a widowed woman with no sons is permitted to legally marry her brother-in-law whose duty it is then to raise children in the name of the deceased father. The daughters of Zelophehad point out that their mother, a widow, should therefore be obligated to marry her dead husband's brother, but, in this case, she did not comply. Why? Because, according to the same law, a child of *either* sex annuls the injunction. In effect, the women were saying: You say that daughters cannot be heirs, but here is a circumstance wherein girls are, indeed, looked upon as heirs!

The women, in defense of their objection, go on to remind Moses that their father had not been involved with the faction that rose up against him, but rather that he had "died in his own sin." Why should our father's name be lost?

27:5 "And Moses brought their cause before the Lord."

NUMBERS RABBAH 21:12: "Moses our Teacher knew this law, but the women came, in the first instance, before the chiefs of ten who said: 'This is a case concerning inheritance and it is not within our scope. It belongs to our superiors.' The women came to the chiefs of fifty. Seeing that the chiefs of ten had shown them honor, the chiefs of fifty said: 'In our case also there are superiors to us.' The same reply was given by the chiefs of hundreds, by the chiefs of thousands, and by the princes. They all answered them in the same strain, for they were unwilling to begin considering it before their superior. So they went to Eleazar and he told them: 'Behold, there is Moses our Teacher!' All parties came before Moses. When Moses saw that each one had shown respect to his superior, he thought: If I tell them the law I shall be appropriating all the greatness. So he said to them: 'I too, have a Superior!' Therefore, 'Moses brought their cause before the Lord.' "

27:7 And the Lord said to Moses, "The daughters of Zelophehad speak right."

NUMBERS RABBAH 21:12: "This indicates that the Holy One, blessed be He, acknowledged the justice of their words."

NUMBERS RABBAH 21:12: In chapter 49 of the Book of Genesis, Jacob, before dying, gathers his sons together. He blesses each one, in turn, and within each blessing is a prophecy, "to tell you that which shall befall you in the end of days." Regarding Joseph, an ancestor of Zelophehad, Jacob makes this pronouncement: "Joseph is a faithful vine . . . its branches run over the walls" (Gen. 49:22). Jacob's words were not merely poetry, but were in all respects prophecy. "The wall," say our rabbis, refers to the Jordan River, which to Moses was like a wall which prevented him from entering the land. "The branches" running over the wall are the five daughters, who, with God's blessing, received portions on both of its sides.

SIFRE NUMBERS 133: How different were the women from the men at that time in Israel's history. The men said, "Let us make a captain and let us return into Egypt!" (Numbers 14:4), but the women demanded, "Give unto us a possession!" (Numbers 27:4).

NUMBERS RABBAH 21:10: "In that generation, the women built up the fences which the men broke down." In the Book of Exodus, Aaron says, "Break off the golden rings which are in the ears of your wives," but the women resist and refuse to participate with their husbands in the creation of the golden calf. In the Book of Numbers, Moses sends off spies who return from the land flowing with milk and honey with a disheartening report, dissuading the embryonic nation from proceeding with its plan. The women refuse to involve themselves with the growing loss of faith. Our rabbis suggest that God's ensuing decree against the populace that they would never reach Canaan, but would instead die in the desert, was levied against only the men! "And there was not left a man of them, save Caleb" (26:65). The text speaks of the men, not of the women. Why? Because, teach the rabbis, the men had revealed their unwillingness to enter the Promised Land. As for the women, however, they "drew near" to ask for an inheritance.

II

The Women of the Books of the Prophets and the Writings

"The Rabbis taught: There have been four women of surpassing beauty in the world—Sarah, Rahab, Abigail, and Esther . . . . Rahab inspired lust by her name; Abigail by merely the memory of her."
—*(TALMUD, Megillah 15a)*

Rahab

The Book of Joshua,
Chapter One.

J oshua 1:1. After the death of Moses, the servant of the Lord, the Lord said to Joshua, son of Nun, Moses' attendant, 2. "My servant Moses is dead. Prepare to cross the Jordan, together with all this people, into the land that I am giving to the Israelites. 3. Every spot on which your foot treads I give to you, as I promised Moses . . . . 5. . . . . As I was with Moses, so I will be with you; I will not fail you or forsake you . . . . 8. Let not this book of the Teaching cease from your lips, but recite it day and night, so that you may observe faithfully all that is written in it. Only then will you prosper in your undertakings and only then will you be successful. 9. I charge you: Be strong and resolute; do not be terrified or dismayed, for the Lord your God is with you wherever you go." 10. Joshua thereupon gave orders to the officials of the people, 11. "Go through the camp and charge the people thus: Get provisions ready, for in three days' time you are to cross the Jordan, in order to possess the land that the Lord your God is giving you as a possession." Chapter 2:1. Joshua, son of Nun, secretly sent two spies out from Shittim, saying, "Go, reconnoiter the region of Jericho." So they set out,

> and they came to the house of a harlot named Rahab
> and lodged there.

At this time, numerous small nations lived on the far side of the Jordan River, residing in cities or on hilltops surrounded by high walls. Joshua and the Israelites were camped east of the Jordan, opposite Jericho, a city with fortifying walls so thick that houses were built in and on top of them. God instructs Joshua to cross the Jordan and invade this seemingly impenetrable city. From there, they could proceed North against the Canaanites and then South against the Amorites. Joshua's first step in the plan is to send two spies on a reconnaissance mission. The place they happen to choose to spend the night belongs to a woman on whom the whole success of their mission will hinge—a prostitute.

There are two conflicting traditions regarding Rahab's actual profession. Some contend that she was not really a prostitute, but rather an innkeeper, although most feel that the Aramaic word used in the Targum and translated as innkeeper or hostess is merely a euphemism.

TALMUD, *ZEBAHIM*: 116b: Not a prince, ruler nor leader had not possessed Rahab the harlot. When the Israelites left Egypt, she was ten years old, and it is said that she played the harlot the whole of the forty years that the Israelites spent in the wilderness [perhaps accounting for her worldliness, her ability to decipher right action from wrong].

When the King of Jericho is alerted of the Israelite spies lodging with Rahab, he immediately sends orders requiring Rahab to surrender them. In response, despite the protection she would have been assured by her own Amorite nation had she complied with the king, she chooses instead to risk treason and hide the two foreign spies on the roof under some stacks of flax. When the king's men arrive, she tells them that the Israelites have already left, and she directs them out of the city on a fruitless chase.

2:8. The spies had not yet gone to sleep when she came up to them on the roof. 9. She said to the men, "I know that the Lord has given the country to you, because dread of you has fallen upon us, and all the inhabitants of the land are quaking before you. 10. For we have heard how the Lord dried up the waters of the Red Sea for you when you left Egypt, and what you did to Sihon and Og, the two Amorite kings across the Jordan, whom you doomed. 11. When we heard about it, we lost heart, and no man had any more spirit left because of you; for the Lord Your God is the only God in heaven above and on earth below. 12. Now since I have shown loyalty to you, swear to me by the Lord that you, in turn, will show loyalty to my family. Provide me with a reliable sign."

The harlot, sacrificing her own nation, sides with the spies whom she perceives as men of God, siding with the spies being akin to siding with God Himself. The men pledge to protect her and her entire family, as long as she does not disclose their mission. With a crimson rope, Rahab lowers the spies through her window, which is situated in the wall of Jericho itself.

2:17. But the men warned her, "We will be released from this oath which you have made us take 18. unless, when we invade the country, you tie this length of crimson cord to the window through which you let us down. Bring your father, your mother, your brothers and all your family together in your house; 19. and if anyone ventures outside the doors of your house, his blood will be on his head, and we shall be clear. But if a hand is laid on anyone who remains in the house with you, his blood shall be on your heads. 20. And if you disclose this mission of ours, we shall likewise be released from the oath which you made us take." 21. She replied, "Let it be as you say."

The men hid for three days in the hills, and when their pursuers gave up the search, the spies crossed over the Jordan and reported to Joshua all that had happened: "The Lord has delivered the whole land into our power—in fact, all the inhabitants of the land are quaking before us" (2:24). The nation of Israelites crossed over the Jordan River with God by their side, witnessing the same miracle that their ancestors had witnessed when leaving Egypt.

Chapter 4:19. The people came up from the Jordan on the tenth day of the first month and encamped at Gilgal on the eastern border of Jericho. 20. And Joshua set up in Gilgal the twelve stones that they had taken from the Jordan. 21. He charged the Israelites as follows: "In time to come, when your children ask their fathers, 'What is the meaning of these stones?' 22. Tell your children: Here the Israelites crossed over the Jordan on dry land. 23. For the Lord your God dried up the waters of the Jordan before you until you crossed, just as the Lord your God did to the Red Sea."

Miracle or no miracle, Divine promise or not, the problem remained; how were the Israelites to enter the city of Jericho, now fortified so tightly against them that no one could enter or leave?

Chapter 6:2. The Lord said to Joshua, "See, I will deliver Jericho and her king and her warriors into your hands. 3. Let all your troops march around the city and complete one circuit of the city. Do this six days 4. with seven priests carrying seven ram's horns preceding the Ark. On the seventh day, march around the city seven times, with the priests blowing the horns. 5. And when a long blast is sounded on the horn—as soon as you hear that sound of the horn—all the people shall give a mighty shout. Thereupon the city wall will collapse, and the people shall advance . . . . 15. On the seventh day they rose at daybreak and marched around the city . . . . 15. On the seventh round, as the priests blew the horns, Joshua commanded the people, "Shout! For the Lord has given you the city." . . . 20. . . . the people raised a mighty shout and the wall collapsed. The people rushed into the city, every man straight in front of him, and they captured the city . . . . 25. Only Rahab the harlot and her father's family were spared by Joshua, along with all that belonged to her, and she dwelt among the Israelites—as is still the case. For she had hidden the messengers that Joshua sent to spy out Jericho.

TALMUD, *ZEBAHIM* 116b: This woman, who had practiced prostitution her entire life, converted to Judaism at the age of fifty. She said to God: "May I be forgiven in reward for the cord, the window, and the flax."

TALMUD, *MEGILLAH* 14b, RUTH RABBAH 2:1: The salvation of this central figure in the story of Joshua's first conquest is considered by the rabbis to be enormous and complete. Some of our Sages claim that Rahab, the former harlot, was ultimately married to Joshua. From this union came "eight prophets who were also priests," among them, Jeremiah. Some of our Sages say that ten priests descended from Rahab and include Ezekiel among them. Some add that even Huldah, one of our seven prophetesses, was a descendant of Rahab the harlot.

> When God changed Abram's name to Abraham, none of the original letters were removed; an additional one was added. But when Sarai was changed to Sarah, one letter, the yud, the smallest of letters, was taken away. And for this Divine act, for having been so callously removed from the name of that beloved woman, the yud had a grievance with God. God considered the yud's case and to rectify the matter He agreed to place the slighted yud in the name of Moses' successor—not at the end, as it was in Sarai, but at the very beginning. In the fourth book of the Bible (Numbers 13:16), Moses changes the name of his successor Hosea, to Joshua, Yehoshua in Hebrew. The name Hosea signified "He has helped"; the added prefix, yud, indicative of the future tense, signified the Divine salvation yet to come. (Genesis Rabbah 47:1)

The BOOK of JUDGES, Chapter 2:8. Joshua, son of Nun, the servant of the Lord, died at the age of one hundred ten years 9. and was buried on his own property . . . in the hill country of Ephraim. . . . . 10. And all that generation were likewise gathered to their fathers. Another generation arose after them, which had not experienced the deliverance of the Lord or the deeds that He had wrought for Israel. 11. And the Israelites did what was offensive to the Lord. They worshipped the Baalim 12. and forsook the Lord. . . . 14. Then the Lord was incensed at Israel, and he handed them over to foes who plundered them.

We enter into the Age of the Judges, chieftains who rose up from within the Israelite nation, delivering them through their wisdom and expertise from their oppressing neighbors. But Scripture teaches that as soon as danger was averted and comfort returned, the Israelites resumed their worship of idols, turning their backs on the guidance of their Divinely inspired leader.

2:18. When the Lord raised up chieftains for them, the Lord would be with the chieftain and would save them from their enemies during the chieftain's lifetime; for the Lord would be moved to pity by their moanings. . . . 19. But when the chieftain died, they would again act badly, even more than their fathers. . . . 20. Then the Lord became incensed against Israel, and He said, "Since that nation has transgressed the covenant that I enjoined upon their fathers and has not obeyed Me 21. I for My part will no longer drive out before them any of the nations that Joshua left when he died. 22. For it was in order to test Israel by them—to see whether or not they would faithfully walk in the ways of the Lord, as their fathers had done—23. that the Lord had left those nations, instead of driving them out at once, and had not delivered them into the hands of Joshua.

Deborah and Jael

The Book of Judges, Chapters 4 and 5.

J udges 4:1. The Israelites again did what was offensive to the Lord . . . 2. And the Lord surrendered them to King Jabin of Canaan, who reigned in Hazor. His army commander was Sisera, whose base was in Haroshethgoiim. 3. The Israelites cried out to the Lord; for he had nine hundred iron chariots, and he had oppressed Israel ruthlessly for twenty years. 4. Deborah, wife of Lappidoth, was a prophetess; she led Israel at that time. 5. She used to sit under the Palm of Deborah, between Ramah and Bethel in the hill country of Ephraim, and the Israelites would come to her for decisions.

YALKUT, JUDGES 42: The rabbis ask: What was so special about Deborah's character that she became qualified to prophesy about Israel and to judge them? What were Deborah's praiseworthy deeds? Deborah's husband was an uneducated man. So what did she do? She made thick candle wicks and told her husband to bring them to the holy site in Shiloh where righteous men studied. The light of his wicks would enable worthy men to study. Her husband complied; he brought the wicks to Shiloh. God smiled upon her actions:

Deborah, your efforts provided ample light for the study of My Torah; I, in turn, will make the light of your prophecy shine throughout all of Israel.

Deborah lived at the southernmost point of the Canaanite kingdom; the palm tree she sat beneath is often popularly identified with Allon-Baccuth, the burial site of Rebekah's nurse, Deborah. The Talmudic Sages tell us that Deborah had great wealth, which allowed her to dispense justice with no need for remuneration (Targum, Judges 4:5).

One day, Deborah chooses to embark upon a military plan to finally free her people from the Canaanite oppression, a seemingly impossible venture given their inferior military might. Deborah summons Barak, a man from the northern tribe of Naphtali, intending to appoint him as military commander of her mission.

Chapter 4:6. "The Lord, the God of Israel, has commanded: Go march up to Mount Tabor, and take with you ten thousand men of Naphtali and Zebulun. 7. And I will draw Sisera, Jabin's army commander, with his chariots and his troops, toward you, up to the Wadi Kishon, and I will deliver him into your hands." 8. But Barak said to her, "If you will go with me, I will go; if not, I will not go." 9. "Very well. I will go with you," she answered. "However, there will be no glory for you in the course you are taking, for then the Lord will deliver Sisera into the hands of a woman."

4:8 "If you will go with me, I will go."

ZOHAR IV:21a: "Barak reasoned thus: Because the Holy Spirit rests upon her, I shall be delivered through her merit and shall come to no harm."

GENESIS RABBAH 40:4: Barak is requesting that Deborah accompany him up to Kadesh wherein, together, they will summon volunteer warriors from the northern tribes. If she agrees, then he has no objection to going with her against the Canaanites in Hazor. He proposes a joint venture. Rabbi Nehemiah explains that Barak's request refers to his desire to have her join him in singing praises to God, with Deborah playing a subordinate role. If she is amenable to this, he is willing to go with her into battle, wherein, he would, likewise, take the lesser role. "Desist from setting conditions," the prophetess warns. "The glory of the song will not be for *your* honor."

The day of battle arrives. Barak ascends Mount Tabor with his troops as Sisera's men move down to the swollen River of Kishon. On Deborah's direction, the Israelites storm Sisera's camps, overwhelming the Canaanite fighters, sending them into a panic as their chariots sink into the mud. Sisera leaps from his chariot and flees the battle site on foot. Every one of his abandoned men are killed. Where did Sisera go? Heber, the Kenite, a descendant of Jethro, Moses' father-in-law, and Jael, his wife, lived in friendly alliance with King Jabin. Sisera heads for Jael's tent, seeking protection and refuge.

4:18. Jael came out to greet Sisera and said to him, "Come in, my lord, come in here, do not be afraid." So he entered her tent, and she covered him with a blanket. 19. He said to her, "Please let me have some water; I am thirsty." She opened a skin of milk and gave him some to drink; and she covered him again. 20. He said to her, "Stand at the entrance of the tent. If anybody comes and asks you if there is anybody here, say, 'No.' " 21. Then Jael, wife of Heber, took a tent pin and grasped the mallet. When he was fast asleep from exhaustion, she approached him stealthily and drove the pin through the temple till it went down to the ground. Thus he died. 22. Now Barak appeared in pursuit of Sisera. Jael went out to greet him and said, "Come, I will show you the man you are looking for." . . . 23. On that day God subdued King Jabin of Hazor before the Israelites.

EXODUS RABBAH 4:2: "If one undertakes to perform a good deed, that good deed will never cease to reappear in his house." Jethro willingly received into his house a redeemer [Moses] who was fleeing from the enemy [Pharaoh]; Likewise, a descendant of his, Jael, received into her house an enemy [Sisera] who was fleeing from the redeemer [Barak]."

4:21 "She approached him stealthily and drove the pin through the temple."

Thus Deborah's prophecy that "The Lord will deliver Sisera into the hands of a woman" was fulfilled. For forty years hence, Israel was in peace, but what of Jael's cruel act?

TALMUD, *HORAYOTH* 10b: "A transgression (committed) with good intent is more meritorious than the performance of a commandment with no intent."

"Most blessed of women be Jael" (5:24), sings Deborah in her song of glory to God.

TALMUD, *NAZIR* 23b: Deborah blessed Jael, and she was considered even greater than Sarah, Rebekah, Rachel, and Leah.

GENESIS RABBAH 48:15: The matriarchs gave birth to

children, but for Jael's action, their children would have been destroyed. Jael is above the women of the generation of the wilderness. They, too, gave birth to children, yet, if not for Jael, their children would have been destroyed.

> Through the window peered Sisera's mother,
> Behind the lattice she gazed.
> "Why is his chariot so long in coming?
> Why so late the clatter of his wheels?"
> The wisest of her ladies give answer;
> She, too, replies to herself:
> "They must be dividing the spoil they have found:
> A damsel or two for each man,
> Spoil of dyed clothes for Sisera,
> Spoil of embroidered cloths
> A couple of embroidered cloths
> Round every neck as spoil."
> —From Deborah's song, recited after Sisera's
> unexpected defeat at the hands
> of Jael, Judges 5:28–30

ZOHAR IV:19b: "There were two women in the world who composed praises to God such as the men never equalled, namely Hannah and Deborah."

ZOHAR IV:19b: Deborah began her song "speaking in the mystery of Wisdom," but when she began to praise herself saying, "Until that I Deborah arose, that I, arose, a mother in Israel!" (5:7), the prophetic spirit departed from her, so that she was forced to admonish herself with, "Awake, awake, O Deborah! Awake, awake, utter a song!" (5:12). "All this happened when the men were sinful and not worthy that the spirit of prophecy should rest upon them. . . ."

Delilah

Samson, the man destined to be the first to deliver Israel from the Phillistines, fell in love with a woman named Delilah. The lords of the Philistines went up to her and said, "Coax him and find out what makes him so strong, and how we can overpower him, tie him up and make him helpless, and we'll each give you eleven hundred shekels of silver." 6. So Delilah said to Samson, "Tell me what makes you so strong. And how could you be tied up and made helpless?" (Book of Judges 16:5–6).

*The name Delilah is based on a root dildelah, meaning "to weaken" or "to dilute." The rabbis taught that even "if her name had not been called Delilah, she was fit that it should be so-called. She weakened his strength, she weakened his heart, she weakened his actions." (Tal-*mud, Sotah *9b)*

Naomi and Ruth

In the Tanakh, the Book of Ruth is included among "The Writings," but it too takes place during the period of the Judges. It is not about heroes like Deborah and Samson; it is about ordinary people who make extraordinary human choices.

Rabbi Zeira said: This scroll tells us nothing either of cleanliness or uncleanliness, either of prohibition or permission. For what purpose then was it written? To teach how great is the reward of those who do deeds of kindness. (Midrash Rabbah Ruth 2:14)

RUTH 1:1. In the days when the Judges ruled, there was a famine in the land; and a certain man of Bethlehem in Judah, with his wife and two sons, went to reside in the country of Moab. 2. The man's name was Elimelech, his wife's name was Naomi, and his two sons were named Mahlon and Chilion. . . . 3. Elimelech, Naomi's husband, died; and she was left with her two sons. 4. They married Moabite women, one named Orpah and the other Ruth, and they lived there about ten years. 5. Then those two—Mahlon and Chilion—also died; so the woman was left without her two sons and without her husband.

Do the very names of the players reveal their fates? Yes, say the Sages.

RUTH RABBAH 1:4, 2:5: The name, Elimelech, highlights the pride of this man which led to his ultimate punishment: "Eli"/"to me," "melech"/"the kingship," that is "to me shall the kingship come!" This man, acknowledged by the rabbis as a notable leader in the tribe of Judah, "one of the sustainers of the generation," abandoned his fellows in a time of despair.

"Now all of Israel will come knocking at my door for help."
So he ran from them; his sons accompanied him to Moab,
the fertile plateau on the far side of the Dead Sea. There,
Machlon was "blotted out"/"nimchu" and Chilion was "destroyed"/"kahlu." What of Naomi, the survivor? The midrash
tells us that she was so named because her actions were
"na'im"/"fine," and "naim"/"pleasant."

When the famine in Judah finally ended, and she and her
daughters-in-law "went forth out of the place" (1:6) the rabbis speak of her departure in the same way they spoke of
Jacob's when he left Canaan at his mother's bidding.

GENESIS RABBAH 68:6, RUTH RABBAH 2:12: "When the
righteous man is in the town, he is its lustre, its majesty, and
its glory; when he leaves it, its lustre, its majesty, and its glory
depart."

> 1:8. But Naomi said to her two daughters-in-law, "Turn
> back, each of you to her mother's house. May the Lord
> deal kindly with you, as you have dealt with the dead
> and with me! 9. May the Lord grant that each of
> you find security in the house of a husband!" And she
> kissed them farewell. They broke into weeping 10.
> and said to her, "No, we will return with you to your
> people."

Naomi's argument is that she is too old to remarry. Even
if she did and even if she bore sons, the women would have
to wait for them to grow up. They would, in effect, cheat themselves of the opportunity to remarry. "Oh, no, my daughters!
My lot is far more bitter than yours, for the hand of the Lord
has struck out against me" (1:13). Within the responses of
Orpah and Ruth to the dejected woman (who looked upon

herself as "the leavings of a meal-offering," which are of no
value at all) we now understand how planted within the names
of these two young Moabite women are couched their essences
and their fates:

> 1:14. They broke into weeping again, and Orpah
> kissed her mother-in-law farewell. But Ruth clung to
> her. 15. So she said, "See, your sister-in-law has
> returned to her people and her gods. Go follow your
> sister-in-law."

RUTH RABBAH 2:9: Orpah returns to her own family, her
old ways. The rabbis teach that she was stiff necked, "she
turned her back on her mother-in-law"; Orpah's name contains within it the letters of the word *ha-oref,* which means
"the nape of the neck." Ruth, on the other hand, understood
the true underlying meaning of her mother-in-law's words and
wish. The clue to her perceptiveness, her ability to perceive
Truth, is found in her name; *ra'athah* means "considered
well," or literally "saw"—the meaning of her mother-in-law's
words.

TALMUD, *BERAKOTH* 7b: Why was she called Ruth? Due
to her merit she earned the privilege of having David issue
from her line—David, who "saturated"/"ruh" the Holy One
with his songs and praise.

1:16. But Ruth replied, "Entreat me not to leave you, to turn back and not follow you."

RUTH RABBAH 2:22: The word for "to entreat" also means
"misfortune" or "plague." Ruth is telling Naomi not to attempt
to turn her away by enumerating her misfortunes to her, that

she is determined to become a convert, no matter what the circumstances.

> 1:16 . . . . For wherever you go, I will go; wherever you lodge, I will lodge; your people shall be my people, and your God my God. 17. Where you die, I will die, and there I will be buried. Thus and more may the Lord do to me if anything but death parts me from you. 18. When Naomi saw how determined she was to go with her, she ceased to argue with her.

RUTH RABBAH 2:23: " 'Thy people shall be my people' in that I will destroy all idolatry within me, and then, 'Thy God shall me be my God,' to pay me the reward of my labor."

RUTH RABBAH 3:5: Once Ruth decided to convert, to align her faith with Naomi's, they are ranked as equals in the eyes of God, this being revealed, say the rabbis, by Scripture's specific wording of verse 18—Ruth went *with* her.

> *Ruth, the Moabitess, was granted a miraculously long life. Our Rabbis teach that she lived to witness the kingdom of Solomon, the son of her grandson! (Talmud,* Baba Bathra *91b)*

> 1:19. And the two went on until they reach Bethlehem. When they arrived in Bethlehem, all the city buzzed with excitement over them. The women said, "Can this be Naomi?"

RUTH RABBAH 3:6: "Is this the one whose actions were fitting and pleasant ('ne' imim')? . . . In the past she wore a cloak of fine wool, and now she is clothed in rags, and you say, 'Is this Naomi?' Before, her countenance was ruddy from abundance of food and drink, and now it is sickly from hunger, and yet you say, 'Is this Naomi?'"

1:20. "Do not call me Naomi," she replied. "Call me Mara," for the Almighty has made my lot very bitter. 21. I went away full, and the Lord has brought me back empty. How can you call me Naomi, when the Lord has afflicted me, and the Almighty has brought misfortune upon me."

Naomi asks that she not be called by a name reflecting "pleasantness," but one that embodies her condition and attitude, "mara," which means "bitterness."

RUTH RABBAH 3:7: "God has afflicted me with His attribute of Justice," He has testified against me—another interpretation of the Hebrew word for "afflicted" being "testified."

> R. Hanina and his wife were extremely poor, and one day, his wife, overcome with their condition of poverty, had an idea. "As a reward for the good deeds you have done," she said to him, "Perhaps, if you pray for it, God will give you, right now, some of the reward that has been reserved for you in the world-to-come. It is time our troubles were ended."
>
> The rabbi prayed, as his wife had asked him to, whereupon a hand reached down from heaven and gave him the golden leg of a golden table . . . . But that night, the rabbi's wife had a dream. In it she saw all the righteous dining at golden tables, each with four golden legs, whereas the table she and her husband dined upon had only three. "Pray again," she begged her husband. "And ask that the leg be taken back." Our Sages say that an

even greater miracle then occurred. When Rabbi Hanina
stretched out his hand to return the golden leg, a hand
descended from heaven and took it back.[36]

1:22. Thus Naomi returned from the country of Moab;
she returned with her daughter-in-law, Ruth the Moabite.
They arrived in Bethlehem at the beginning of the barley harvest.

RUTH RABBAH 3:6: On the day that Naomi and Ruth arrived in Bethlehem was the very day that all the neighboring
townspeople gathered together to celebrate the reaping of the
Omer, a measure of barley that would be offered up as a sacrifice on the second day of Passover. "O Lord God of
Hosts . . . who brings things about in their due season. The
wife of Boaz died on that day, and all Israel assembled to pay
their respects, and just then, Ruth entered with Naomi. Thus
one was taken out when the other entered."

Chapter 2:1. Now Naomi had a kinsman on her
husband's side, a man of substance, of the family of
Elimelech, whose name was Boaz. 2. Ruth the Moabite
said to Naomi, "I would like to go to the fields and glean
among the ears of grain, behind someone who may show
me kindness." "Yes, daughter, go," she replied; 3. and
off she went. She came and gleaned in a field, behind

---

36. For variations on this tale see: M. J. Bin Gorion, *Mimekor*
Yisrael (Bloomington and Indianapolis: Indiana University
Press, 1990), 564–565; M. Gaster, *Ma'aseh Book* (Philadel-
phia: Jewish Publication Society, 1929), 60–61; H. Goldin, *The*
Book of Legends—Talmudic Period (New York: Hebrew Pub-
lishing Co., 1929), 173–174.

the reapers; and as luck would have it, it was the piece
of land belonging to Boaz, who was of Elimelech's family. 4. Presently Boaz arrived from Bethlehem.

Biblical law commanded that whatever accidentally or un-
consciously fell from the hands of a reaper had to be left behind for the poor to gather for themselves. Such was Ruth's
intention. The field she randomly chooses to gather remnants
from belongs to a relative of Naomi's husband, and therefore
of Ruth's deceased husband, Mahlon. Sheer coincidence or
is it the inception of God's plan? Naomi, herself, attributes
this stroke of luck to God, "who did not withhold his
kindness from the living and dead" (2:20). This sentiment,
these words are found in only one other place in the Bible;
they were uttered by Abraham's servant, Eliezer, upon being
led to Rebekah, God's choice for Isaac. "Blessed be the Lord
who has not withheld his steadfast kindness from my master.
For I have been guided on my way by the Lord" (Genesis
24:27).

Ruth chooses the field of a man who is described here as
"a man of substance" or, in other translations, "a mighty man
of valor."

RUTH RABBAH 4:3: "If a giant marries a giantess, what do
they produce? Mighty men. Boaz married Ruth. Whom did
they produce? David, of whom it is said, 'Skillful in playing,
and a mighty man of valor, and a man of war, and prudent
in affairs (he could deduce one matter from another), and a
comely person and the Lord is with him' (Samuel I 16:18)."

2:5. Boaz said, "Whose girl is this?"

RUTH RABBAH 4:6: Boaz is immediately drawn to Ruth, her
beauty and the modesty of her demeanor.

2:8. Boaz said to Ruth, "Listen to me, daughter. Don't go to glean in another field. Don't go elsewhere, but stay here close to my girls. 9. Keep your eyes on the field they are reaping, and follow them. I have ordered the men not to molest you. And when you are thirsty, go to the jars and drink some of the water that the men have drawn." 10. She prostrated herself with her face to the ground, and said to him, "Why are you so kind as to single me out, when I am a foreigner?" 11. Boaz said in reply, "I have been told of all that you did for your mother-in-law after the death of your husband, how you left your father and mother and the land of your birth and came to a people you had not known before. 12. May the Lord reward your deeds. May you have a full recompense from the Lord, the God of Israel, under whose wings you have sought refuge!" 13. She answered, "You are most kind, my lord, to comfort me and to speak gently to your maidservant—though I am not so much as one of your maidservants."

2:12 "May the Lord reward your deeds . . . under whose wings you have sought refuge."

RUTH RABBAH 5:4: "Come and consider how great is the power of the righteous, and how great is the power of righteousness [or charity, the same word expresses both ideas in Hebrew], and how great the power of those who do kindly deeds, for they shelter neither in the shadow of the morning, nor in the shadow of the wings of the earth, nor in the shadow of the sun, nor in the shadow of the wings of the Hayyoth, or the cherubim or the seraphim [hierarchies of angels], but under whose wings do they shelter? Under the shadow of Him at whose word the world was created."

2:13 "You are most kind . . . to speak gently to your maidservant."

RUTH RABBAH 5:5: "He said unto her, 'Heaven forfend! Thou art not as one of the handmaidens (amahoth), but as one of the matriarchs (imahoth)!' "

When Ruth returns home to Naomi and reports to her the day's events, Naomi sees the prospect for her daughter-in-law of a "levirite marriage." Naomi would offer for sale a piece of land that belonged to her deceased husband, Elimelech. Boaz was a close relative of Elimelech, and Naomi felt that he might be willing to redeem the family property and marry Ruth, Elimelech's daughter-in-law, the wife of the deceased son. In this way, the family name would be carried on in accordance with the ancient patriarchal duty. Naomi advises Ruth to continue gleaning in Boaz' field, but it isn't until the barley and wheat harvests are over that she instructs Ruth with the heart of her plan. "I will do everything you tell me," answers Ruth (3:5).

3:6. She went down to the threshing floor and did just as her mother-in-law had instructed her. 7. Boaz ate and drank, and in a cheerful mood went to lie down beside the grainpile. Then she went over stealthily and uncovered his feet and lay down. 8. In the middle of the night, the man gave a start and pulled back—there was a woman lying at his feet! 9. "Who are you?," he asked. And she replied, "I am your handmaid Ruth. Spread your robe over your handmaid (a formal act of espousal), for you are a redeeming kinsman.

3:8 "In the middle of the night . . ."

RUTH RABBAH 6:1: Ruth startles Boaz with her unexpected

and uninvited presence, and out of fear, Boaz might have rashly pronounced a curse upon her, but "whoso putteth his trust in the Lord shall be set on high" (Proverbs 29:25); and "God put it in his heart to bless her."

RUTH RABBAH 6:1: "She clung to him like ivy, and he began to finger her hair. 'Spirits have no hair,' he thought, so he said, 'Who art thou, a woman or a spirit?' She answered, 'A woman.' 'A maiden or a married woman?' She answered, 'A maiden.' 'Art thou clean or unclean? [ritually]. She answered, 'Clean.' 'And behold, a woman,' purest of women, 'lay at his feet.' "

> 3:10. He exclaimed, "Be blessed of the Lord, daughter! Your latest deed of loyalty is greater than the first, in that you have not turned to younger men, whether poor or rich. 11. And now, daughter, have no fear. I will do in your behalf whatever you ask, for all the elders of my town know what a fine woman you are. 12. But while it is true I am a redeeming kinsman, there is another redeemer closer than I . . . .

Boaz is desirous of and willing to redeem Naomi's land and then to marry Ruth, but according to the levirite tradition, the nearest kinsman to the deceased must get the first right of refusal.

> 4:1. Meanwhile, Boaz had gone to the gate and sat down there. And now the redeemer whom Boaz had mentioned passed by.

RUTH RABBAH 7:7: "Was he [the other kinsman] then standing, waiting, behind the gate? [The coincidence appears to be that extraordinary]. Rabbi Samuel b. Nahman answered:

Had he been at the uttermost ends of the earth, the Holy One, blessed be He, would have caused him to fly and would have brought him there in order that that righteous man [Boaz] should not grieve while sitting there . . . . Rabbi Eliezer said: Boaz played his part, and Ruth played hers, and Naomi played hers, whereupon the Holy One, blessed be He, said, 'I, too, must play Mine.' "

Boaz offers the option of redeeming the land to Elimelech's closest kinsman. At first he accepts the proposal. When he finds the deal includes marriage to Ruth, and therefore the property and the money expended would ultimately pass onto any sons born to Ruth, he states that he is unable to afford the proposition and will be forced to decline. Boaz takes over the right of redemption, being the next one in line. To validate this transaction, one "drew off his shoe" and gave it to the other, as was the practice in Israel at that time.

4:9. And Boaz said to the elders and to the rest of the people, "You are witnesses today that I am acquiring from Naomi all that belonged to Elimelech and all that belonged to Chilion and Mahlon. 10. I am also acquiring Ruth the Moabite, the wife of Mahlon, as my wife, so as to perpetuate the name of the deceased upon his estate, that the name of the deceased may not disappear from among his kinsmen and from the gate of his home town. You are witnesses today." 11. All the people at the gate and the elders answered, "We are. May the Lord make the woman who is coming into your house like Rachel and Leah, both of whom built up the House of Israel! . . . 12. And may your house be like the house of Perez whom Tamar bore to Judah—through the offspring which the Lord will give you by this young woman."

RUTH RABBAH 6:2: The rabbis speak of the power of prayer. R. Johanan comments that Boaz was already eighty years of age and had not yet been granted children. When the righteous Naomi prayed for him, "Blessed be he of the Lord" (2:20), he was immediately graced with a child. Resh lakish said that Ruth was now forty years old, and as long as she was married to Mahlon, she had never been granted children. As soon as the righteous Boaz prayed for her, "Be blessed of the Lord, daughter" (3:10), she conceived. The rabbis said that both Boaz and Ruth were favored with a son only as a result of the blessings of the righteous elders.

4:12 ". . . Which the lord will give you by this young woman."

RUTH RABBAH 7:14: May all the children which the Lord will give you, be from this woman, from Ruth, and not from another. This recalls the Rabbinic interpretation of Genesis 25:21, "And Isaac entreated the Lord for his wife, because she was barren." The literal translation of "for" is "opposite"; Isaac prostrated himself in one corner, say the rabbis, and Rebekah in the other, and Isaac prayed to God that all the children he was destined to father be from his righteous wife. Again, in the story of Elkanah and Hannah, the future parents of Samuel, the priest Eli blesses the couple, saying, "May all the children which the Holy One, blessed be He, will give you, be of this righteous woman" (I Samuel 2:20).

A wealthy man is he who has a virtuous wife, beautiful in deeds. (Talmud, Shabbat *25b)*

4:13. So Boaz married Ruth; she became his wife, and he cohabited with her. The Lord let her conceive, and she bore a son. 14. And the women said to Naomi,

"Blessed be the Lord, who has not withheld a redeemer from you today! May his name be perpetuated in Israel! 15. He will renew your life and sustain your old age; for he is born of your daughter-in-law, who loves you and is better to you than seven sons." 16. Naomi took the child and held it to her bosom. She became its foster mother, 17. and the women neighbors gave him a name, saying, "A son is born to Naomi!" They named him Obed; he was the father of Jesse, father of David.

4:17 "A son is born to Naomi."

Just as with Bathyah, the daughter of Pharaoh who raised Moses, Scripture speaks of Naomi as though she actually gave birth to Ruth's son, Obed, because she was the one who raised him.

Ruth and Boaz are the great grandparents of David, but Scripture tells us that the line leading to his birth began with Tamar and Judah. Both episodes conclude with the rendering of the genealogy of the unborn king. The similarities and links between both stories are more striking than that. The sons born of Tamar and Judah (namely Perez of the line of David) and Obed, the son born of Ruth and Boaz, were conceived by virtue of levirate marriages. In both instances, it was neither the brother-in-law nor even the nearest relative who performed the duty. Furthermore, following the deaths of their first husbands, both Tamar and Ruth achieved the marriage unions of their choice by breaking with the commonly accepted societal rules of behavior. In addition, neither Tamar nor Ruth were born into the faith; they were "outsiders," Tamar being a Canaanite and Ruth, a Moabite. The link between the two couples is further emphasized by the elders themselves within the words of their blessing to Boaz and

Ruth: "May your house be like the house of Perez, whom Tamar bore to Judah."

ZOHAR II:188a–188b: King David, King Solomon, and the Messiah would all descend from the Tribe of Judah due to the actions of two women, Tamar and Ruth. "Tamar was the daughter of a priest, and it can hardly be imagined that she set out with the intention of committing incest with her father-in-law, since she was by nature chaste and modest. She was indeed virtuous and did not prostitute herself, and it was out of her deeper knowledge and wisdom that she approached Judah, and a desire to act kindly and faithfully (towards the dead). And it was because her act was based on a deeper knowledge that God aided her and she straightway conceived. So that it was all ordained from on high. If it is asked, why did not God cause those sons to be born from some other woman, the answer is that Tamar was necessary for this purpose, and not any other woman .... Now we do not ask why Obed was not born from another woman, for assuredly Ruth was necessary for that purpose to the exclusion of any other woman. From these two women, then, the seed of Judah was built up and brought to completion, and both of them acted piously . . . and God aided them in that work, and all was done fittingly."

> *Rebekah's son, Jacob, attained firstborn status through a cunning plot, and Perez, the son of Tamar, attained it through force as the twins fought to leave the womb. Both of the "rejected" brothers, Rebekah's son Esau and Tamar's son Zerach, are later connected with the nation of Edom, the notorious enemy of David—the King who springs from the line of Judah and Tamar and Boaz and Ruth.*

The Age of the Judges had closed, and the tribes of Israel, divided one from another, were independently occupied with defending themselves against the oppressing Philistines. In the hill country of Ephraim, a man named Elkanah, a Levite, lived with his two wives, Hannah and Peninnah. "Peninnah had children, but Hannah was childless" (I Samuel 1:2). Despite her condition, so familiar in our biblical studies, Hannah was the more beloved of the two, just as Rachel was in the eyes of Jacob.

The Book of Samuel opens with the story of Hannah, her name meaning graciousness or favor. Locked inside her many unhappy days as a taunted, barren woman, she did not know that she would go down in the Rabbinic annals as one of the seven named prophetesses of the Bible. In time, she would bear a son who would lead the Israelites towards the establishment of the first Jewish kingdom, a child who would hear the word of God in an age when, Scripture tells us, vision and prophecy was extremely rare.

Hannah

Samuel I, Chapter 1.

Every year, Elkanah and his family traveled to the Temple in Shiloh to offer ritual sacrifices.

Samuel I 1:4. He used to give portions to his wife Peninnah and to all her sons and daughters, 5. but to Hannah he would give one portion only—though Hannah was his favorite—for the Lord had closed her womb. 6. Moreover, her rival, to make her miserable, would taunt her that the Lord had closed her womb. 7. This happened year after year. Every time she went up to the House of the Lord, the other would taunt her, so that she would weep and would not eat. 8. Her husband Elkanah said to her, "Hannah, why are you crying, and why aren't you eating? Why are you so sad? Am I not more devoted to you than ten sons?"

PESIKTA RABBATI 43:6: The rabbis tell us that, like Sarah, it was only upon Hannah's instigation that her husband took a second wife, having lived together for ten years and being unsuccessful in their efforts to bear a child.

When this second wife conceives, she, like Hagar, treats the childless woman with derision, ceaselessly reminding her of her infertility.

1:8 "Hannah, why are you crying?."

PESIKTA RABBATI 43:7: Sarah, who was also barren, did she weep all day? Rebekah was barren, did she act this way? Rachel, too, was barren, did she sit all by herself and cry? "Am I not more devoted to you than ten sons?" (1:7), her husband asks. In the Book of Ruth, the ten generations leading up to the birth of David are enumerated. The rabbis take Elkanah's remark to be a prophetic one, intimating that his wife would soon have a son more worthy than all those ten generations taken together.

1:5 ". . . one portion only."

PESIKTA RABBATI 43:8: Peninnah plagued the childless Hannah with one upsetting taunt after another." 'Why don't you rouse yourself and wash your children's faces, so they are fit to go to their schoolmaster?' And at twelve o'clock she would say, 'Why don't you rouse yourself and welcome your children who are about to return from school?' . . . When they sat down to eat, Elkanah would give each of his children his proper portion. But what would Peninnah do? Intentionally to vex Hannah (by calling attention to the fact that Hannah was childless), she would say to Elkanah, 'Give this son of mine his portion and to this son of mine you have not yet given his portion.' Why did Peninnah speak thus?" "To make her miserable" [or "to irritate her"/"hariymah"], says the text. The Hebrew word can also be interpreted as "to make her thunder," that is "to make her thunder against God in prayer on her own behalf!" "Thereupon the Holy One, blessed be He said to Peninnah, 'Thou makest her thunder against Me. As thou livest, there are no thunders that are not followed by rain! I shall remember her at once.' "

The Most Desirable Thing

A married couple lived together for ten years, but were unsuccessful in their efforts to bear a child. Not wishing to neglect the duty of begetting children, they decided to part from one another. For consultation in the matter they paid a visit to Rabbi Simeon ben Yohai, who told the couple that even as they were paired over food and drink, so also must they be parted over food and drink.

Following the Rabbi's advice, the couple prepared a terrific feast for themselves, and while celebrating, the woman gave her husband a bit too much to drink. In his resulting jovial mood he looked at his wife and said to her, "My dear, pick anything at all in my home that you desire, and take it with you when you return to your father's house." Soon after, the man fell fast asleep. While he slept, the woman instructed her servants to pick her husband up, couch and all, and to carry him off to her father's house.

The man woke from his sleep in the middle of the night, and sobriety returning to him, he asked her where he was. "You are in my father's house," she replied. "But what am I doing in your father's house?" She reminded him of what he had said to her. "Did you not say to me, "Pick anything you desire and take it with you when you return to your father's house? Well, there is no desirable article in the world that I care for more than for you!" The couple returned to Rabbi Simeon ben Yohai who stood and prayed for them, and God remembered the couple, and they were granted children.

—Song of Songs Rabbah 1:4

1:9 After they had eaten and drunk at Shiloh, Hannah rose and stood before the Lord. The priest Eli was sitting on the seat near the doorpost of the Temple of the Lord. 10. In her wretchedness, she prayed to the Lord, weeping all the while. 11. And she vowed a vow and said, "O Lord of Hosts, if You will look upon the suffering of Your maidservant, and will remember me and not forget Your maidservant, and if You will grant Your maidservant a male child, I will dedicate him to the Lord for all the days of his life; and no razor shall ever touch his head." 12. As she kept on praying before the Lord, Eli watched her mouth. 13. Now Hannah was praying in her heart; only her lips moved, but her voice could not be heard.

What was the nature of Hannah's "thunder against God?"

TALMUD, *BERAKOTH* 31b: "Sovereign of the Universe, among all the things that Thou hast created in a woman, Thou hast not created one without a purpose, eyes to see, ears to hear, a nose to smell, a mouth to speak, hands to do work, legs to walk with, breasts to give suck. These breasts that Thou hast put on my heart, are they not to give suck? Give me a son, so that I may suckle with them."

PESIKTA RABBATI 43:3: "Master of the Universe, there is a host above, and there is a host below. The host above do not eat, nor drink, nor procreate, nor die, but they live forever; and the host below eat and drink and procreate and die. Now I do not know of what host I am, whether I am of the host above or the one below. If I am of the host above, I should not be eating, nor drinking, nor possibly bearing children, nor dying, for I should live forever, just as the host above live forever. But if I am of the host below, then not only should I be eating and drinking, but I should be bearing children and eventually dying, even as the host below eat, and drink and procreate and die." To which host do I belong?

TALMUD, *BERAKOTH* 31b: "Rabbi Eliezer said: From the day that God created His world, there was no man who called the Holy One, blessed be He, 'Lord of Hosts,' 'Zebaoth,' until Hannah came . . . . Said Hannah before the Holy One, blessed be He: Sovereign of the Universe, of all the hosts and hosts that Thou hast created in Thy world, is it so hard to give me one son?"

An ancient ritual, "the ordeal of water," is described in chapter 5 of the Book of Numbers, wherein a suspected adulteress is brought before the priest and asked to drink a concoction said to have an ill effect on only the guilty. If the woman is found innocent, "she shall be cleansed and conceive seed." In Hannah, the rabbis paint a picture of a woman, who, in her desperate longing even volunteers to feign adultery to force God's hand.

TALMUD, *BERAKOTH* 31b: "Hannah said before the Holy One, Sovereign of the Universe, if Thou wilt look upon the suffering of Thy maidservant, it is well, and if Thou wilt not look, I will go and shut myself up with someone else in the knowledge of my husband, Elkanah, [so he will become suspicious and test me], and as I shall have been alone, they will make me drink the water of the suspected wife, and Thou cannot falsify Thy law, which says, 'She shall be cleansed and bear seed.'

In exchange for the longed-for blessing of a child, Hannah vows to return him to God, to dedicate him to the Temple, for God's exclusive use.

For the first time in Scripture we meet with the idea of praying silently, not for the ears of other men. Eli, witnessing this strange activity, accuses Hannah of being intoxicated.

> 1:14. "... How long will you make a drunken spectacle of yourself?"... 1:15. And Hannah replied, "Oh, no, my lord! I am a very unhappy woman. I have drunk no wine or other strong drink, but I have been pouring out my heart to the Lord."

1:15 "... Oh, no, my Lord."

TALMUD, *BERAKOTH* 31a–31b: Hannah actually meant: You are not a Lord at all! In taking the harsher rather than the more lenient perspective of my conduct, you demonstrated that the Shekhinah, the Holy Spirit, does not accompany you.

Eli stands corrected, and in place of his chiding, he offers his own blessing to support Hannah's urgent pleas. "May the God of Israel grant you what you have asked of Him" (1:17). Scripture tells us that after her discourse with God and the priest's additional blessing, Hannah's demeanor completely changed.

> 1:18. The woman left and she ate and was no longer downcast. 19. Early next morning they bowed low before the Lord, and they went home to Ramah. Elkanah knew his wife and the Lord remembered her. 20. Hannah conceived, and at the turn of the year bore a son. She named him Samuel meaning, "I have asked him of the Lord."

PESIKTA RABBATI 43:5: "The refining pot is for silver, and the furnace for gold; and a man is tried according to his praise" (Proverbs 27:21). "Even as the refiner puts silver into the fire and gold into the furnace, but does not keep them in the fire or in the furnace beyond the time necessary to refine them, so also does the Holy One, blessed be He, refine the righteous, each one of them, according to their strength . . . according to what his praiseworthy deeds have proved him to be. You find that it was so with Sarah. For twenty-five years, from the time she came to the Land of Israel, the Holy One, blessed be He, tried her. It is written that, 'Abram was seventy-five years old when he departed from Haran,' and Sarah at that time sixty-five years old, he older than she by ten years. At the age of ninety she gave birth to a child, Abraham being one hundred years old when Isaac was born . . . . Thus you find that the Holy One, blessed be He, tried her according to HER strength.

And Rebekah also—the Holy One, blessed be He, tried her according to HER strength—tried her for twenty years.

And Hannah—her also the Holy One, blessed be He, tried according to HER strength. And how long did He try her? Nineteen years, according to our Masters . . . . There were the ten years that she lived with Elkanah when she did not bear any children; then he took Peninnah who bore him ten sons . . . . Now if you allow eight years for the times Peninnah was pregnant, and allow one year for the time Hannah was pregnant with Samuel, you have a total of nineteen years that God tried Hannah. And after that, He remembered her."

Why is the prayer of the righteous compared to a hind? To tell you that just as with the hind, as long as it grows, its antlers form additional branches every year, so with the righteous, the longer they abide in prayer, the more will their prayer be heard. (Talmud, Yoma 29a)

Hannah did not go up to Shiloh again with Elkanah until the boy was weaned.

> 1:24 .... and though the boy was still very young, she brought him to the House of the Lord at Shiloh. 25. After slaughtering the bull, they brought the boy to Eli. 26. She said, "Please, My lord! As you live, my lord, I am the woman who stood here beside you and prayed to the Lord. 27. It was for this child I prayed; and the Lord granted me what I asked of Him. 28. I, in turn, hereby lend him to the Lord. For as long as he lives he is lent to the Lord." And they bowed low there before the Lord.

1:27 ". . . for THIS child I prayed."

TALMUD, *BERAKOTH* 31b: The rabbis find significance in Hannah's demonstrative words, and the Talmud offers an explanation. Eli called for a priest to perform the ritual slaughter of a bullock, but the child, Samuel, intervened. He questioned Eli's request, claiming that a commoner's slaughter would be just as valid. Scripture states that the priest's obligation actually begins *after* the actual slaughter. Although the child's answer was an intelligent and valid one, Eli points out that he is now guilty of wrongly giving a decision in his teacher's presence, an action punishable by death. At this point, Hannah stood up and cried "I am the woman who stood here beside you." In response, Eli said that if she allowed the child to be punished that he would pray to God to give her an even better one! "For THIS child I prayed," Hannah said.

Hannah, having been granted her wish and having followed through with her difficult end of the bargain which was declared privately to God, again turns to her Creator, but this time with gratitude and praise.

> 2:3–8. Let no arrogance cross your lips! For the Lord is an all-knowing God .... Men once sated must hire out for bread; men once hungry, hunger no more. While the barren woman bears seven, the mother of many is forlorn. The Lord deals death and gives life .... The Lord makes poor and makes rich .... He raises the poor from the dust . . . setting them with nobles, granting them seats of honor. For the pillars of the earth are the Lord's.

Hannah would see her beloved son only once a year, during the annual pilgrimage. While there, "Eli would bless Elkanah and his wife and say: May the Lord grant you offspring by this woman in place of the loan she made to the Lord."

RUTH RABBAH 7:14: As Isaac asked of God in regard to his wife, Rebekah, as the elders asked of God regarding Ruth and her new husband, Boaz, Eli now asks of God regarding Elkanah and Hannah: "May all the children which the Holy One, blessed be He, will give you, be of *this* righteous woman."

The once-barren woman bears five more children, three sons and two daughters. "Young Samuel, meanwhile, grew up in the service of the Lord" (2:21).

PESIKTA RABBATI 43:2: "Because the Holy One, blessed be He does not wish to bring frustration to the spirit of righteous men when they pray to Him, the Holy One, blessed be He, grants what they request of Him .... When the Holy One, blessed be He, saw David in continuing distress on account of the [site of] the Temple, at once he sent to him the prophet Gad, who showed him the site for the Temple. David went at once . . . . And there he found the altar to which Adam had brought offerings—Noah also had brought offerings to it, Abraham had also brought offerings to it . . . .

It is thus shown that the Holy One, blessed be He, does not frustrate the spirit of the righteous by withholding the reward due them. He grants them whatever they desire . . . . To whom else was granted what she desired? To Hannah, who prayed before the Holy One, blessed be He; at the conclusion of her prayer, the Holy One, blessed be He did not let her go forth empty-handed. For the Holy One, blessed be He, heard her prayer and granted all that she asked of Him."

Abigail

Samuel I, Chapter 25.

A woman named Abigail makes her appearance in the first Book of Samuel. She is married to a tactless man named Nabal, but no clues to her genealogy are given. Stemming from a rather brief encounter with David, who has not yet become King, she earns the respect and admiration of our rabbis who name her as one of the Bible's seven prophetesses and who count her among the four most beautiful women in the entire world.

A t the time Abigail and David meet, Saul is King over Israel. David, mortally endangered by Saul's vengeful jealousy of him, has been living as an outlaw, fleeing Saul's repeated attempts on his life. In the wilderness of Ein Gedi, David proves his righteousness and goodness when he spares Saul's life even when he is given an easy opportunity to take it.

Samuel I, Chapter 25: The prophet Samuel has just died, and David, with his band of followers, retires to the wilderness of Maon where Abigail and her husband, Nabal, happen to live. Nabal is a wealthy man; he owns thousands of goats and sheep which his workers shear in the open fields at Carmel. David and his stronghold never interfere with the shepherds, never infringe on Nabal's property. In exchange for this courtesy and protection, David sends a message to Nabal, asking for a gift of provisions. Nabal's response to the messengers is filled with contempt: "Who is David? Who is the son of Jesse? There are many slaves nowadays who run away from their masters. Should I then take my bread and water and the meat that I slaughtered for my own shearers and give them to men who came from I don't know where?" (25:10–11). When David receives Nabal's response, he is filled with unbridled anger and decides to exact his due by force, threatening to plunder Nabal's possessions and to murder Nabal and all his men. "He has paid me back evil for good. May God do thus and more to the enemies of David, if by the morning I leave a single male of his" (25:21–22). Now, as it happened, Abigail was privately informed of her husband's spurn.

> Samuel I 25:18. Abigail quickly got together two hundred loaves of bread, two jars of wine, five dressed sheep, five saehs of parched corn, one hundred cakes of raisin and two hundred cakes of pressed figs. She loaded them on asses 19. and told her young men, "Go on ahead of me, and I'll follow you"; but she did not tell her husband, Nabal . . . . 23. When Abigail saw David, she quickly dismounted from the ass and threw herself facedown before David, bowing to the ground. 24. Prostrate at his feet, she pleaded, "Let the blame be mine, my lord, but let your handmaid speak to you; hear your handmaid's plea. 25. Please, my lord, pay no attention to that wretched fellow Nabal. For he is just what his name says: His name means 'boor,' and he is a boor."

Abigail offers David her gift of provisions, acknowledging her awareness that he "is fighting the battles of the Lord," and suggesting to him that to pursue his current course would be antithetical to his purposes. "Do not let this be a cause of stumbling and of faltering courage to my lord that you have shed blood needlessly" (25:31). David praises her for restraining him from his rash impulses, and he promises to respect her wishes. When Abigail returns home, she finds her husband feasting and drinking, and so she says nothing to him of her meeting with David.

> 25:37. The next morning, when Nabal had slept off the

wine, his wife told him everything that had happened; and his courage died within him and he became like a stone. 38. About ten days later the Lord struck Nabal and he died. 39. When David heard that Nabal was dead he said, "Praised be the Lord who championed my cause against the insults of Nabal and held back His servant from wrongdoing; the Lord has brought Nabal's wrongdoing down on his own head." David sent messengers to propose marriage to Abigail, to take her as his wife . . . . 41 . . . she immediately bowed low with her face to the ground and said, "Your handmaid is ready to be your maidservant, to wash the feet of my lord's servants."

Abigail followed David's messengers, and she became his wife. Together, they will have a son, Chileab, also known by the name of Daniel.

TALMUD, *MEGILLAH* 14a–14b: When encountering David for the first time, Abigail calmly puts a ritual question to him. When David responds that he will not be able to investigate the matter until the following morning, Abigail suggests that he, likewise, postpone the death sentence pronounced upon her husband. When David protests that Nabal is a rebel, deserving punishment, she retorts, "You are not yet king." Not *yet* King? The rabbis teach that this first meeting with David revealed not only Abigail's wisdom, but her divine powers of prophecy.

Abigail goes on to predict David's future sin with a woman named Bathsheba, warning him that this present matter with Nabal is a small one in comparison to a grief that will come upon him in the future. (While reigning over Israel, King David will be pierced with desire for a beautiful woman named Bathsheba. Upon finding that she is already married, he has her husband placed into the front lines in a war being waged against the Ammonites. When her husband is subsequently killed in battle, David sends for Bathsheba and marries her. The prophet, Nathan, prophesied that as punishment, their first child would die when only seven days old. Indeed, it came to pass.)

A Rare Find

"A tale is told of Rabbi Meir that while he was sitting and expounding in the academy on a Sabbath afternoon, his two sons died. What did their mother (Beruriah) do? She left them both lying on their couch and spread a sheet over them. At the close of the Sabbath, Rabbi Meir came home from the academy, and he asked her, 'Where are my two sons?' She replied, 'They went to the academy.' He said, 'I looked for them at the academy, but did not see them.' She silently handed him the cup of wine for the Habdalah benediction (recited at the end of the Sabbath), and he pronounced it. Then he asked her again, 'Where are my two sons?' She replied, 'Sometimes they go someplace ("maqom") first ("maqom" means "place" as well as "the Omnipresent." In a hidden manner, she was admitting the truth of the boys' deaths without openly revealing it—mourning is prohibited on the Sabbath.); they will be back presently,' she said. She served him his meal, and he ate.

After he recited the Grace after Meals, she said to him, 'Master, I have a question to ask you.' He replied, 'Ask your question.' She said, 'Master, some time ago a certain man came by and left something on deposit with me. Now he has come to reclaim this deposit. Shall I return it to him or not?' He replied, 'My daughter, is

---

not one who holds a deposit obligated to return it to its owner?' (that is, surely you know that you are obligated!). She said, 'Without your opinion on the matter, I would not give it back to him.' What did she do then? She took him by the hand, led him up to the children's room, brought him to the bed and removed the sheet so that Rabbi Meir saw them both lying on the bed dead. He burst into tears, saying, 'My sons, my sons! My masters, my masters! My natural born sons and my masters who enlightened me with their learning in Torah!' At this point Rabbi Meir's wife said to him, 'Master, did you not just now tell me that we must return a pledge to its owner?' To which he replied, 'The Lord has given, and the Lord has taken away; blessed be the name of the Lord.'" (Job 1:21)

Rabbi Hanina said: In this manner she comforted him and brought him solace, hence it is said, "What a rare find is a capable wife!" (Proverbs 31:10)

Rabbi Meir and his wife, Beruriah, lived in Palestine in the second century c.e., a period of Roman persecution. Many great rabbis, including Beruriah's father, were martyred during this time. (Midrash on Proverbs, chapter 31)

The Woman of Tekoah

Samuel II, Chapter 14.
Among the twenty-three good women of Israel—
The Woman of Tekoah.

After Saul's death, and "according to the word of the
Lord through Samuel" (Chronicles I 11:3), David is
anointed king over the House of Judah. Meanwhile,
Saul's son Ish-bosheth is anointed king over the
northern kingdom of Israel. The two houses war with
each other for a time, but the House of David grows
stronger as the House of Saul weakens. David, finally
triumphant, is anointed king over a united Israel
where he reigns for the next thirty-three years. Dur-
ing his reign, the king will endure some grievous
personal events. Within the royal family, bitter jeal-
ousies will arise between his wives, each one desirous
of obtaining the throne for her own son. David's sons
themselves will not be immune from vengeful quar-
rels. His eldest son, Amnon, will violate his half-sister,
Tamar, and Absalom will avenge his brother's crime
by resorting to murder. Fleeing the city of Jerusalem,
Absalom will live in exile for three years, fearing to
face the unabating wrath of David, his father.

S amuel II 14:1. Joab (a loyal aide of King David) . . . could see that the king's mind was on Absalom; 2. so Joab sent to Tekoah and brought a clever woman from there. He said to her, "Pretend you are in mourning . . . act like a woman who has grieved a long time over a departed one. 3. Go to the king and say to him thus and thus." And Joab told her what to say.

The unnamed woman, praised by the Sages, dons mourning attire and acts the part of a mother, heartbroken over the murder of one of her two quarreling sons and now threatened by the vengeful pursuit of her remaining son, the accused killer. She begs the king to intervene in the situation and to offer protection of her only son. The king compassionately agrees, and the woman continues to speak with convincing eloquence, praising his wisdom and further securing his promise—"My lord the king is like an angel of God, understanding everything, good and bad" (14:17). David is gently led into the realization that all is not what it seems. "Is Joab in league with you in all this?" (14:19). David, shamed into doing for his own son what he has just promised to do for the imaginary son of the wise woman of Tekoah, grants Absalom a safe return home.

"Let sins be consumed and let the wicked be no more"
— *Psalms 104:35*

In Rabbi Meir's neighborhood there lived a group of men who participated in delinquent, criminal activity. Upset and annoyed by their very presence, the Rabbi prayed for them to die. But his wife, Beruriah, chastised him: "The psalm does not state that sinners should be consumed, but rather that all sins should be no more! Don't pray for their death, pray that they repent!" He prayed for them, and they turned in penitence. (Talmud, Berakhot *10a)*

When David is an elderly man, his son, Solomon, succeeds him to the throne where he reigns for the next forty years over a united Israel. Under the rule of Solomon's son, Rehoboam, heir to the throne following his father's death, the kingdom once again breaks up into two separate factions, with Rehoboam ruling the southern kingdom of Judah and Jeroboam the northern kingdom of Israel. Numerous kings subsequently rule in both Judah and Israel. The two separate kingdoms become vulnerable to attack, weakened as a result of their disunification and, as Scripture teaches, because they had fallen under the leadership of men who shunned the practices of their fathers and did what was displeasing in the eyes of the Lord.

In time, the northern kingdom of Israel would be conquered by the Assyrians, the ten tribes comprising it, disappearing from history. Soon after, the kingdom of Judah would fall to the Babylonians who vanquish Jerusalem and exile its inhabitants, the two tribes of Judah and Benjamin. It was during these troubled times that the great prophets arose, fabled teachers of the word of God, men such as Elijah and his disciple, the kind prophet, Elisha.

The Shunammite

Kings II, Chapter 4.
Among the twenty-three good women of Israel—
The Shunammite

"One day Elisha visited Shunem. A wealthy woman lived there, and she urged him to have a meal..."

As it happened, the prophet Elisha made it his practice to always visit this particular woman's home and to be refreshed there with a meal before continuing on his way. One day, the woman urges her husband to build an enclosed chamber with a bed, a chair, and a lamp for the prophet's use. She does nothing more. So why is she lauded by the Sages?—For her perception and her willingness to act upon it. "I am sure it is a holy man of God," she says to her husband (4:9). Elisha seeks to reward his hostess.

Kings II 4:11. One day he came there; he retired to the upper chamber and lay down there. 12. He said to his servant Gehazi, "Call that Shunammite woman . . . . Tell her, 'You have gone to all this trouble for us. What can we do for you? Can we speak in your behalf to the king or to the army commander?' She replied, "I live among my own people." 14. "What then can be done for her?" he asked. "The fact is," said Gehazi, "she has no son, and her husband is old." 15. "Call her," he said. He called her, and she stood in the doorway. 16. And Elisha said, "At this season next year, you will be embracing a

---

son." She replied, "Please, my lord, man of God, do not delude your maidservant."

As prophesied, the woman conceives and bears a son at the same season the following year. We can only ponder the possible myriad of inner meanings to this scriptural story that bears such likeness to that of Sarah—the heralding of a miraculous birth to a woman standing in a doorway!

Some years later, while still a child, the boy complains of a pain in his head. At noon that day, he dies in his mother's lap. The woman lays him down on the bed prepared for the prophet, and she shuts the door. She summons Elisha. He enters the room alone and prays to God.

4:34. Then he mounted the bed and placed himself over the child. He put his mouth on its mouth, his eyes on its eyes, and his hands on its hands, as he bent over it. And the body of he child became warm . . . . 35. The boy sneezed seven times and . . . opened his eyes.

The Shunammite woman is mentioned one more time, four chapters later. It was prophetically revealed to Elisha that a seven-year famine would plague the land. Elisha again remembers the goodness of his hostess, personally advising her to immediately take her family elsewhere until the lean times pass. The woman lives among the Philistines for seven years. When she returns, she approaches the king to appeal for the return of her abandoned property. Why should the king respond favorably to this unnamed woman? It so happened that at the very moment she appeared, Elisha's servant, Gehazi, was conversing with the king about all "the wonderful things" that the prophet had done and was specifically speaking about the miracle accorded the Shunammite woman.

8:5. "My lord, king," said Gehazi, "this is the woman and this is her son whom Elisha revived. 6. . . . "Restore all her property, and all the revenue from her farm from the time she left the country until now," says the king.

Such were the rewards for a woman who recognized Holiness when it silently passed before her.

It is for her fear of the Lord that a woman is to be praised (Proverbs 31:30).

After the northern kingdom of Israel was overthrown by the Assyrians, the Judeans began to fear for their own survival; Hezekiah is now the king of Judah. The prophet Isaiah warns of the strength of the Babylonians and the probable duplicity of its leaders, but his warnings go unheeded. King Hezekiah is slain, and his son Manasseh, heir to the throne, makes it his practice to persecute and silence the admonishing prophets. After Manasseh's death, Amon, his son, rules Judah, and after him, Josiah.

Josiah deviates from the path of his most recent predecessors. During Josiah's twelfth year of rule, he takes steps to purge Judah and Jerusalem of all its idolatrous shrines. In his eighteenth year, he begins renovation of the holy Temple in Jerusalem which had suffered much debasement as a result of the idolatrous rituals practiced within its walls under previous reigns.

Kings II 22:1. Josiah was eight years old when he became king, and he reigned thirty one years in Jerusalem . . . . 2. He did what was pleasing to the Lord and he followed all the ways of his ancestor, David; he did not deviate to the right or to the left.

Josiah sends his scribe to the Temple with instructions for the High Priest. He is to weigh the silver that was collected from the people and deposited in the Temple, and then to arrange payment for all the workmen laboring to repair the "House of the Lord." When the scribe arrives at the Temple, the High Priest delivers some compelling news—"I have found a scroll of the Teaching in the House of the Lord" (22:8). The scribe, himself, reads the unearthed book and then rapidly returns to the king.

Huldah

Kings II, Chapter 22—
one of the twenty-three good women of Israel and
one of its seven prophetesses

22:11. When the king heard the words of the scroll of the Teaching, he rent his clothes. 12. And the king gave orders to the priest . . . the scribe . . . and the king's minister: 13. "Go, inquire of the Lord on my behalf, and on the behalf of the people, and on behalf of all Judah, concerning the words of this scroll that has been found. For great indeed must be the wrath of the Lord that has been kindled against us, because our fathers did not obey the words of this scroll to do all that has been prescribed for us."

Some scholars believe that the hidden book was the entire collection of the Five Books of Moses, others feel it was only the fifth, the Book of Deuteronomy. Either way, its effect was dramatic. Whom did the messengers of the king choose to consult?

PESIKTA RABBATI 26:1–2: In that generation, three prophets prophesied—Jeremiah, Zephaiah, and a woman named Huldah. "Jeremiah prophesied in the city squares, Zephaniah in the Temple and in synagogues, and Huldah among the women."

TALMUD, *MEGILLAH* 14b: It is Huldah, alone, that the messengers choose to consult, feeling that the greater compassion of a woman would be an asset. She would be more willing to intercede with God on the king's behalf. The Sages teach that both Huldah and Jeremiah were descendants of Rahab the harlot. Because they were related, the messengers felt that Jeremiah would not resent being excluded.

> *The Kabbalists assign the letter yud to the second sefirah or quality of Chakmah-Wisdom, and the letter heh to the third sefirah, Binah-Understanding. The Hebrew word for "woman"/"ishah," contains within it both the letter heh and the letter yud, whereas the word for "man"/"ish" contains only the yud. From this, the Sages derive the teaching that Woman was endowed by God with greater Understanding than was Man. (Talmud, Nidah 45b, Genesis Rabbah 18:1)*

TARGUM, KINGS 22:14, RASHI: What do the Sages teach about Huldah? In the Talmud, a certain "Gate of Huldah" is mentioned in relation to the Temple. The rabbis teach that this had previously been the gate which led to Huldah's school!

Scripture writes that Huldah was married to a man named Shallum, whom the rabbis teach was a noble and compassionate man. Everyday he would carry a pitcher of water outside the city limits and offer each and every passing traveler a drink. It was as a reward for his deeds that his wife was granted the ability to prophecy. . . . [It is interesting to note that Deborah, another one of the seven prophetesses, inspired and instructed her uneducated husband also in the performance of a simple good deed—carrying candles to the Holy Temple in Shiloh—

and was also rewarded with a gift of prophecy that would be heeded throughout Israel.]

If he be worthy she shall be a help-meet for him; if not, she shall be against him, to fight him. (Pirke de Rabbi Eliezer, chapter 12)

What did Huldah prophesy?

22:15. "Say to the man who sent you to me: 16. Thus said the Lord: I am going to bring disaster upon this place and its inhabitants .... 17. Because they have forsaken Me and have made offerings to other gods and vexed Me with all their deeds, My wrath is kindled against this place and it shall not be quenched."

Because of the king's humble and repentant response to the words of the Law, Huldah also prophesies that God will spare him the promised punishment; before adversity strikes, he will have been laid peacefully to rest.

With determination, King Josiah cleanses the Temple of all its idolatrous shrines, and everything throughout the country that represents pagan practice is, likewise, destroyed. Not since the days of Samuel was the Passover ritual celebrated so fully, with so much vigor, as it was under Josiah's rule. Despite his efforts, history was relentlessly catching up with Huldah's prophecy of doom.

News reaches the kingdom of Judah that the powerful Assyrians, the vanquishers of the northern kingdom of Israel, had themselves been conquered by the Babylonians. When Josiah's son ascends the throne after his father's death, despite warnings by the prophet Jeremiah, troops are sent against the mighty Babylonians. Josiah's son is deposed after a reign that lasts only three months. The three kings to follow all lived and ruled in ways that were, as Scripture teaches, displeasing in the eyes of God.

The last king to rule Judah is Zedekiah. In the ninth year of his reign, Nebuchadnezzar, emperor of Babylonia, attacks Jerusalem. Two years later, on the ninth day of the eleventh month of Av, Nebuchadnezzar captures and decimates the city—the royal sons are murdered, the king himself is blinded and imprisoned. The city's leaders, priests, and most of the population in and around Jerusalem are exiled to Babylon. Heeding the advice of Jeremiah, the exiles choose to become law-abiding citizens, rather than rebels, in their new home. The Babylonian civilization was itself to fall, and the new governors of the exiled Israelites would be the Persians.

> On three occasions the Ministering Angels wished to utter song before the Holy One, blessed be He, but he would not let them . . . at the destruction of the generation of the flood, at the overthrow of the Egyptians in the Red Sea, and at the destruction of the Temple. (Lamentations Rabbah, proem 24)

For a time, life in Persia is uneventful for the exiles. Then, in the year 485 B.C.E., a new king ascends the throne. The royal throne of King Ahaseurus was in the fortress city of Shushan, but he reigned over one hundred and twenty-seven provinces, all the way from India to Nubia. In the third year of his reign, the king decided to give a banquet.

> Esther 1:4. For no fewer than a hundred and eighty days he displayed the vast riches of his kingdom and the splendid glory of his majesty. 5. At the end of this period, the king gave a banquet for seven days in the court of the king's palace garden for all the people who lived

in the fortress Shushan, high and low alike . . . . 9. In
addition, Queen Vashti gave a banquet for women, in
the royal palace of King Ahaseurus. 10. On the seventh
day, when the king was merry with wine, he
ordered . . . the seven eunuchs in attendance . . . 11. to
bring Queen Vashti before the king wearing a royal
diadem, to display her beauty to the peoples and the
officials . . . . 12. But Queen Vashti refused to come at
the king's command . . . . The king was greatly incensed,
and his fury burned within him.

The Sages warned that the Queen's disobedience would
breed disdain among all wives for their husbands.

1:19. If it please Your Majesty, let a royal edict be issued
by you . . . that Vashti shall never enter the presence of
King Ahaseurus. And let Your Majesty bestow her royal
state on another who is more worthy than she.

Esther

The story of Esther,
one of the twenty-three good women of Israel,
one of its seven prophetesses,
and in the eyes of our rabbis, one of the four most
beautiful women in the entire world.

W hen the king's anger subsided and he realized what he had done, he endeavored to find a solution. The king's servants suggested that beautiful young virgins be sought out for the king, and that the one most appealing be chosen as a replacement for Vashti.

Esther 2:5. In the fortress Shushan lived a Jew by the name of Mordecai, son of Jair, son of Shimei, son of Kish, a Benjaminite. 6. Kish had been exiled from Jerusalem in the group that was carried into exile . . . by King Nebuchadnezzar of Babylon. 7. He was foster father to Hadassah—that is, Esther—his uncle's daughter, for she had neither father nor mother. The maiden was shapely and beautiful; and when her father and mother died, Mordecai adopted her as his own daughter. 8. When the king's order and edict was proclaimed, and when many girls were assembled in the fortress Shushan, . . . Esther, too, was taken into the king's palace . . . . 10. Esther did not reveal her people or her kindred, for Mordecai had told her not to reveal it. 11. Every single day Mordecai would walk about in front of the court of the harem, to learn how Esther was faring and what was happening to her. 12. When each girl's turn came to go to King

Ahaseurus at the end of the twelve month's treatment prescribed for women (for that was the period spent on beautifying them . . .) whatever she asked for would be given her to take from the harem to the king's palace . . . . 15. When the turn came for Esther . . . to go to the king, she did not ask for anything but what . . . the king's eunuch, guardian of the women, advised. Yet Esther obtained favor in the sight of all who looked upon her. 16. Esther was taken to King Ahaseurus, in his royal palace, in the tenth month . . . in the seventh year of his reign. 17. The king loved Esther more than all the other women, and she won his grace and favor more than all the virgins. So he set a royal diadem on her head and made her queen instead of Vashti. 18. The king gave a banquet for all his officials and courtiers, "the banquet of Esther." . . . 20. But Esther did not reveal her kindred or her people, as Mordecai had instructed her.

Mordecai watches his adopted daughter suddenly elevated from exile and poverty to the highest position imaginable, that of queen over the mightiest empire on the planet. Nowhere in the Scroll of Esther is God's name mentioned, but the story is, in itself, a revelation of Divine Providence, silently and relentlessly directing from the wings.

From the Book of Lamentations (5:1–3): "Remember, O Lord, what has befallen us . . . . Our heritage has passed to aliens . . . . We have become orphans, fatherless, our mothers are like widows."

MIDRASH RABBAH ESTHER 6:7: "As you live," God says in response to the exiles, "the deliverer whom I shall raise up for you in Media shall have no father nor mother!"

MIDRASH RABBAH ESTHER 6:5, TALMUD, *MEGILLAH* 13a: The rabbis teach that Esther's mother died soon after her birth, and her father, soon after her conception.

Who is this Esther, this orphan destined for greatness, this orphan whose courage will be tested, whose obedience and responsibility to needs higher than her own will be triumphantly demonstrated?

Scripture tells us that this orphan girl, Esther, was also called by another name, Hadassah.

TALMUD, *MEGILLAH* 13a: R. Nehemiah said that Hadassah was her real name, but everyone called her Esther because she was reminiscent of Venus, "Ishtar" being the Goddess's Persian name. Hadassah means "myrtle," and R. Joshua b. Korha commented that Esther's complexion was sallow, a light green, like a myrtle leaf, but she was endowed with a touch of grace— the literal translation being that "a thread of grace was drawn about her."

TALMUD, *MEGILLAH* 7a: Regarding her alluring beauty, R. Eleazar said that she appeared to every man as a member of his own people.

MIDRASH RABBAH ESTHER 6:9: "R. Judah said: She was like a statue which a thousand persons look upon and all equally admire. R. Nehemiah said: They put Median women on one side of her and Persian women on the other, and she was more beautiful than all of them."

2:15 "Esther obtained favor in the sight of all them that looked upon her."

MIDRASH RABBAH ESTHER 6:9: She obtained favor not only in the sight of all earthly beings, but in the sight of all heavenly beings, as well.

What of her actions even at this early point in her startling new-found position of power and royalty?

TALMUD, *MEGILLAH* 13a: Hadassah was her name; she was called Esther because she concealed (mastereth) the truth about herself and her origins. Heeding Mordecai's instruction, "Esther did not reveal her people or her kindred" (2:10).

TALMUD, *MEGILLAH* 13a: The king "made a feast for her, and still she did not tell him who she was. He remitted taxes, and she did not tell him. He sent gifts, and she still did not tell him."

MIDRASH RABBAH ESTHER 6:12, TALMUD, *MEGILLAH* 13b: Esther "put a ban of silence on herself like her ancestress, Rachel, who also put a ban of silence on herself. All the greatest of her descendants forced themselves to be silent. Rachel put a ban of silence on herself when she saw her wedding presents in the hand of her sister and said nothing."

MIDRASH RABBAH ESTHER 6:8: After Esther had been taken from him, Mordecai, concerned for her welfare, "walked everyday in front of the court of the harem, to learn how Esther was faring" (2:11). In light of events yet to unfold, the rabbis chastise the young woman's uncle. "God said to him: You have inquired of the welfare of one person, to know how Esther fared. I swear that in the end, you will seek the welfare of a whole nation!"

So our story unfolds.

Chapter 2.21: At that time, when Mordecai was sitting in the palace gate, Bigthan and Teresh, two of the king's eunuchs who guarded the threshold, became angry, and plotted to do away with King Ahaseurus. 22. Mordecai learned of it and told it to Queen Esther, and Esther reported it to the king in Mordecai's name. 23. The matter was investigated and found to be so, and the two were impaled on stakes. This was recorded in the book of annals at the instance of the king.

This seemingly coincidental event would prove to be an essential element in the downfall of the enemy who was soon to rise to power in King Ahaseurus' realm.

MIDRASH RABBAH ESTHER 6:13, TALMUD, *MEGILLAH* 15a: The two officials had been replaced by Mordecai, an individual whom they regarded as a barbarian.

The post required the assigned official to inform the king of any conspiracies against him. To prove their superiority over Mordecai, the two eunuchs plotted to assassinate Ahaseurus. Mordecai, said to have been schooled in seventy languages, understood the native Tarsean in which the plotters conversed. The entire event—the plot, the punishment, and Mordecai's part in saving the king—were all entered into the king's chronicles for future reference. From this event originated the Talmudic axiom: Whoever reports a saying in the name of the one who said it, its originator, brings deliverance to the world . . . . "And Esther told the king in Mordecai's name."

Chapter 3:1. Some time afterward, King Ahaseurus promoted Haman, son of Hammedatha the Agagite; he advanced him and seated him higher than any of his fellow officials. 2. All the king's courtiers in the palace gate knelt and bowed low to Haman, for such was the

king's order concerning him; but Mordecai would not
kneel or bow low.

Mordecai's disobedience enraged Haman. When it was
brought to his attention that Mordecai was a Jew, Haman plotted to do away with every Jew living anywhere within
Ahaseurus's kingdom. Haman approaches the king, explaining to him that a certain group of people inside his kingdom
subscribed to a set of laws different from those of other
people. It would not be in the king's interest to tolerate their
disobedience to the king's ordinances. The king was per-
suaded.

> 3:13 .... Written dispatches were dispatched by couri-
> ers to all the king's provinces to destroy, massacre, and
> exterminate all the Jews, young and old, children and
> women, on a single day, on the thirteenth day of the
> twelfth month—that is, the month of Adar (determined
> by the casting of lots)—and to plunder their posses-
> sions .... 15. The king and Haman sat down to a feast,
> but the city of Shushan was dumbfounded. Chapter 4:1.
> When Mordecai learned all that had happened,
> Mordecai tore his clothes and put on sackcloth and
> ashes .... 3. Also, in every province that the king's com-
> mand and decree reached, there was great mourning
> among the Jews.

Esther was unaware of the cause of the mass distress outside the palace; Mordecai instructed one of her attendants to
bring her a copy of the king's new proclamation.

> 4:8 .... he bade him show it to Esther and inform her,
> and charge her to go to the king and to appeal to him
> and to plead with him for her people.

Esther sent back a refusal to Mordecai.

4:11. "All the king's courtiers and the people of the
king's provinces know that if any person, man or woman,
enters the king's presence in the inner court without
having been summoned, there is but one law for him—
that he be put to death. Only if the king extends the
golden scepter to him may he live. Now I have not been
summoned to visit the king for the last thirty days." 12.
When Mordecai was told what Esther had said, 13.
Mordecai had this message delivered to Esther: "Do not
imagine that you, of all the Jews, will escape with your
life by being in the king's palace. 14. On the contrary,
if you keep silent in this crisis, relief and deliverance will
come to the Jews from another quarter, while you and
your father's house will perish. And who knows, perhaps
you have attained to royal position for just such a crisis." 15. Then Esther sent back this answer to Mordecai:
16. "Go, assemble all the Jews who live in Shushan and
fast in my behalf: Do not eat or drink for three days,
night or day. I and my maidens will observe the same
fast. Then I shall go to the king, though it is contrary
to the law; and if I am to perish, I shall perish.

MIDRASH RABBAH ESTHER 8:5: When Esther was just a
child, and Ahaseurus was in the second year of his rule,
Mordecai dreamed a strange and disturbing dream. In it, he
saw two dragons [representing Mordecai and Haman] rise up
against one another and prepare for battle. In his dream,
Mordecai saw one small nation among all the nations of the
world singled out for obliteration. The dragons fought, the
world recoiled in fear, and the one small nation prayed to
God. Then suddenly something new happened. A small stream

of water [Esther] passed between the two dragons, separating them from one another. The stream grew into a great sea that flowed over the entire planet. Once again, Truth reigned, there was Light, and all was set right.

"And it came to pass that from that day Mordecai kept in mind the dream which he had dreamed, and when Haman vexed him he said to Esther, by her messenger, 'Here is the dream which I related to you in your childhood. Now rise and pray for mercy from God and come before the king and supplicate for your people and your kindred.' "

4:14 "if you keep silent in this crisis . . ."

MIDRASH RABBAH ESTHER 8:6: "If you keep silent now and refrain from pleading for your nation, in the end you will be silent in the time to come and you will not be able to justify yourself, because you had the opportunity of doing good in your lifetime and you did not do it."

4:16 "Fast in my behalf."

MIDRASH RABBAH ESTHER 8:6: The fast days that Esther requests of Mordecai and the Jews were the thirteenth, fourteenth, and fifteenth of Nissan. Mordecai sends back word to her that she has erroneously chosen a time that includes the first day of Passover! Esther replied: Why is there a Passover? Without an Israel there is no need for a Passover! Mordecai assented to her request and did as she had asked.

MIDRASH RABBAH ESTHER 8:6: Esther took off her royal robes and ornaments and she fasted and she prayed before God to favor her efforts with success. "And do Thou, father of orphans, stand at the right hand of this orphan who trusts in Thy loving kindness, and make this man mercifully disposed towards me, for I am afraid of him, and cast him down before me, for Thou bringest low the proud."

Chapter 5:1. On the third day, Esther put on royal apparel and stood in the inner court of the king's palace, facing the king's palace, while the king was sitting on his royal throne in the throne facing the entrance of the palace. 2. As soon as the king saw Queen Esther standing in the court, she won his favor. The king extended to Esther the golden scepter which he had in his hand, and Esther approached and touched the tip of the scepter. 3. "What troubles you, Queen Esther?" the king asked her. "And what is your request? Even to half the kingdom, it shall be granted you." 4. "If it please your Majesty," Esther replied, "let Your Majesty and Haman come today to the feast that I have prepared for him." 5. The king commanded, "Tell Haman to hurry and do Esther's bidding." So the king and Haman came to the feast that Esther had prepared.

5:1 "Esther put on royal apparel."

MIDRASH RABBAH ESTHER 9:1: She put on "her most beautiful robes and her riches and ornaments, and she took with her two maidens, placing her right hand on one of them and leaning on her, as is the royal custom, while the second maiden followed her mistress bearing her train so that the gold on it should not touch the ground. She put on a smiling face, concealing the anxiety in her heart."

The literal translation of the first verse of this chapter is not that Esther put on "royal apparel," as the Scripture is often popularly rendered, but rather that she put on "royalty."

TALMUD, *MEGILLAH* 15a: "This tells us that the Holy Spirit clothed her."

MIDRASH RABBAH ESTHER 9:1: When the King saw Esther, unsummoned standing before his throne, his face reflected a furious wrath. The Queen, sensing his anger, lost courage, and her head sank onto the maiden who supported her.

TALMUD, *MEGILLAH* 15b: Until Esther reached the King's throne, the Divine Presence was with her. When she entered his chamber of idols, it departed. "My God, my God," she cried, "Why hast Thou forsaken me?" (Psalms 22:2). My association with the king was forced upon me. Will you punish my inadvertent offense in the same way you would an offense committed willingly?

MIDRASH RABBAH ESTHER 9:1: "But our God saw and had mercy on His people, and He took note of the distress of the orphan who trusted in Him and He gave her grace in the eyes of the King and invested her with new beauty and new charm."

TALMUD, *MEGILLAH* 15b: "Three ministering angels were appointed to help her at that moment; one to make her head erect, a second to endow her with charm [literally 'to draw a thread of grace over her'] and a third to stretch the golden scepter."

MIDRASH RABBAH ESTHER 9:1: " 'Esther, my Queen, why dost thou tremble? For this law which we have laid down does not apply to thee, since thou art my beloved and my companion.' He also said to her, 'Why, when I saw you, did you not speak to me?' Esther replied, 'My lord, the King, when I beheld you I was overcome by your high dignity.' "

5:4 "Let your Majesty and Haman come today to the feast that I have prepared for him."

TALMUD, *MEGILLAH* 15b: The question: What was Esther's reason for inviting Haman? The rabbis respond: To keep Haman always on hand in the event that the opportunity to accuse him should suddenly arise; to persuade the king to change his mind about his decree while Haman is with them, and not provide the fickle king with the time to change his mind, again; to make the king and all the princes jealous of Haman; to set a trap; to make God notice her and to what ends she is being forced to go—perhaps He'd be moved to perform a miracle. It is said that Rabbah b. Abbuhu once came across the prophet Elijah and he asked him: Which of the reasons given actually convinced Esther to act as she did? Elijah replied: Esther was influenced by all of the reasons given by all the Tannaim and all the Amoraim.

With their poison I will prepare their feast. (Jeremiah 51:39)

May their table be a trap for them, a snare for their allies. (Psalms 69:23–24)

If your enemy is hungry, give him bread to eat; If he is thirsty, give him water to drink. You will be heaping live coals on his head, and the Lord will reward you. (Proverbs 25:21–22)

Pride goeth before destruction. (Proverbs 16:18)

5:9. That day Haman went out happy and lighthearted. When Haman saw Mordecai in the palace gate, and Mordecai did not rise or even stir on his account, Haman was filled with rage at him. 10. Nevertheless,

Haman controlled himself and went home. He sent for his friends and his wife Zeresh, 11. and Haman told them about his great wealth and his many sons, and all about how the king had promoted him and advanced him above the officials and the king's courtiers. 12. "What is more," said Haman, "Queen Esther gave a feast, and besides the king she did not have anyone but me. And tomorrow, too, I am invited by her along with the king. 13. Yet all this means nothing to me every time I see that Jew Mordecai sitting in the palace gate." 14. Then his wife Zeresh and all his friends said to him, "Let a stake be put up, fifty cubits high, and in the morning ask the king to have Mordecai impaled on it. Then you can go gaily with the king to the feast."

MIDRASH RABBAH ESTHER 9:2: Haman had three hundred sixty-five counsellors, one for each day of the year, but not one of them could give counsel like his wife, Zeresh. She warns Haman that if this man who disturbs him, Mordecai, happens to be a Jew, he cannot be successfully prevailed against unless they move against him in a way that no Jew has ever before encountered. "If you throw him into a fiery furnace, Hananiah and his companions [Book of Daniel] have already been delivered from this; if into a lion's den, Daniel has already escaped from one. If you imprison him in a dungeon, Joseph has already escaped from one . . . . If you banish him into the wilderness, his ancestors have already been fruitful and multiplied in the wilderness, and they underwent many trials there and they withstood them all and were delivered. If you put out his eyes, there was Samson who killed ever so many souls of the Philistines when he was blind. Hang him, therefore, on a gallows, for we have not found one of his people who was delivered from that."

MIDRASH ON PROVERBS, CHAPTER 11: "He who is bent on evil, upon him it shall come . . . . He who trusts in his wealth shall fall, but the righteous shall flourish like foliage" (Proverbs 11:27–28).

R. Levi taught that there were two extremely wealthy men in the world, one a Jew and one a Gentile. The Jew was Korah and the Gentile was Haman. Both were deposed from power as a result of heeding the counsel of their wives.

Korah appears in chapter 16 of the Book of Numbers. He and a group of followers are rebelling against the authority of Moses and Aaron. Rabbi Levi asks, How did it happen that Korah fell as a result of listening to his wife? The midrash he tells is as follows: Returning home from the Academy one day, Korah's wife asks him to tell her about the ruling that Moses had expounded. "He explicated to us the law of the blue fringes," he answered. "What are these blue fringes?" she asked. Korah went on to recount how Moses was instructed by God to tell all the men to put four blue fringes on the four corners of their garments. ["Look at and recall all the commandments of the Lord and observe them, so that you do not follow your heart and eyes in your lustful urge. Thus you shall be reminded to observe all My commandments and to be holy to your God."—Numbers 15:39–40] Upon hearing this ruling, Korah's wife burst out laughing, asserting that Moses was making fun of all of them. "A garment with blue fringes? Why not simply a garment that is blue all over?" When Moses saw the blue garment that she had made, he demanded an explanation. Korah's reasoning [borrowed from his wife] enraged Moses, and he questioned him further. "The ruling says to place a mezuzah [containing the words of the Teaching] on the doorposts of your house (Deuteronomy 6:9). Does a house filled with Torah scrolls [also] require a mezuzah?" When Korah responded in the affirmative, Moses declared, 'Let your ears hear what your mouth is saying! O Korah, you have transgressed God's commandments because you have grown haughty in your wealth.' Thereupon Moses stood before God and spoke up before him saying, 'Master of the Universe, if my words are to stand, pray, issue a decree in their behalf.'

In the Scriptural account of the rebellion of Korah and his followers, we find Moses declaring aloud, "If these men die as all men do . . . it was not the Lord who sent me. But if the Lord brings about something unheard of, so that the ground opens its mouth and swallows them up with all that belongs to them . . . you shall know that these men have spurned the Lord." Scripture continues, "Scarcely had he finished speaking all these words when the ground under them burst asunder and the earth opened its mouth and swallowed them up with their households." The phrase, "their households" indicates to our commentators that Korah's wife was even more at fault than Korah himself. What was this newly created thing that Moses speaks of? "It was the entryway to Gehenna" (Hell).

"The wisest of women builds her house, but folly tears it down with its own hands. (Proverbs 14:1)

The Hebrew word for "husband"/"ish" is spelled aleph, yud, shin; "wife"/"isha" is spelled aleph, shin, heh. In common, they share the letters aleph and shin, which together spell the word for "fire"/"esh"; the distinguishing letters are yud in husband, and heh in wife, which when placed together form the Divine Name, Yah. The Sages taught that if the couple is worthy, the Divine Presence dwells between them and blesses them. If unworthy, the Presence departs, and what is left behind is a devouring fire that will destroy them both. (Talmud, Sotah 17a)

MIDRASH ON PROVERBS, CHAPTER 11: The rabbis tell us that Haman's wife, Zeresh, and all his friends participated in the advice given. Based on their counsel, the next morning Haman decided to approach the king with the intention of maligning Mordecai. "The wicked Haman said to himself, 'Once I am seated with the king at the banquet, I will advise him to have Mordecai impaled on the stake.' The Holy Spirit responded, 'O wicked one, your evil thoughts will be turned upon your own head.' . . . To all his plotting the Holy Spirit kept responding, 'Not according to your planning, but according to My planning,' as it is said, 'For My plans are not your plans, nor are My ways your ways, declares the Lord (Isaiah 55:8).' "

> 5:14 . . . The proposal pleased Haman, and he had the stake put up. Chapter 6:1. That night, the sleep of the king was disturbed, and he ordered the book of records, the annals, to be brought; and it was read to the king. 2. There it was found written that Mordecai had denounced Bigthana and Teresh, two of the king's eunuchs who guarded the threshold, who had plotted to do away with King Ahaseurus. 3. "What honor or advancement has been conferred on Mordecai for this?" the king inquired. "Nothing at all has been done for him," replied the king's servants.

6:1 "That night, the sleep of the king was disturbed."

TALMUD, *MEGILLAH* 15b:—Not just the sleep of the King of Persia, but the sleep of the King of the Universe, the angels above, and the sleep of all Israel, below.

6.1 "He ordered the book of records."

TALMUD, *MEGILLAH* **15b:** The king suddenly had a troubling thought. What is Esther's reason for inviting Haman? Perhaps they are planning to kill me! But have I no friends who would tell me? Perhaps there is someone in my kingdom who has shown me a kindness and I've been remiss in rewarding him. Agitated by these thoughts, the king immediately ordered that the annals be brought.

6:4. "Who is in the court?" the king asked. For Haman had just entered the outer court of the royal palace, to speak to the king about having Mordecai impaled on the stake he had prepared for him. 5. "It is Haman standing in the court," the king's servant answered him. "Let him enter," said the king. 6. Haman entered, and the king asked him, "What should be done for a man whom the king desires to honor?" He said to himself, "Whom would the king desire to honor more than me?" 7. So Haman said to the king, "For the man whom the king desires to honor, 8. let royal garb which the king has worn be brought, and a horse on which the king has ridden and on whose head a royal diadem has been set . . . . And let the man whom the king desires to honor be attired and paraded on the horse through the city square, while they proclaim before him: "This is what is done for the man whom the king desires to honor!" 10. "Quick then!" said the king to Haman. "Get the garb and the horse, as you have said, and do this to Mordecai the Jew, who sits in the king's gate. Omit nothing."

Haman followed through on the king's command, returning home to his wife, his head covered in mourning.

6:13. His advisors and his wife Zeresh said to him, "If Mordecai, before whom you have begun to fall, is of

---

Jewish stock, you will not overcome him; you will fall before him to your ruin." 14. While they were still speaking with him, the king's eunuchs arrived and hurriedly brought Haman to the banquet which Esther had prepared.

MIDRASH RABBAH ESTHER 6:14: "If a record in a book of a human being can have such an effect, how much more so a record in the Book of the Holy One, blessed be He."

Chapter 7:1. So the king and Haman came to the feast with Queen Esther. 2. On the second day, the king again asked Esther at the wine feast, "What is your wish, Queen Esther? It shall be granted you. And what is your request? Even to half the kingdom, it shall be fulfilled." 3. Queen Esther replied, "If it pleases Your Majesty, let my life be granted me as my wish, and my people as my request. 4. For we have been sold, my people and I, to be destroyed, massacred, and exterminated. Had we only been sold as bondmen and bondwomen, I would have kept silent...." 5. Thereupon, King Ahaseurus demanded of Queen Esther, "Who is he and where is he who dared to do this?" 6. "The adversary and enemy," replied Esther, "is this evil Haman!"

MIDRASH RABBAH ESTHER 6:5: "Just as the myrtle (hadassah) has a sweet smell but a bitter taste, so Esther was sweet to Mordecai, but bitter to Haman."

Chapter 7:7. The king, in his fury, left the wine feast for the palace garden, while Haman remained to plead with Queen Esther for his life, for he saw that the king had resolved to kill him. 8. When the king returned from the palace garden to the banquet room, Haman was lying prostrate on the couch on which Esther reclined. "Does he mean," cried the king, "to ravish the queen in my own palace?" No sooner did these words leave the king's lips than Haman's face blanched. 9. Then . . . one of the eunuchs in attendance on the king said, "What is more, a stake is standing at Haman's house, fifty cubits high, which Haman made for Mordecai—the man whose words saved the king." "Impale him on it!" the king ordered. 10. So they impaled Haman on the stake which he had put up for Mordecai, and the king's fury was abated.

MIDRASH ON PROVERBS, CHAPTER 9: "She has prepared the feast, mixed the wine and also set the table" (Proverbs 9:2). This verse is a reference to Queen Esther. "She has prepared the feast—When great trouble befell Israel in the days of Mordecai, what did she do? She prepared a banquet for Ahaseurus and the wicked Haman and got them very drunk with wine. The wicked Haman thought to himself that she was paying him honor and did not realize that she had spread a net to trap him, for in getting them drunk with wine she had preserved her people unto eternity. She has also set the table—she furnished for herself a table in this world and a table in the world to come. What sort of table is this? It is the good name which she acquired both in this world and in the world to come, for all holy days will be annulled in the (messianic) future, but Purim will never be annulled, as it is said, 'These days of Purim shall never cease!' (Esther 9:28)"

MIDRASH RABBAH ESTHER 9:2: At the moment Haman ordered the gallows to be made, God called together all the trees of creation, and He asked which of them would offer itself for Haman, himself, to be hanged upon. The figtree, pomegranate, nuttree, citron, the myrtle, the olive tree, the apple tree, the palm tree, the acacia and fur tree, the cedar, the palm and the willow all came forward and said: Choose *me*, because the children of Israel are compared to me! Finally, the thorn bush stepped forward, offering itself as the most appropriate instrument for the task, " 'because my name is thorn and he is a pricking thorn, and it is fitting that a thorn should be hanged on a thorn . . . So they found one of these and they made the gallows. When they brought it to Haman, he set it up at the entrance to his house and measured himself on it to show his servants how Mordecai should be hanged on it. A Bath Kol (a voice descending from Heaven) answered him: For thee is the tree fitting—the tree has been made ready for thee from the beginning of the world."

"Woe to him who as his house is destroyed, is hanged from his own beam."

Chapter 8:1. That very day King Ahaseurus gave the property of Haman, the enemy of the Jews, to Queen Esther. Mordecai presented himself to the king, for Esther had revealed how he was related to her. 2. The king slipped off his ring, which he had taken back from Haman, and gave it to Mordecai . . . 3. Esther spoke to the king again, falling at his feet and weeping, and beseeching him to avert the evil plotted by Haman the Agagite against the Jews. 4. The king extended the golden scepter to Esther, and Esther arose and stood before the king. 5. "If it please Your Majesty," she said, "and if I have won your favor and the proposal seems right to Your Majesty, and if I am pleasing to you—let dispatches be written countermanding those which were written by Haman."

On the twenty-third of Sivan, letters were written and sent to every province, from India to Ethiopia, to this effect:

8:11. The king has permitted the Jews of every city to assemble and fight for their lives; if any people or province attacks them, they may destroy, massacre, and exterminate its armed force, together with women and children, and plunder their possessions 12. on a single day in all the provinces of King Ahaseurus, namely on the thirteenth day of the twelfth month, that is the month of Adar (the very day chosen by Haman). 17. And in every province and in every city, when the king's command and decree arrived, there was gladness and joy among the Jews, a feast and a holiday. And many of the people of the land professed to be Jews, for the fear of the Jews had fallen upon them. Chapter 9:5. So the Jews struck at their enemies with the sword, slaying and destroying; they wreaked their will upon their enemies.

At Esther's request, the Jews in Shushan were allowed on the following day, the fourteenth of Adar, to again act as they had on the previous day. So they did, resting and celebrating on the fifteenth.

9:20. Mordecai recorded these events. And he sent dispatches to all the Jews throughout the provinces of King Ahaseurus, near and far 21. charging them to observe the fourteenth and fifteenth days of Adar, every year— 22. the same days on which the Jews enjoyed relief from their foes and the same month which had been transformed for them from one of grief and mourning to one of festive joy.

Queen Esther herself wrote a second letter, confirming all that Mordecai had decreed.

9.32 And Esther's ordinance validating these observances of Purim was recorded in a scroll.

TALMUD, *MEGILLAH* 7a: Esther sent word to the Wise Men requesting that they establish and commemorate her for future generations. They replied that this action would incite the ill will of the other nations who would accuse the Jews of rejoicing at the remembrance of the downfall of their neighbors. Esther sent back a reply—"I am *already* recorded in the chronicles of the kings of Media and Persia!" [see Esther 10:2].

MIDRASH ON PSALMS 22:3, 4, 10, TALMUD, *YOMA* 29a: During the night, we have the light of the moon, the light of the stars and the planets. After the moon sets and the stars and planets vanish from sight, in that hour before dawn, there is a darkness deeper than night. It is in that hour, out of this deepest darkness, that God brings forth the light of the dawn. Esther means "the hidden one"; she remained hidden until the instant her light was needed in the world. Then she came forth, like the dawn. Just as the dawn marks the end of the whole night, so, too, is the story of Esther the end of all recorded miracles in these sacred Scriptures.

References

Antonelli, Judith S. *In the Image of God: A Feminist Commentary on the Torah.* New Jersey: Jason Aronson, 1995.

Bialik, Hyman Nahman and Yehoshua Hana Ravnitzky. *The Book of Legends.* New York: Schocken Books, 1992.

Bin Gorion, Micha Joseph. *Mimekor Yisrael.* Ed. Emanuel Bin Gorion. Trans. I. M. Lask. Bloomington and Indianapolis: Indiana University Press, 1990.

Braude, William G. *The Midrash on Psalms.* New Haven: Yale University Press, 1959.

———— *Pesikta Rabbati.* New Haven and London: Yale University Press, 1968.

Buber, Martin. *Tales of the Hasidim: The Later Masters.* New York: Schocken Books, 1947.

Chavel, Rabbi Dr. Charles B. *Ramban (Nachmanides): Commentary on the Torah.* 5 Vols. New York: Shilo, date per volume.

———— *Ramban: His Life and Teachings.* New York: Philipp Feldheim, 1960.

Epstein, Rabbi Dr. I. *The Babylonian Talmud.* 17 Vols. London: Soncino Press, date per volume.

Freedman, R. Dr. H. and Maurice Simon. *The Midrash Rabbah.* 4 Vols. London, Jerusalem, New York: Soncino Press, 1977.

Friedlander, Gerald. *Pirke de R. Eliezer.* New York: Sepher-Hermon Press, 1981.

Gaster, Moses. *Maaseh Book*. Philadelphia: Jewish Publication Society, 1929.

Ginzberg, Louis. *Legends of the Bible*. Philadelphia: The Jewish Publication Society, 1956.

Glazerson, Matityahu. *Letters of Fire*. Translated by S. Fuchs. Spring Valley, New York: Feldheim Publishers, 1991.

Goldin, Hyman E. *The Book of Legends*. 3 Vols. New York: Hebrew Publishing Company, 1929.

Hertz, Dr. J. H. *The Pentateuch and Haftorahs*. London: Soncino Press, 1956.

Holtz, Barry. *Back to the Sources—Reading the Classic Jewish Texts*. New York: Summit Books, 1984.

Kaplan, Aryeh. *The Bahir*. York Beach, ME: Samuel Weiser, 1979.

———— *Inner Space*. Brooklyn: Moznaim Publishing, 1990.

———— *Sefer Yetzirah*. York Beach, ME: Samuel Weiser, 1990.

Kugel, James L. and Rowan A. Greer. *Early Biblical Interpretation*. Philadelphia: Westminster Press, 1986.

Lauterbach, Jacob Z. *Mekilta de Rabbi Ishmael*. Philadelphia: The Jewish Publication Society, 1949.

Newman, Jacob. *The Commentary of Nachmanides on Genesis, Chapters 1–6*. Leiden, E. J. Brill, 1960.

Rosenbaum, Rev. M. and Dr. A. M. Silbermann. *Pentateuch with Rashi's Commentary: Genesis and Exodus*. New York: Hebrew Publishing Company, date per volume.

Roth, Cecil, editor-in-chief. *Encyclopedia Judaica*. Jerusalem: Keter Publishing House, 1972.

Scholem, Gershom. *Zohar: The Book of Splendor, Basic Readings from the Kabbalah*. New York: Schocken Books, 1977.

Sperling, Harry and Maurice Simon. *The Zohar*. 5 Vols. London: Soncino Press, 1984.

Strack, Hermann Leberecht. *Introduction to the Talmud and Midrash*. New York: Meridian Books, 1959.

Tanach—The Holy Scriptures. Philadelphia: Jewish Publication Society, 1985.

Tishby, Isaiah. *The Wisdom of the Zohar.* 3 Vols. New York: Oxford University Press, 1989.

Townsend, John T. *Midrash Tanhuma—S. Buber Recension.* Hoboken, NJ: Ktav, 1989.

Visotzky, Burton. *The Midrash on Proverbs.* New Haven and London: Yale University Press, 1992.

Index

About the Author

Barbara L. Thaw Ronson divides her time between the practice of optometry and her first love, writing. Most recently, she and her husband co-authored *The Armchair Magician*, a beginner's book on the psychology and performance of magic. Prior to this endeavor, Dr. Ronson enjoyed years in the theater as a playwright. Long interested in the hidden meanings of the Torah, she now looks forward to incorporating this knowledge with the performance of magic and storytelling. Dr. Ronson lives with her husband in New York City.